**TRAVELERS
AND
TRAVEL LIARS**
1660-1800

TRAVELERS AND TRAVEL LIARS
1660-1800

BY PERCY G. ADAMS

DOVER PUBLICATIONS, INC., NEW YORK

This Dover edition, first published in 1980, is an unabridged, slightly corrected republication of the work first published by the University of California Press, Berkeley and Los Angeles, in 1962. The author has written a new Preface especially for the present edition.

International Standard Book Number: 0-486-23942-X
Library of Congress Catalog Card Number: 79-8906

Manufactured in the United States of America
Dover Publications, Inc.
180 Varick Street
New York, N.Y. 10014

To Polly
and
Our Three Thoroughbred Travelers,
Andrea, Dick, and Elise

PREFACE TO THE DOVER EDITION

IT GIVES me great pleasure to have Dover reprint *Travelers and Travel Liars: 1660–1800*. The book has proved to be more enduring and useful than I had dared hope; several reviewers, in fact—in France, in Germany, in the United States—called it seminal or pointed out that it fits on the shelf beside Marjorie Nicolson's *Voyages to the Moon* and Philip Gove's *The Imaginary Voyage in Prose Fiction*. Normally I would be happy to have the opportunity to correct typographical errors, but, because of the excellence of the first printing, I have in fourteen years been able to find only three such errors, all of which are now set right.

Also in fourteen years any author who remains with his subject, as I have, will learn much more about it, from friendly and knowledgeable readers of his book, from the many new books and articles related to it, and from new discoveries. And to be sure, if I were writing *Travel Liars* now I could make it much longer; but I am not certain it would be a better book. We have, for example, more evidence today for a study of Defoe's techniques as a real traveler and as a fireside traveler, but the conclusions we draw are not different from those found here. And *Travel Liars* never did pretend to be exhaustive, for I knowingly omitted certain accounts of seventeenth- and eighteenth-century travel books that sometimes, or often, passed for real when they were either wholly or partly invented. One good example is John Campbell's *The Travels and Adventures of Edward Brown, Esq.*, which fooled few people and stirred up little controversy. Nevertheless, it is an intriguing

v

"novel" and has been reprinted recently (1973). What is far more important to me is one correction, or addition, that needs to be made. When I wrote *Travel Liars,* scholars and librarians were in almost complete agreement that Charles Swaine and Theodore Drage were two influential travel writers of the 1740s and, although hesitantly, I accepted that as a fact (pp. 68–72). But later I was able to prove to my satisfaction, and I believe to that of others, that Drage and Swaine were the same man, a seaman, a trader in Pennsylvania, a friend of Franklin, and finally a missionary for the Society for the Propagation of the Gospel.

Finally, while I think that the period 1660 to 1800 is especially fruitful for a study of travel lies and their influence, such a book as this one could be written about any period. One scholar has, in fact, been threatening to do a companion volume for the nineteenth century, and I myself would delight to do it for the Renaissance, which has not only such wonderful fabrications as Vicente Espinel's *La Vida de Marcos de Obregón* and the anonymous author's ". . . lettre envoyée de la Nouvelle France, par le sieur de Combes," but also such controversial travel writers as Fernão Mendes Pinto who, although a close friend and companion of St. Francis Xavier, was often given the middle name of "Mendax" because his delightful adventures, as he wrote them, seemed to be mendacious. But then Lucian's *True History* had, centuries before, satirized such travelers and helped make all travelers suspect forever after. A great number of the best travel writers of the seventeenth and eighteenth centuries, seldom if ever suspect, have been reprinted by Dover. Among them are Chaplain Walter with George Anson, Captain Cook, John Esquemeling the buccaneer, John Bartram, and others, all together filling up a shelf that goes well with *Travelers and Travel Liars: 1660–1800.*

P.G.A.

PREFACE TO THE FIRST EDITION

"The Trav'ler leaping o'er those bounds,
The credit of his book confounds."
JOHN GAY, *Fables*

THIS IS *not* a book about imaginary or extraordinary voyages. The story of the Gullivers, of the Munchausens, of the Cacklogallinians is a fascinating and important one in the history of fiction and satire, but that is another story. Dog-birds, flights to the moon, people with tails, tribes of Amazons—with such as these we have almost nothing to do; they belong to the realm of the incredible, and readers of the eighteenth century were usually able to recognize that fact.

This book deals rather with authentic travel accounts that in an Age of Reason told untruths, with pseudo voyages that were designed to make the public believe them real, with charges and countercharges of lying, with the reasons that brought these falsehoods, these fake travels, and these charges into existence, with the devices that writers of travel books used in fooling or attempting to fool readers, and with the amazing results that these devices achieved. Our book, then, is concerned not with the use of the marvelous to amuse and instruct but with the employment of deception for the sake of money, pride, or a point of view.

One is aware of the danger involved in pursuing such a path. No reader of a study of incredible voyages would come away from it believing that all travel accounts were filled with Lilliputs, Utopias, or Lunar societies, but one who reads only of travel lies may obtain a perspective that lacks enough truth. For, in spite of the popular contemporaneous accusation that all travelers were liars, the eighteenth century was a time that both sought and gave the truth, and voyagers of the day often attempted to follow the directions of the Royal Society and return with facts and drawings that would enlighten both the scientist and the general reader. But science was young in the eighteenth century, and with its Halleys and Sloanes, its Buffons and Lavoisiers, it produced many less notable figures, among them the projectors that Swift and others could ridicule. In the same fashion, by no means did all travelers always advance the cause of truth. Furthermore, there is a sort of paradox that provides the present work with one *raison d'être:* Because the eighteenth century was so avid in its search for data about man and his physical surroundings, it was inclined to be gullible and fall victim to facts that were not facts and to travel books that were partly, even completely, false.

There are, of course, other reasons for writing this book, the chief one being that I have long felt the need of a broad survey of voyage literature, one that would not limit itself to a single nation. The sources and the libraries of Temple, Defoe, and Swift, for example, reveal that they knew the French travelers as well as they knew the British; and great collections and immediate translations made the journals of all nations accessible to Montesquieu and Sir Hans Sloane alike. Yet scholars in this field, because of the great amount of spadework that had to be done, have so far been forced to restrict themselves rather carefully. Robson-Scott has studied the Germans who came to England, Parks has treated travelers in Italy, and Frantz has considered the British voyagers of the late seventeenth and early eighteenth centuries. The English in France, the French in England, the French in Spain, the British in America, the French in Egypt, the French in America—all these, and more, have been studied thoroughly. But now, because of the careful documentation that has been going on, the time has come for the broad perspective. Although the present survey is not by any means the definitive and all-inclusive one that will be written, it does attempt a synthesis so far not attempted.

It has taken over a dozen years for me to gather the facts presented here, and many people have helped. Among them, of course, have been authors of books in the same or a related field: E. G. Cox, whose bibliography, although badly in need of revision, is still standard; J. R. Moore, A. W. Secord, and M. Foulché-Delbosc, whose techniques have taught me much; H. R. Wagner, G. Atkinson, Philip Gove, Gilbert Chinard, Jean Delanglez, Louis Martz, and J.-M. Carré.

My friends and associates have offered helpful suggestions— Win and Roderick Thaler, Reinhold Nordsieck, John Hansen, Bailey McBride, Paul S. Lietz, Coulton Storm, and Wright Howes. Editors of periodicals, as well as certain other specialists, have read portions of the book and made fruitful comments, among them George B. Parks, Dean Kenneth L. Knickerbocker, Nicholas B. Wainwright, and Leonard W. Labaree. The most extended reading of the manuscript has been that by Professor Gary Dunbar of the Department of Geography at the University of Virginia; my debt to his knowledge, thoroughness, and generosity is incalculable. Most of all, I thank Theodore Hornberger, now of the University of Pennsylvania, who introduced me to Crèvecoeur and other travelers, and Stanley Pargellis, Director of the Newberry Library, for conversations about the eighteenth century, for criticism of the text, and for considerable financial aid. No one of these friends or acquaintances, however, is to be held responsible for any faulty logic, omissions, or errors that may be found in my account of travel lies. In fact, I have sometimes gone contrary to their wishes and must beg their forgiveness.

There are three other groups whose help I am happy to acknowledge. First there are the editors who have granted me permission to reprint portions of certain articles which they have published for me in their periodicals—*American Literature,* the *Newberry Library Bulletin,* the *Princeton University Library Chronicle,* the *North Carolina Historical Review,*

PREFACE TO THE FIRST EDITION

Pennsylvania History. Then there are the staffs of the libraries where I have worked—the Universities of North Carolina, Ohio State, Aix-en-Provence, Grenoble, Paris, and, especially, the Duke University Library, the University of Texas Library, the Bibliothèque Nationale, the Newberry Library, and the University of Tennessee Library. And finally, there are the five sources which, through their financial assistance, have made this book possible—the University of Tennessee, the Duke University Graduate School, the Fulbright Exchange Program, the Newberry Library, and the American Council of Learned Societies.

John C. Hodges, Chairman of the Department of English at the University of Tennessee, has generously arranged for the typing of the manuscript, and Mrs. Irene Davis has done that typing beautifully.

P. G. A.

CONTENTS

ILLUSTRATIONS

I will say in advance this one true thing, to wit,
I am going to tell you lies.

LUCIAN

Wenn einer eine Reise tut, denn kann er was
erzahlen.

OLD PROVERB

Et surtout ne haïssez pas le mensonge; sans lui
vous ne seriez rien.

ETIENNE REY

CHAPTER
I

THE VOYAGE BEGINS:
Travelers
and Travel Liars

"He who will tell a lie from idle vanity will not scruple
telling a greater from interest." [1]

THE DUBLIN EDITION of *Gulliver's Travels* begins with "A
Letter from Captain Gulliver to His Cousin Sympson," the first
sentence of which speaks of another cousin named Dampier. If
the fictitious recipient of this letter was inspired by one William
Symson, as many people believe, then in a sentence Jonathan
Swift was knowingly or unknowingly introducing posterity to
the three kinds of travel books of the eighteenth century. William Dampier's *A New Voyage round the World* (1691) is one
of the most admired of true travel accounts. The story of Gulliver is itself the great English example of the imaginary, or
extraordinary, voyage. And William Symson's *A New Voyage to
the East Indies* (1715) [2] is a suitable representative of the third
group, one that is now known to have been larger and more
important than Swift's contemporaries would have suspected.
This group can be called the travel lies, a name that the eighteenth century would have liked.

A travel lie may be defined as a tale told by a traveler or
pseudo traveler with intent to deceive. But that is much too

simple. In the first place, just as all classicists were not utterly devoid of romanticism—Pope, for example, placing exotic grottoes in his gardens at Twickenham—those men who told untruths about their journeys, the journeys of others, or no journeys at all, did not usually avoid reality. In fact, as we shall see, they knew the importance of the dictum, "Be careful to mix some truth with your lies." [3] In the second place, the authors of travel deceptions are to be separated as completely as possible from the writers of imaginary voyages, a type of literature almost as popular in the eighteenth century as were the authentic travel accounts. Perhaps the separation can be made clearer by an image.

Let us place the hundreds of true travel books, like the journals of the circumnavigators Bougainville and Captain Cook, the account of the European tour of the English farmer Arthur Young, and the *Travels* of New England's Timothy Dwight, in the conservative center of our image. To the right range the imaginary voyages—realistic, philosophical, satirical, utopian, in short, all those fictitious tales that deceive almost no one. Close to the center on this right side we would place *Robinson Crusoe,* but with some hesitation, since Defoe succeeded so well in his attempts at verisimilitude that some readers were at first deceived. Beyond these imagined books that are so like the true accounts would belong the Rasselases, the Gullivers, and the Candides, fictional travelers who went to unbelievable lands and had amazing adventures but whose stories are placed in a realistic framework. Far out to the right are discovered the peregrinations of the mendacious Baron Munchausen, the subterranean and submarine voyage, such as that of Peter Wilkins, and the trip to the moon or the sun, like that in Defoe's *Consolidator.* To complete the collection on this right-hand side of the image, one should add all those many eighteenth-century novels that include fictional travels, such as *Tom Jones* or *Humphrey Clinker,* and the many varieties of the picaresque, such as *Gil Blas.*

Now for the radical left of center. Here, arranged in order, are the deceivers, beginning with the authors of travel books that tell few or insignificant lies and extending to those that tell many or very influential ones. On the near left, closest to center, we meet with some important, even indispensable, travelers, such as Chateaubriand and Jonathan Carver. One made people believe that he had visited in the southern part of what is now the United States; the other supplied vocabularies of Indians he never saw, gave habits of animals he never knew, and perhaps described places he had never been. But neither of the two men can be spared from any collection of voyages, Chateaubriand because of his importance in belles-lettres, Carver because numerous other travelers depended on him, and both because they have provided so many scholars with puzzles to solve. On the extreme left of our picture, we discover the anarchists, whose books almost completely destroy truth, like the adventurer Benyowski and the novelist Defoe. Benyowski invented love affairs, arranged all incidents to make a hero of himself, and altered times and places, even changing the year of his birth in order to claim that he had fought in a war which came too early for his actual career. Daniel Defoe, by reading the accounts of real travelers, remained comfortably in his London room and hoaxed the public, only briefly with *A New Voyage round the World,* and almost enduringly with the story of Captain Singleton, which over a century later was supplying a historian with descriptions of the Nile Basin. These writers of the left did not fool everyone, but they were accepted in their day more than the ancients believed in Pliny or the Middle Ages in the fictitious Sir John Mandeville.

At least two questions could be asked concerning this pictorial arrangement. First, what is the difference between books on the extreme left like Defoe's *A New Voyage round the World* and books on the extreme right like *Baron Munchausen's Narrative of his Marvelous Adventures?* While the Library of Congress system does not find a need for distinguishing between Defoe's book and Raspe's, listing them both under "Voyages, Imaginary," a distinction should be made. From the point of view of the authors, both books are fictional, imaginary; but from the point of view of the readers, one was real and the other was not.

The contents, even the title, of the famous Munchausen attempted to fool no one, while Defoe's *New Voyage* not only was intended to deceive but was for a while accepted as the report of an authentic trip to the southern oceans and lands. The real problem here is to decide how long or how widely these false accounts should be accepted as true before they are placed among the travel lies. Some, as we shall see, were exposed quickly, some fooled the public for several decades, others were considered authentic for fifty, one hundred, even two hundred years before a particularly inquisitive scholar inquired more closely into the facts.

The second question is more difficult: What shall we do with travel accounts that contain errors and report legends, that give false impressions through ignorance or bad judgment on the part of the traveler? It is a more difficult question because it leads to complications and disagreements. For example, there has always been the problem of what constitutes a lie. One authority, the medieval Church, distinguished between the wilful sin, or lie direct, and the intellectual error, or mistake due to ignorance; and since the general acceptance of utilitarian ethics, modern practice, one writer complains, "is strangely lenient whenever 'ignorance' can be pleaded—as if ignorance was not often wilful, or reckless indifference to truth." The eighteenth century, however, was sometimes more plain-spoken and less lenient. One famous traveler of the day, James Boswell, has reported of his equally famous fellow traveler, "Johnson had accustomed himself to use the word *lie,* to express a mistake or an errour in relation . . . though the relater did not mean to deceive." If Dr. Johnson did use the word in such a fashion, he has not been alone. In the same century one finds De Pauw, author of copious histories, speaking of writers who lie out of stupidity. And a recent scholar, apparently agreeing with Johnson and De Pauw, includes lies of ignorance as one of five types.[4] Such a meaning for the word is, nevertheless, not generally acceptable, even though it comes from a lexicographer and has such fine backing, and we shall not apply the word so broadly to our travelers.

But obviously one cannot always be sure whether a lie is the result of ignorance or intention. Fontenelle once told his marquise that the good philosopher must have a curious mind and bad eyes,[5] characteristics that belong to many travelers. But bad eyes can be organic or they can be blurred by their owner's mind or heart. Furthermore, if Pascal was correct in believing that *"Le coeur a ses raisons que la raison ne connait point,"* those travelers who reported falsely as the result of careful planning should perhaps be separated from their brothers who were guilty of following their hearts, that is, their emotions and prejudices. Such a separation is hard to make since it is often impossible to tell how much heart and how much reason, even how much physical blindness, entered into a traveler's false report. And so, in general, if the evidence points to any kind of a motive behind the error, let us call the error a lie and the reporter a travel liar. However, such a distinction need not rule out the fact that while many untruths are mortal sins others may be simply venial.

Perhaps we can agree to call the venial lies "white lies," an expression that seems to have orginated in the eighteenth century. In the *Gentleman's Magazine* of 1741, there appeared this note by the editor: "A certain Lady of the highest Quality . . . makes a judicious Distinction between a white Lie and a black Lie. A white Lie is that which is not intended to injure any Body in his Fortune, Interest, or Reputation but only to gratify a garrulous Disposition and the Itch of amusing People by telling them wonderful stories." [6] This lenient attitude on the part of the editor and his "Lady of highest Quality" was not however, to be generally accepted, even in the eighteenth century. For example, Paley's *Moral Philosophy* of 1785 complained [7] that "white lies always introduce others of a darker complexion." And while later times have retained the expression, they have reshaped the definition offered by the *Gentleman's Magazine*. But whether the present study is concerned with travelers infected by a harmless garrulity, or those infested with the itch to tell wonderful stories, or those inflicted with the desire to report lies "of a darker complexion," its author hopes to show how important some of them have been in history.

The eighteenth century, the beginning of which social and literary historians often place at about 1660, is the best period to use for a study of untruthful travelers, their reasons for lying, and their influence, even though voyagers have invented lies as far back as those writers satirized by Lucian in the *True History* and as recently as those who, like Richard Halliburton, have flourished on the modern reader's love of fabulous adventures. For the eighteenth century sent out thousands of travelers on whom it depended heavily for information as well as for pleasure. In fact, in the history of ideas no other period seems to have felt so much the influence of these unofficial reporters. There are many reasons why this is true.

In the first place, the oceans of the earth became better highways for travelers. Although the great era of geographical discovery had been the late Renaissance, the eighteenth century produced many important findings in all parts of the Pacific Ocean, in spite of the fact that it was a period more specifically devoted to the exploration, settlement, and scientific study of new lands. After Portugal, Spain, and Holland, lured by the gleam of gold, had paved the way by finding new continents and planting colonies in them, France under Louis XIV and Louis XV and England under Charles II, William of Orange, and the Georges assumed a lead, not to be relinquished, in making discoveries and settling great territories while following another kind of gleam, the power of empires that would bring not only wealth in trade but strength in arms. Between 1660 and 1800 those two nations were at war with each other almost as much as they were at peace, and when not shooting they indulged their antipathies and their competitive spirits in cold wars of territorial acquisitions in the Pacific Ocean and the Western Hemisphere and in scientific expeditions to the Arctic region, the Austral waters, and the land of the great Pyramids. During that time, Russia, with its voyages to the North Pacific, was the only nation to provide competition for the two leaders. All these mariners and explorers of the eighteenth century were far wanderers. In earlier periods ships had sailed dangerously by

inaccurate calculations and guesswork; but after the perfection
of the sextant in the time of Hadley, the improvement of the
marine chronometer with Harrison, and the great strides taken
in cartography by such giants as Coronelli, Guillaume Delisle,
and Herman Moll, pilots could determine their longitude as
well as their latitude and locate themselves on maps that were
more and more trustworthy. And so the century produced
dozens of Dampiers and Ansons, of Berings and Bougainvilles,
of Cooks and Laperousses, who unveiled the oceans of the world
to the eyes of Europe.

While the ocean was becoming a better highway, the interiors
of unknown continents were being opened up. Peter the Great
not only went west to observe the culture of France and England; he sent ambassadors and explorers east through Siberia
to China and Kamchatka. When the Franco-Spanish rivalry in
North America slowed down, the French and English began
their scramble for the Mississippi Valley and the Great Lakes
country; and after its successful Rebellion, the newly created
United States sent its colonists and its trappers south to the
Gulf of Mexico and west along the Ohio Valley and toward
the Rockies, preparing the way for its Lewises, its Clarks, and
its Pikes, who were quickly to follow. By the end of the century, only the interiors of Africa and Australia remained unexplored and dark; and in the larger of these two continents,
Egypt and much of the southern extremity had been seen and
described by curious Europeans. No group of travelers was more
important in opening up these lands than were the Jesuit
missionaries. In the time of the young Louis XIV and his farsighted minister Colbert, these daring pioneers had gone out to
convert and educate the pagans of China, Egypt, and Canada.
But by the end of the Sun King's reign they had made only a
small start. It was the eighteenth century that sent forth the
Jesuits in such great numbers and that received the full force
of their influence in religion, politics, and science; for not until
then were most of the hundreds of journals and letters they
wrote given to the public in great collections or in individual
publications.

In the period we are studying, the more adventurous travelers were the missionaries, the circumnavigators, the fighters, and the scientists who made great and exhausting journeys by ship and horse, by canoe and camel. But there were also less venturesome travelers, both men and women, who went to the civilized nations of Europe or the seaboard areas of North America and spent their time in cities, visiting the symbols of progress and conversing with cultured people in clubs and salons. These were the Addisons and Montesquieus, the Lady Montagus and Madame de Staëls. The eighteenth was the century of the Grand Tour, such as the very extensive one taken by Lord Chesterfield's natural son; and if a man did not have the means to complete his early education with a visit to neighboring nations accompanied by a tutor, he very possibly visited them in middle age. Perhaps he went for pleasure, like young Boswell or Sophie von la Roche. Perhaps he went as a political refugee, like François Misson, or as an invalid, like Laurence Sterne. Perhaps he was an intellectual seeking for knowledge of men and institutions, like Montesquieu and Locke; a student seeking a course of study, like Henry Fielding; a minister seeking a congregation, like Pastor Wendeborn; or a ruler seeking ideas that would improve his nation, like Peter, czar of all the Russias. Perhaps he was looking for new fields to conquer, whether in the offices of finance with John Law, in the boudoir with Giacomo Casanova, in the music hall with George Frederick Handel, in bloody battles with Alexander de Bonneval, or in theological battles with Karl Friedrich Bahrdt. Perhaps he was a diplomat carrying out an assignment, like Edward Wortley Montagu. Or he may have traveled simply to gather observations for a journal, as did Béat de Muralt and Tobias Smollett. But whatever their reason for going, these men and women almost invariably found it profitable to report their journeys.

And so the eighteenth century was a time in which people and ideas moved about. In this age of geographical exploration and intellectual activity, men wrote their travel accounts to satisfy the scientific curiosity of a century of reason or to satisfy the idle curiosity and the escapism found in all centuries; and other men, profiting from the interest in traveling, contrived fictional voyages that likewise appealed to the intellect and the imagination. It was the age of gold for travelers, both real and imaginary. And, as a result, it was the age of opportunity for travel lies.

A great many eighteenth-century wanderers took advantage of their opportunity and stretched or sliced or varnished the truth. In fact, for even the most conscientiously correct of them, a certain amount of editorializing was deemed desirable. Three examples will help to show what standards the century set up for those who reported their journeys. One is taken from the highly respected historian-traveler François Charlevoix, the first page of whose *Histoire et description générale de la Nouvelle France* of 1774 presents the theory that while a writer must sift the false sources from the true, he is permitted to write two kinds of history; a serious, dignified, factual kind when dealing with the ancient nations and civilizations; and a lighter, more entertaining kind—such as that presented by Charlevoix himself—when treating the new and unsettled countries. Another statement, found in the preface to Henry Fielding's *Journal of a Voyage to Lisbon,* offers the opinion that "some few embellishments must be allowed to every historian," and "it is sufficient that every fact should have its foundations in truth." He further believed that "to make a traveller an agreeable companion to a man of sense, it is necessary, not only that he should have seen much, but that he should have overlooked much of what he hath seen." These two writers would not condone gross tampering with the truth, but both the historian and the man of literature would permit certain colorings, omissions, editorializings. The third opinion, given by Rudolph Erich Raspe, one who traveled more by imagination than by some costlier means of locomotion, states that "a traveller has a right to relate and embellish his adventures as he pleases, and it is very impolite to refuse that deference and applause they deserve." The author of this opinion is not so well known as his creation Baron Munchausen, from whose mouth the quotation is taken,[8] and who was invented primarily for the purpose of ridiculing real travelers and their tall tales.

While a certain amount of editorializing was condoned, some travelers colored their reports and mishandled the truth more than Fielding or Charlevoix would have liked. There were various reasons for doing so. Fielding believed that "vanity of knowing more than other men" is the chief cause of lying, an opinion that Dr. Johnson had offered one year earlier in *The Adventurer*. In the twentieth century, Geoffroy Atkinson, who has written two books on travelers before 1720, says substantially the same thing: "Those who make long trips owe it to their self-esteem to insist on the beauty of far away places." [9] Someone has written a creed for liars which recognizes the importance that vanity assumes in their character; it is a creed that would have been appropriate for a number of eighteenth-century travelers: "The great attraction of the lie is that it is something personal. It belongs to you, it is your work . . . When you lie you intervene in the order of things, you change them, you dispose them as it seems good to you . . . You are a poet, you are a god . . . One is the master of the lie, one is the slave of the truth." [10]

In spite of its importance, vanity was not the only motive for travel lies in the eighteenth century. At least two other causes stand out. After vanity, perhaps cupidity was the most influential; for travelers desired to find publishers who would pay them handsomely, and both publisher and writer often seemed to honor the ancient opinion that there is nothing more stupid than a straight line, nothing more uninteresting than the truth. A third motive for the lies of travelers was their prejudice, whether political, religious, personal, national, or philosophical. One eighteenth-century traveler, Brissot de Warville, who kept his head better as a writer than as a revolutionist, laid down a set of rules to be observed by those who hoped to publish reports of their journeys.[11] He particularly warned against vanity and prejudice, which are closely related and both of

which he himself had in some quantity, but he failed to recognize the influence of money.

So the authors of travel lies filled their pockets, pleased
the public, and satisfied their own biases and vanity. They
invented facts about the savages of America and the South
Seas. They found evil in their nations' enemies and good in
their allies. Some travelers were violent Anglophobes, like the
German Andreas Riem, or gushing Anglophiles, like his coun-
try-woman Sophie von la Roche. If they were Jesuit missionaries,
they could exaggerate their successes among the pagans; if they
were Récollets, they might give the lie to the Jesuits; and if
they were deists or revolutionists, they were liable to find
princes in Madagascar or Indian chiefs in the wilds of Canada
who could present all the contemporaneous theories of rational
religion or arguments for anarchy. Voyagers sometimes reported
falsely about people—their characters, their ages, their sizes.
If one of them vilified a Delaware flirt, another could be found
to "give him the Lye and follow his Lye with a stab." [12] If one
inspected New England graveyards and reported that Americans
died at remarkably early ages, another visited the same graveyards and found that Americans lived much longer than Europeans. If one claimed that in Argentina he saw a race of men six
feet tall, another might give the same men nine feet. There were
travelers who invented or changed geography, and animals, and
plants. One fabricated a tale of a fabulous river—not the
Missouri—that connected the Rockies with the Mississippi; another told of a serpent in Egypt that when cut into a dozen parts
could rejoin those parts and glide away; and still another
advertised a Louisiana plant, the juice of which, somewhat like
Louisiana liquids of later times, made Indians live over a hundred years.

But that is not all. Some travelers invented stories about
other travelers. They even made false statements about their
own books or about themselves. They naïvely or knowingly repeated legends as facts. They pretended to have visited places
they never saw. It was an age of plagiarism, and travel liars ap-

propriated material from other travelers and, ironically, from other travel liars. It was a century of great freedom in translating and editing; and publishers, translators, and editors often made travel lies out of reports that were originally truthful. In fact, some writers, like Tobias Smollett, edited themselves into the category of travel liars. It was the day of the "honored adventurer," as Goldoni called him, and adventurers like the German Bahrdt, the Frenchman Bonneval, the Hungarian Benyowski, the Spaniard Torres y Villaroel, and the Italian Casanova left memoirs and journals and letters that force us to call their authors untruthful. But no one of them, perhaps, could live a better lie than that most intriguing of adventurers, Guiseppe Balsamo—the "Divine Cagliostro," as Houdon entitled the bust —who convinced the people of Paris that he was immortal and that he had known Jesus Christ personally.

The esteem which travelers like Cagliostro might receive in their own lifetime was often only part of their total compensation, since the public of later times was also prone to honor them with attention. We have always been quite ready to forgive a liar his sins if he entertains us and if his inventions do not hurt us personally—our pocketbooks, our pride, or our own prejudices. The general opinion is perhaps that expressed by a noted student of travel literature who said of Captain John Smith, that traveler of another century, "He may have been, as it was once the fashion to proclaim, an inordinate liar, but whatever the historians say, the certain fact is that what he wrote was read in his own day and has ever since been read by thousands." [13] One classic story of the rewards in popularity that accrued to an eighteenth-century travel liar is of the Hungarian Benyowski, who filled a travel book with inventions of all sorts and thereby made himself so famous that after his death he became the subject of an opera, a long poem, a novel, and a play by the well-known dramatist Kotzebue.

In spite of the rewards they were offered in money, notoriety, or immortality, by no means did all travelers of the eighteenth century falsify what they saw. Nevertheless, in their day and until the end of the century, as a group they were frequently accused of doing so. In France, Diderot's very influential encyclopedia cited Strabo, as an authority whose judgment was still correct, that voyagers almost always embellished what they saw and what they read, that "every man who describes his travels is a liar." A judge not so respected as the noted encyclopedist was Corneille De Pauw, a disciple of Buffon, a prodigious reader, user, and misuser of travel books, who concluded that all Europeans writing from China were liars and all travel books, whether ancient or modern, had both errors and falsehoods. The same writer expressed the opinion that "some travelers have told fables, others have travestied the truth through imbecility, or have violated it out of malice, and still others, overcome by the vertigo of their enthusiasm, have seen things so badly, that out of respect for reason they should have abstained from describing them." These adverse opinions on the veracity of voyagers were, of course, countered by positive ones, especially in England. Early in the period we are studying, John Locke urged all gentlemen to study history, geography, and travel books; and Sir William Temple, the patron-teacher of Jonathan Swift, believed that by reading travelers one would conclude that "the fundamental moral beliefs . . . are shared by all men." At the end of the eighteenth century, the English historian John Adams advised young people to read travel literature because in reading it "one is struck by the differences between the customs of his own country and those of other nations. Then penetrated by that difference, one seeks the reason for it, and there for him is the beginning of political, commercial, and moral combination." [14] And so the two traditions existed side by side, one a continuation of the ancient unfavorable opinion of Strabo and Lucian, the other a product of the optimism of an Age of Enlightenment.

It would be interesting to find all the eighteenth-century comments on travel falsehoods and arrange those comments by countries, in order to come to some conclusion as to which nations were most lenient in judging them. Some correlation might be found between a country's leniency of judgment and the number of such falsehoods it produced. But it is much easier to show that those nations which raised most of the travelers harvested most of the deceivers. As England and France of the eighteenth century were rivals for world leadership in the arts and the sciences, and as they fought each other to build the mightiest world empire, so they vied in the production of travel literature and travel lies. One Frenchman has recently contended that "south of the Loire River, lying is a form of Sociability." He believes that "the sun causes lying to flourish. The races of the South have always passed for being the greatest liars. Those of the North love only the truth . . . They know neither the light nor the joy of living." [15] Thomas Carlyle, who, since he came from one of those sunless, northern races, may be considered a Victorian judge of the art of falsifying, would perhaps have agreed that southerners are most adept at that art—at least, he proposed the title "Prince of Liars" for the Italian Cagliostro, a traveler of the eighteenth century. Nevertheless, in the period we are dealing with, Carlyle's own England had its share of untruthful travelers, and some of the falsehoods they told were as important historically as any of those recounted by their southern friends—or rivals.

The first step in studying travel lies is to ferret them out and determine their extent. In such a pursuit the detective is offered many clues and much direct help from the detectives who have preceded him, from the newspapers and journals of the time, and, more particularly, from the voyage literature itself. One of the most amusing stories that involve exposing frauds, both by book and by journal, is that concerning Hispanophobe Jean-Marie-Jérome Fleuriot. In 1784, at Saint-Malo, he published anonymously and in one volume *Le Voyage de Figaro en Espagne*. Sarcastic and spiteful, frank and romantic at the same time, this travel book was immediately answered by an anonymous Hispanophile who called himself "Le Véritable Figaro" and his book *Dénonciation au public du Voyage d'un soi-disant Figaro en Espagne*. In it the "true Figaro," following exactly the table of matters employed by Fleuriot, quoted from and denounced every part of the original. Undaunted, Fleuriot republished his book the next year, nobody knows where, this time in two volumes and under a new title, simply *Voyage en Espagne,* and on the title page called himself "le Marquis de Langle." But the ambitious and aggressive author could not escape his persecutor. On November 14, a matter of weeks later, the *Journal de Paris* contained a letter by the same "véritable Figaro" that exposed the second, revised edition. The nature of Fleuriot's book can be judged in part by its title in English translation, *A Sentimental Journey through Spain,* and by the fact that in France it was burned by the public hangman, thus increasing its popularity and forcing it into a number of printings.

The best clues, then, can be found by comparing the various accounts of one particular trip or of different trips to the same place—in short, by setting one traveler against another. In spite of the claim that "if one liar confronts another liar, it is no longer a game, it is the height of disloyalty," [16] there were those treacherous travelers who broke faith with the fraternity. As a group, the voyagers wrote prefaces or dedications setting forth their intentions. Usually they defended the purity of their own books; just as often they damned their fellow travelers. Sometimes their charges turn out to be true, but the more a writer pointed an accusing finger at someone else, the more a reader is inclined to suspect that the man was protesting too much and should himself be investigated. Examples are numerous. Jean Carré, who went to the East Indies, announced with pride that he would avoid the false fables and legends that filled up the voyage literature of his day, and then he himself told sentimental and amorous tales of Amazons in mountain castles and harems who had to be put to death in the middle of deserts. One French work on America contains a dedication to a great lord who, we are told, praised the authenticity of the report; and then in that report we read how in Virginia one often sees twin children, one white and one black, born of women who in the same night were caressed by men of different colors.[17]

But simply to convict travelers of untruths is not the object of this book. Such a practice would produce a distorted image, since we must continually remind ourselves that there were hundreds of honest, conscientious voyagers in the eighteenth century whose reports deserved the high praise which we have seen was accorded them by John Locke, Sir William Temple, and John Adams. Our object is rather to study the travel fabrications of the period and from them derive certain laws and learn certain facts that will make us better readers of voyage literature. For one possible benefit, a knowledge of the methods and motives of the fabricators may make us more perceptive, more careful, in using all travel accounts and may lead more quickly to the exposure of any of them that still need to be exposed. There are, it is hoped, benefits of another kind.

Much has been done by social historians in evaluating the importance of the traveler, especially since 1913 when Gilbert Chinard complained that the time had not yet come to determine the influence that the discovery of the physical universe had exercised on the thought of the seventeenth and eighteenth centuries.[18] But much more needs to be done in estimating that influence, and the present work aspires to make its contribution by trying to ascertain the effects of the many travel deceptions of the period. The result of the deception and the reason for it were often related, particularly in the realm of hopes, such as those concerning the Northwest Passage, or ideas, such as those concerning the character of the Noble Savage; for a traveler could distort appearances to make them conform with a set of notions derived from previous travelers and theorists, and then his report would become part of a myth, self-fed but not self-consumed. When this close relationship prevails, one finds it impossible to discuss the falsehood, or the falsifier, alone. We must go before the man and his story and we must follow after him and his book when he returns.

In such a study various approaches seem obvious. One of the most important leads to the influence of travel lies on geography. Explorers of the eighteenth century were especially useful in bringing back information that would aid in the mapping and analyzing of relatively unknown areas of the world, and, as a result, such voyagers had a grand opportunity to leave their impressions on history by moving bodies of water, exaggerating distances or heights, even inventing topography or nations of people. Another approach takes us to that growing company of men who pretended to go somewhere or who altered the accounts of actual travelers. These are the fireside travelers, like Daniel Defoe and the anonymous inventor of the voyage of Admiral de Fonte. One of the distinctive features of eighteenth-century literature of all sorts was the quite liberal attitude to the borrowing of other writers' works. Travel writers were the most "liberal" of them all, even the honored ones, like Careri and Commodore Byron, culling their predecessors for facts to use in making an account more nearly complete. Because the prevalence of this practice has always been recognized, the present work will restrict its treatment of the subject to a discussion of a type of plagiarism that seems to have been peculiar to travelers, a type that made some of them liars twice over, and a type that has turned out to be astoundingly effective. Still another approach is to consider the group of travelers who did not tell their stories immediately after returning but waited until old age had starved their memories or fed their imaginations. Other sections of the study concern the prejudices that often made voyage literature untrustworthy and the controversies that aroused antagonisms and thereby produced distortions of the truth. For an entirely different approach, one must also consider the fact that some travelers were unjustly condemned because many others, less honest than they, had conditioned the public to doubt any marvelous story of a far country. Finally, after studying a great number of particularly representative, broadly influential, or lasting falsehoods found in the great body of eighteenth-century voyage literature, one will not only understand why and how they were produced and thereby be better prepared to recognize the true travels but one will see how important the lies themselves have been.

And they have been important, so important that one of them caused the newspapers of the world to use up a small river of ink in reporting a race of nine-foot giants in Patagonia; so important that another of them could persuade the Academy of

Sciences in Paris to spend hours discussing a spurious Northwest
Passage; so important that historians quoted them, cartographers
changed maps to conform to them, wits like Voltaire used them,
readers were entertained by them, and philosophers like Buffon
depended on them. These lies mingled with the truth to form
the eighteenth century's picture of the world. But before classifying them, it would be well to take one falsehood that was particularly important, trace its origin, determine its immediate
cause, and find its effect; for many such fabrications have histories so long and involved that a single volume cannot do full
justice to all of them. This one lie, therefore, can serve as an
example.

CHAPTER

II

THE PATAGONIAN GIANTS
or
The Drama of the Dolphin

"Nobody was more lied of." [1]

IN 1766 THE FIRST VOLUME of another of the many eighteenth-century collections of voyages appeared. In it the editor, John Callander, after gathering the journals of the more famous European seamen, made this comment about the Spaniard Sarmiento's tales of a race of gigantic men in southern Argentina: "It will appear, that these stories give the first ground to the fabulous report of these savages being giants in stature, though none of the subsequent navigators think them taller than other men." [2] The concluding words of this statement were not at all correct, for other navigators before and after Sarmiento had reported giants in Patagonia. Moreover, as Callander sat at his desk phrasing the sentence, a little sailing vessel named the *Dolphin* was hurrying toward an anchorage in the Downs, carrying men who were dramatically to disprove the statement and force its author to publish a retraction.

The commander of the *Dolphin* was Commodore, later Admiral, John Byron, "Foul-Weather Jack," who fifty years later, as that "certain relative of mine," was to be immortalized by his famous poet grandson. But for a decade after he returned from circumnavigating the globe, Admiral Byron's name was

perhaps as famous as was to be the poet's later, not so much for
having commanded men who went around the world, although
that brought honor enough, but for having commanded men
who, in books and newspapers and by word of mouth, announced to all the world that there was a race of nine-foot giants
in Patagonia. There were skeptics who argued and scoffers who
laughed, but within a matter of months most of the dissenting
voices were stifled—some even recanted—and the people of
Europe and America believed in the giants, from the man in
the street, who accepted his newspaper's report without a pro-
test, to the best-known scientists and philosophers, who were—
some quickly, some hesitatingly—won over by a mass of evidence.

Why, in an Age of Reason, was the world still so ready to
accept stories like these? In order to answer the question, we
must start by trying to understand that although they were the
only eyewitnesses to have done so in many decades, Byron's men
were not the first to tell such tall tales of tall Patagonians.
While until this time the people of the eighteenth century had
doubted the existence of a tribe of southern giants or had left
the question open, they had read many testimonies of travelers
from older times who had seen the fabulous race. Philosophers
and scientists had sometimes referred to these reports, and historians had occasionally reviewed their evidence; but after the
return of the *Dolphin,* Magellan, Drake, Sarmiento, and many
other mariners, from the well-known Dutch navigators of about
1600 to some unknowns of the early eighteenth century, were
restored to life that they might corroborate the English account
of 1766. They were quoted and misquoted and handled in very
unscholarly ways; but, especially in the first months of enthusiasm, few people worried about scholarship, and everyone believed the witnesses who claimed to have seen the giants, preferring to think that those travelers who reported seeing none
had not been to exactly the right place or had not met the
right Patagonians. In good eighteenth-century fashion, let us
review the evidence too, in order to understand why people of

Admiral Byron's day were so ready to accept the nation of giants as a fact.

John Callander had been wrong in saying that navigators subsequent to Sarmiento had disproved the legend. He was also wrong in believing that the Spaniard had started it. As most historians have known for a good four centuries, that honor must be given to Antonio Pigafetta, an Italian who sailed around the world on the *Vittoria,* one of Magellan's ships. At least half a dozen early sixteenth-century versions of this first circumnavigation of the globe are known, four of them apparently by men who made the voyage, but none by Magellan himself. Of the four eyewitness accounts, Pigafetta's journal is the fullest and the longest. This journal tells us [3] that at 49½° South Latitude, while the fleet was spending the winter of 1520 at Port Saint Julian, "One day we suddenly saw a naked man of giant stature on the shore of the port, dancing, singing, and throwing dust on his head." When the crew landed, this colossus was led before Magellan. "He was so tall," Pigafetta wrote, "that we reached only to his waist, and he was well proportioned." The man was friendly and was given presents. Then other natives came bringing their wives, who, Pigafetta said, "were not so tall as the men but are very much fatter . . . Their breasts are one-half *braza* long." [4] Two weeks later four "giants" appeared, two of which were captured only to escape by running; for, the journal says, "of a truth these giants run swifter than horses and are exceedingly jealous of their wives." This last bit of information was added to explain what, to Pigafetta, seemed an uncalled-for, angry refusal of one captured Patagonian to let the ship's pilot sleep with his wife. The journal supplied many facts about these very tall South Americans, their habits, their clothes, their weapons, their nomadic life, their language, and even their religion. Magellan gave them the name "Patagons" apparently because of their big feet, or at least because their feet looked big encased in the animal hides which the savages used for shoes. Their appearance and their god Setebos, as described by Pigafetta, were, in part, the inspiration for Caliban and Setebos in *The Tempest*. In studying Pigafetta's record, so much referred to by the eighteenth century, nowhere are we told that he or any of Magellan's men actually measured the Patagonians, although one of the natives was reported to be so tall that the Europeans reached only to his waist. Continually, the narrator referred to them as "giants."

When we look into the other eyewitness accounts of the same voyage,[5] most of which were never mentioned during the revival of interest at the time of Admiral Byron, we discover a lack of agreement about the "giants" reported in Pigafetta's much more popular journal. Three of the reports agree with Pigafetta's that the savages of Port Saint Julian were fast runners and had good physiques; but only one says that the men were tall, and that one disagrees about the size of the women.

We have little opportunity to check the credibility of any of the journals but Pigafetta's, which is of some length. He, we discover, was superstitious and addicted to the marvelous, delighting to record wonders and exaggerations. His sixteenth-century eyes turned St. Elmo's fire into a holy phenomenon, observed curious sea birds that laid eggs on one another's backs, and at the Rio de la Plata saw "giant" cannibals with bull-like voices who took prodigious steps. In Brazil he met people who lived to be one hundred and forty years old; off Argentina three saints appeared to quell a storm; and at Port Saint Julian the Patagonians, instead of using purgatives, rammed arrows half-way down their throats. All of these marvels make us wonder about the accuracy of Pigafetta's claim concerning a race of giants in Argentina; and the doubt is increased when we learn from the same journal that Magellan, desiring to give a present to the largest, most terrible of all the natives, chose to give him the shirt and breeches worn by an ordinary European seaman!

The second mariner to have seen the gigantic Patagonians, according to many eighteenth-century writers, was Sir Francis Drake,[6] whose famous voyage around the world brought him to Port Saint Julian in 1578. His nephew, exactly fifty years later, published the first account of the circumnavigation, taking his material from several sources, depending for the first part of the voyage upon a manuscript left by Francis Fletcher, chaplain on board Drake's own ship, the *Pelican*. Concerning the size of the Patagonians, the nephew reported:

> Magellane was not altogether deceived in naming them Giants, for they generally differ from the common sort of men, both in stature, bigness, and strength of body, as also in the hideousness of their voice . . . but yet they are nothing so monstrous or giantlike as they were reported, there being some English men as tall as the highest of any that we could see; peradventure the Spaniards did not think that ever any English man would come thither to reprove them, and thereupon might presume the more boldly to lie; the name *Pentagones*, Five Cubits, viz., 7 foote and a half, describing the full height (if not somewhat more) of the highest of them.

On comparing this version made by Drake's nephew with that of Fletcher, the eyewitness, we discover that the published account was much different from the source. Nowhere did Fletcher refer to Magellan, give the incorrect history of the word *Patagon* as meaning five cubits, or announce any exact height for the natives, although he did continually refer to them as "giants."

Within a matter of weeks after Drake passed through the Strait of Magellan, Pedro Sarmiento de Gamboa navigated it coming from the other direction.[7] His mission was twofold—to intercept the English ships and to chart the Strait. He was too late to succeed in the first assignment, but while carrying out the second, he several times encountered many natives of southern Argentina. His description of these Indians, as it was used by eighteenth-century writers, has made him famous as one of the chief witnesses in the growth of the legend. Like Pigafetta and Fletcher before him, Sarmiento did not report measuring any Patagonians. He did call them "giants," however, and managed to capture one of them whose "limbs were very large" and take him back to Spain as a present for Philip II.[8] On the whole, Sarmiento seems much more credible than Pigafetta, the most marvelous incident he recounted being that of a Patagonian's ramming an arrow down his throat even deeper than in the Italian's earlier story. It must be remembered that this Spanish journal had not itself been published before Byron's time, although it was famous in a version that, as we shall see, was much mangled.

One of the most popular of the preservers of the legend was Anthonie Knivet, a seaman with Sir Thomas Cavendish on that mariner's 1591 visit to the South Atlantic. Knivet spent twelve years among the Indians of South America after being one of fifty Englishmen captured by the Portuguese in Brazil. On returning to England, he published a book of travels, "in comparison to which," one modern editor says,[9] "the adventures of Baron Munchausen are as everyday occurrences." And they almost are. At Port Famine, in Argentina, after a cold southern night, this traveler wrote,[10] "The next morning I was [so] nummed, that I could not stir my legs, and pulling off my stockings, my toes came with them." Further on, while the ship was in the Straits, we are told, "Here one Harris a Goldsmith lost his nose; for going to blow it with his fingers he cast it into the fire." After reading of these wonders, we are not much surprised to hear that at Port Desire in Patagonia Knivet measured two dead bodies which were twelve feet long and that he knew a Patagonian boy, captured at Port Saint Julian, whose height was over nine feet. Knivet's book reported a number of marvels, but when it was quoted out of context and when the quotes were placed beside those from other accounts written before and after him, he was considered not an early Munchausen but another of the many reporters who saw giants in South America. Furthermore, his words were often given dignity by being credited to his commander Cavendish, just as the words of Pigafetta and Fletcher attained more credence by being attributed to Magellan and Drake.

In the early seventeenth century the Dutch were much interested in opening up trade routes and in exploring the southern waters. From 1598 to 1643 a great many of their daring sailors visited South America en route to the Pacific and returned with stories that gave support to the popular opinion that there was a race of Goliaths in Argentina. One Dutch mariner told of warriors ten to twelve feet tall in canoes; another captured a boy who described a race of giants ten to eleven feet high; and a third reported that on the shore of Tierra del Fuego, just south of Patagonia, "a human being of very big stature" made "his appearance several times, sometimes climbing up some eminence or little hill the better to see us." [11] The most publicized Dutch circumnavigation was that of William Schouten and Jacob le Maire. Their two ships sailed through the Strait of le Maire in 1615, but the report of this discovery of a new way from the Atlantic to the Pacific was almost overshadowed by their story that on an island near Tierra del Fuego they landed and "on the highest part of the hilles we found some burying places, which were heapes of stones, and we not knowing what they meant, pulled the stones of [sic] from one of them, and under them found mens bones of 10 and 11 foote long." [12] Many of the earliest editions of this journal contained a picture showing the uncovered grave and a very long skeleton.[13] Looking into the grave, in order to provide the contrast in sizes, is a group of sailors. These eyewitnesses from Holland had much to do with the eighteenth-century readiness to accept new reports of Patagonian giants, even though no one of them claimed to have measured a live giant.

After the time of the Dutch, and until the excitement aroused by Byron's return, no published journal of any visit to the Austral waters tells of someone actually seeing giants or giant footprints or giant bones. Writers of other kinds of books, however, assisted in keeping the legend alive and, what is more, in increasing the size of the Patagonians. Of these writers the most influential were the Spaniard Argensola and the Frenchman Frézier. Even though Argensola had a reputation for being one of the worst of liars, those people of Byron's day who believed in giant Patagonians quoted his seventeenth-century "history" in support of their arguments. Whereas early travelers never reported specific sizes for their "giants," Argensola calmly stated that Magellan's men captured natives who towered twelve feet in the air; that Sarmiento fought with Patagonians more than ten feet high; and, worst of all, that Drake's crew saw "eight giants, by the side of whom the tallest Englishmen seemed quite small." [14]

While Argensola was not usually considered a reliable witness, even though he was popular, Frézier was always referred to as a scholar and a man of integrity. During a visit to Chile and Peru in the second decade of the eighteenth century, he became interested in the stories of the Patagonians reported by sailors and by natives of Peru and, in the 1716 edition of his travels,[15] included all the information he could find on this race of giants. Since he had not seen any of them and had not been in their part of South America, he relied on printed sources, chiefly Argensola, although he thought that some of the heights given in the earlier book were probably a "slight exaggeration." Altogether he summarized seven different published accounts, all of which seemed to support his belief in the existence of a race of ten-footers, and supplied new evidence in the form of oral reports received from the crew of the *Jacques*, a ship from Saint-Malo that was in the southern waters in 1704. Furthermore, he recounted the stories he had read and heard in western South America of the race of giants that had figured so prominently in the myths and legends of Peru, stories which he felt must have some basis in fact because of the Patagonians, who were possible descendants of those ancient men of great stature. Frézier's long defense of the "giant" legend acquired an aura of respectability when, in the middle of the century, it was cited by three of the most famous of Frenchmen—Buffon, Maupertuis, and Debrosses.

The first two of these were philosophers and scientists. Buffon quoted Frézier at great length,[16] noted that the mariners who reported giants disagreed on the height, and expressed doubts that there could be men ten feet tall, since the volume of such a Gulliver would create a food problem; but he concluded that if the tribe of giants did exist they must be few in number because so many visitors to Argentina had not seen them. Maupertuis, even more credulous, accepted Frézier's evidence completely and, in a "Letter on the Progress of the Sciences," advocated an expedition to the land of the Patagonians in order to study their habits and their minds.[17] The third man, a philosopher and historian, had more to do with our legend than either of the others.

Debrosses' collection of *Navigations aux terres australes,* published in 1756, owes its origin to the eighteenth century's concern with the possible existence of a continent in the South Pacific, the legendary "Terre Australis," a concern that led to the real discovery and exploration of Australia. But Debrosses' research among the travelers to the South Seas involved him in the question of the Patagonians. At first skeptical about the giants, he gradually became less hostile as he progressed in his compilation from Pigafetta to Frézier, even making one mistranslation from the journal of John Narbrough which considerably increased the size of the Patagonians and placed that English captain in the ranks of the supporters of the legend.[18] At the end of his edition of voyages, after studying all the accounts, Debrosses was quite open-minded about the whole matter, honoring Frézier's report, summarizing all the evidence for and against the existence of a race of giants, and concluding, like Maupertuis before him, that a study of the Patagonians would help decide the question of the influence of climate on the size of people. His book was translated into several languages and went throughout Europe; he was praised and used by other editors; and he was honored by the King of France and by his peers among writers and thinkers, who would have elected him to the Academy if he had not committed the unpardonable sin of disagreeing with the great Voltaire.

In England there were also writers who popularized the Patagonian giants, but none was so important as were Buffon, Maupertuis, and Debrosses in France. Dalrymple, whose collection of voyages to the South Seas appeared in London three years before Byron sailed, borrowed all of Debrosses' summaries and conclusions; but John Harris was more prominently a disciple of the legend. His two-volume edition of travels was one of the most widely read, appearing first in 1705, again in 1744, and finally in 1764, the year in which Byron left for the South Seas. But Harris' scholarship was poor. Not only did he give

Cavendish and Magellan credit for the stories published by their sailors Knivet and Pigafetta; but, contradicting Callander's less popular claim that later travelers to South America failed to corroborate the early accounts of giants, Harris insisted that those reports were "not falsified by any of our subsequent travellers." [19]

All these scientists, historians, and philosophers, both French and English, were important in preparing the way for a popular acceptance of the tales brought back by the *Dolphin* in 1766, but there were other factors almost as important. Man's love for the marvelous in any form has always been fed by travelers and pseudo travelers, by historians and pseudo historians, and among the marvels reported before Byron's return were many accounts of giants. The Old Testament, the ancient history of Peru, the myths of North American Indians—all of these contained stories of giants. Historians of Seville told of a legendary giant founder of that city. Ulrich Schmidt and Alvar Nuñez, who lived for years in South America in the mid-sixteenth century and who wrote spiteful books against each other, agreed on one fact at least, that in central Brazil there were whole tribes of men with gigantic bodies. Tasman, in his voyage of 1642, had reported evidences of a race of giants at Blackman's Bay, concluding, "There can be no doubt that there must be men here of extraordinary stature." Almost exactly one hundred years before Byron, a Dutchman named Henry Schouten had written of his discovery in the South Pacific of a little utopian island inhabited by twelve-foot men and women. And much closer home, the west Europeans of the eighteenth century believed that all Russians were inhumanly large; for Peter the Great had towered over the men of London as he walked down Regent Street in the days of William and Mary, and Frederick and his predecessors on the throne of Prussia had sent to the land of the czars for most of the men in the famed Riesengarde.

Giants, then, had a strong hold on the popular imagination, and the stage was set for the drama of the *Dolphin*. It made little difference that the properties for that stage were hastily gathered and flimsy of structure; they were colorful. Nor was it a matter for much concern that the plot of the play was of spurious authorship; it was exciting. And so the drama lived on until the color faded and the excitement subsided, until the properties broke and the authors were exposed. But before it departed the scene, it enjoyed a longer run than any contemporaneous play produced by Covent Garden or the Comédie française.

The play opened when the newspapers of London rolled back the curtain. Under the date of May 9, 1766, this notice appeared in the *Gentleman's Magazine:*

> Commodore Biron, in his Majesty's ship *Dolphin,* arrived in the Downs from the East Indies. She has been out upon discoveries and the papers say, has found out a new country in the East, the inhabitants of which are eight feet and a half high.[20]

In the following month the same magazine reported that the men of the *Dolphin*'s crew had received double wages, that the object of the ship's voyage was not determined, and that all journals on board had been delivered up on oath in order that the official account would be the only one published. But the editor had somewhere gained information that made him skeptical about the giants, for he concluded the announcement by saying, "The reports in the papers of men 9 feet high being seen, are all fictitious." [21] And for almost a year the *Gentleman's Magazine* maintained an austere silence in the matter, refusing to mention "Foul-Weather Jack" Byron, the Patagonians, or the flood of newspaper articles that during that time made the *Dolphin*'s drama so popular.

One of the newspapers that became involved, typical of those in England except that it was larger and more influential than most, was the *London Chronicle.* It came on the stage late, not mentioning giants until July 12, two months after the return of the *Dolphin,* when it reported, "We are informed, that the giants found by Commodore Byron, measured from 8 feet and ½ to 10 feet in height, and every way stout in proportion. The men's feet measured 18 inches." The *Chronicle* chided scientists for having so long doubted the existence of a race of giants and quoted a letter written by Dr. Maty, Secretary of the Royal

Society, to M. de la Lande in Paris for transmission to the
Academy of Sciences there. Dr. Maty's letter, in part, said:

> The existence of giants is here confirmed. Between 4 and 500
> Patagonians of at least 8 or 9 feet in height, have been seen and
> examined by the company of one of our ships just returned from
> a voyage round the world; the Captain of which, who is himself 6
> feet high, could hardly reach the chin of one of these men with
> his hand.[22]

About two weeks later the lead article in the *Chronicle*
consisted of a letter from a certain "Y. Z." who had taken from
Dr. Harris' collection of voyages a number of reports concerning races of giants, including five early accounts of the Patagonians, a subject which the paper said had "lately engaged
the attention of the public." [23] The five accounts were claimed
to be those of Magellan, Cavendish, and the Dutch mariners
Van Noort, De Weert, and Spilbergen. Then the editor added
this comment: "It seems highly incredible, that so many great
and famous men who have traveled and written in such distant
periods of time should all conspire to agree in a lie, which could
be of no manner of use to them." But the naïve editor was not
aware that "Y. Z." was not quoting Magellan but the journal of
the superstitious exaggerator Pigafetta, and that the information said to have come from Sir Thomas Cavendish had really
come from Cavendish's man Anthonie Knivet, the Munchausen-
like sailor. Nor were the other three reports any more reliable:
Van Noort had not seen his ten- or eleven-foot men but had
heard of them from a captured Indian boy; Sebald de Weert's
giants had been sitting down in canoes some distance away; and
Joris van Spilbergen's one colossus had been observed even
farther away, running up and down hills. The *Chronicle*, concluding that it was now "impossible to admit of the least degree
of doubt with respect to the truth of it," continued to publicize
the drama of the Patagonians to the extent that during the next
two years it printed over a dozen articles about them, including
news items, book reviews, and letters, all of which tended to
increase the public's faith in the legend.

One of the books reviewed was a small octavo written by

the Abbé Gabriel-François Coyer and entitled *Lettre au Docteur Maty sur les Géants Patagons.*[24] The Abbé was a friend of great people, prominent enough to have been driven from Voltaire's home by a joke, a member of several academies, including the Royal Society, and the author of a number of volumes of humor, philosophy, and travel. His book apparently had two purposes —to publicize the reports of nine-foot men in South America as sent to him by his fellow member of the Royal Society, Dr. Maty, and to satirize European society by presenting an imaginary Utopia, the citizens of which were the giant Patagonians.

The second book reviewed by the *London Chronicle* was called *A Voyage round the World, in his Majesty's ship the Dolphin, commanded by the Hon. Comm. Byron.*[25] Like Coyer's smaller book, it was important enough to draw space in two issues; but, unlike Coyer's book, it was written by an eyewitness, not Byron himself but "an officer aboard the *Dolphin*" who had to remain anonymous because his journal of the circumnavigation had not been given up at the request of the Admiralty. This volume was extremely popular, since for over seven years it was the only published report of the circumnavigation; but its popularity was increased many times because it had a frontispiece showing a Patagonian man and woman holding a huge baby and towering over an English seaman, and because it had a nine-page account of the giants, who were reported to average eight feet in height with "an extreme of nine feet and upwards." The anonymous officer's journal appeared first in French and then immediately in four other languages, the nine pages on the size and habits of the giants occupying the attention of the reviewers while the rest of the book went practically unnoticed.[26]

This book, which so capably backed up the evidence publicized by Dr. Maty's letter and the Abbé Coyer's satirical essay, was enough to entice the *Gentleman's Magazine* to take up its part again after almost a year of silence. In the April issue of 1767, that magazine pronounced the journal of the *Dolphin*'s officer to be genuine and extracted from it for publication every word on the Patagonians. After this energetic reappearance on the stage, the *Gentleman's Magazine* continued to play a prominent role in the English version of the drama, publishing five pieces on the Patagonians in little over a year. Other British monthlies followed its lead, the *London Magazine* and the *Monthly Review*, for example, including some eight articles during the same period of time.

The French version of the *affaire des Patagons* was much like the English, although in France the public was apparently more skeptical and certainly more volatile. The news of the *Dolphin's* return and of its discovery of a race of giants came swiftly to Paris in the letter to M. de la Lande, President of the Academy of Sciences. This letter, written by Dr. Maty, the Secretary of the Royal Society, not only inspired the Abbé Coyer's satirical little book; it was reviewed, quoted, and discussed in the Paris newspapers and journals. One of the first of these to treat the story was *L'Avant-Coureur*. On June 23, 1766, in its section entitled "Histoire Naturelle," it gave excerpts from the letter which, it said, "confirmed" the existence of a race of men "at least" eight or nine feet high and concluded with the corroborating report that Milord H——, visiting in Paris at the time, had seen and talked with Admiral Byron and his crew, all of whom, Milord said, attested to the fact. Other periodicals took up the news, including the dignified, very influential *Journal des Sçavans*, which ran an article on Dr. Maty's letter in the July issue, its first after France received the news of the return of the *Dolphin*.[27]

But there was controversy on this side of the Channel. It began in the *Journal Encyclopédique*, one of the most important publications in France—important enough that within a year of Byron's return it published letters dealing with another controversy and written by Hume, Rousseau, Voltaire, and Walpole. This journal held off until August and then entered the scene only long enough to print a letter from a reputable scientist and academician named M. de La Condamine, who announced, "I have learned today that the story of the discovery of the Patagonian Giants is a hoax and that the English spread this rumor in order to cover up their motive for arming four ships which are being sent to Argentina to exploit a mine that they discovered there."[28]

The *Journal Encyclopédique* continued to play a hostile role, but at the same time giving the Patagonians free advertising by publishing two book reviews, one a very misleading appraisal of the Abbé Coyer's pro-giant satire, the other a favorable report on another satire, *An Account of the Geantz recently discovered, addressed to a friend*,[29] written, we now know, by the witty Horace Walpole. The reviewer of the English book was particularly delighted with two of the author's suggestions: that Byron should have brought back some of the Patagonian women to be used in improving the English breed; and that in order to settle all questions about size, some Englishwomen should be sent to make researches into the nature and structure of the South Americans. These reviews, in such an influential periodical, were no doubt irritating to believers in the legend, but the *Journal Encyclopédique* did most damage by publishing Condamine's hoax charge and by calling attention to the evidence of the explorer Bougainville.

Bougainville's part in the affair derived from his two voyages to the Moluccas in 1763–1765 and, more particularly, from voyages made by his lieutenants, Guyot and Giraudais, in the two following years. While at the height of the furor few people knew of Bougainville's own statement, "We made contact with these so-famous Patagonians and found them to be no taller . . . than other men,"[30] the journals of his two officers were much publicized and helped to cause a delay in the general acceptance of the story in France because they reported a meeting with seven Patagonians, the shortest of whom was only five feet, seven inches, by French measure, while "the others were much taller."[31] Although some French gazettes considered these figures conclusive evidence, the *London Chronicle*[32] attempted to reconcile the French and English reports by pointing out that Patagonia was so big it could easily contain both the giants and the "degenerate" race seen by Bougainville's officers.

While it was possible in this way to satisfy many doubters

concerning the reports of Bougainville's men, there was still the question of Condamine's hoax charge. After the charge first appeared in the *Journal Encyclopédique,* other periodicals accepted it as true and denounced their own gullibility, one of these being the *Avant-Coureur,* which bravely advertised its mistake under the lead sentence, "An error destroyed is a truth reëstablished." Seven months later, however, the same paper [33] announced that further researches had caused another change of opinion. The *Avant-Coureur*'s was not the only retraction. Condamine himself publicly recanted, but not in the pages of the *Journal Encyclopédique,* which had printed his accusation that the whole story was a fable. That periodical, apparently disgruntled and defeated, maintained a morose silence. It was the even more important *Journal des Sçavans* that published Condamine's new letter apologizing because he had *"appeared to doubt* the existence of the giants." This "doubt" had now been "completely destroyed" by new correspondence from Dr. Maty, who had spoken with eyewitnesses.[34]

Back in England some of these eyewitnesses were being published. In May, September, and November of 1767 the *London Chronicle* printed three letters written at Port Famine in Argentina by men aboard the *Dolphin* on its second trip around the world, this time commanded by Wallis, Byron's former lieutenant. All three letters reported that Wallis' crew saw the same Patagonians that Byron had visited in 1764, and all three disagreed about them. One writer saw three hundred giants; another, "some thousands." One gave them an average of seven feet, another gave them seven and one-half feet, and the third said they ranged from seven to eight feet.

These letters from Wallis' ship were all made public before a fourth and more influential one written by Charles Clarke, an officer aboard the *Dolphin* with Byron. This account, dated November 3, 1766, was sent to Dr. Maty at his request, included in the *Transactions* of the Royal Society,[35] and exploited by the newspapers in 1768. Mr. Clarke claimed that his report had "the embellishment of truth." He gave many details of the visit with the people of what he called "gigantic stature."

We were with them near 2 hours at noon day, within a very few yards, . . . and some of them are certainly of 9 feet if they don't exceed it. The Commodore who is very near six feet could but just reach the top of 1 of their heads, which he attempted on tip toes. . . . There was hardly a man amongst them less than 8 feet, most of them considerably more. The women, I believe run from 7½ to 8.[36]

Mr. Clarke's report corroborated that of his shipmate, the anonymous author of *A Voyage round the World, in his Majesty's ship the Dolphin*. And it might also have shown that the dozens of stories out of South America contained many elements begging to be exaggerated; but apparently no one remembered that, two years before, Dr. Maty and the periodicals of France and England had claimed that Commodore Byron was able to touch only a Patagonian chin—not the top of a head, as Mr. Clarke was now saying.

While these eyewitnesses were being published, England enjoyed reading what amounted to a retraction similar to Condamine's in France. The historian-editor Callander had insisted, in the first volume of his collection of voyages, published in the year of the *Dolphin*'s return, that navigators after Sarmiento had not seen any giant Patagonians. In 1768 the third and final volume of his collection appeared. The last entry therein was a reproduction of part of *A Voyage round the World, in his Majesty's ship the Dolphin*, the part which told of South Americans nine feet tall.

Although the European countries pursued the intriguing drama of the *Dolphin*, the English colonies in North America were so preoccupied with matters of taxation and troops that they had little time for anything but the play of politics. New England, in particular, slighted the *Dolphin*, preferring to dedicate its newspaper columns to sympathizing with General Paoli, the Corsican patriot, or to condemning merchants who sold British goods. But in Philadelphia the *American Magazine, or General Repository*, running for nine monthly issues in busy 1769 and having space for only one article on travel literature, devoted that article to a very long consideration of the size of the Patagonians.[37] Periodicals of the South, such as the *Maryland Gazette* [38] and the *Virginia Gazette,* were most interested in Admiral Byron, his ship, and the tall South Americans. The *Virginia Gazette* for August 6, 1767, for example, drew a religious conclusion that must have been a favorite one in fundamentalist America. "This voyage," the editor commented,

> fully confirms and establishes the truth of there being a nation of people of monstrous bulk, and that are in general from nine to ten feet high. What use Divines may make of this we do not know but it certainly proves what is recorded in Scriptures, and even in Heathen authors, that there was, and still is, a race of giants.

All during the affair of the giants, whether in America or in Europe, one of the most bothersome facts was that the English and French writers often forgot that their countries used slightly different standards of measurement, six French feet being equal to six feet, four and one-half inches, by English measure. For example, when Suard translated *A Voyage round the World* into French, he made no attempt to convert the many figures taken from the three officers aboard the *Dolphin.* Consequently, the nine-foot Patagonians reported in that book appeared seven inches taller to the French reader.[39]

While there seemed to be a variety of opinions about the Patagonians, by the middle of 1768, two years after the beginning of the drama, the reading world had apparently accepted them as giants. And it was not just the man-in-the-street reader. The *Gentleman's Magazine* and the *Journal des Sçavans,* both of which adopted the nine-foot version, were literature for the intellectuals; and Dr. Maty, de la Lande, Condamine, and the Abbé Coyer, all of whom were involved in the story, were prominent in scientific and philosophical circles. Nor was the *Dolphin*'s report just a matter for news—it went everywhere and affected many aspects of life.

Perhaps most of all it affected the publishing business. In addition to those books already discussed that played prominent roles in the drama, there were others less directly connected which owed their existence to the public's interest in Admiral Byron, in the Patagonians, and in giants in general. Some of these books had been published before and were brought out again as being of topical interest, among them the Spanish journal of Sarmiento [40] and a seventeenth-century account of an island of twelve-footers in the South Pacific. The most popular of the resurrections was the *Narrative of the hon. John Byron.* This was not the story of Byron's circumnagivation of the world on the *Dolphin* but of his much earlier adventures in South America as a midshipman aboard the *Wager,* one of Admiral Anson's ships. This book, which twenty-five years before had been considered too unimportant for publication, was now thrown to the ravenous public, who scanned it eagerly but unsuccessfully for further information about the giants. Certainly one reviewer was disappointed when he wrote, "In this book there is a fund of entertainment very seldom found, but no mention is made of people on the coast of Patagonia of an uncommon height." [41]

One of the new books published because of the *Dolphin* drama was *The Literary Life of the Late Thomas Pennant* (1771). This little volume contained a short biography and eight essays by Pennant, one of which was a "New Account of the Patagonians." Pennant tried to reconcile all conflicting accounts by classifying the natives of southern South America into four groups: people of normal height, those a few inches or a head taller than Europeans, the race of giants reported by Magellan and eight or nine others, and a class consisting of a mixture of the other three. Then he produced a personal letter from Admiral Byron which argued that the English sailors were justified in believing the Patagonians to be nine and ten feet tall because no one had actually measured them. Byron concluded, however, "I do suppose many of them were between seven and eight, and strong in proportion." Pennant was popular because his book could be quoted by more than one faction—those who scoffed at the ten-foot extremists, and those whose definition of *giant* was satisfied with the figures "seven and eight."

Not only were old books revived and new books published because of the *Dolphin* affair; a great many travel accounts of all kinds were issued during the years immediately following

Byron's return. And the book notices of the time offer evidence of their popularity. For example, the Abbé Delaporte's *Le Voyageur français* was so much in demand in 1766 that before volumes three and four could be printed, volumes one and two were sold out, forcing an immediate reprinting,[42] And when the impatiently awaited official journals of Byron, Wallis, Carteret, and Cook were finally given to the public in 1773, "the edition was exhausted in London, the day even of the publication." [43] Much of this popularity of travel literature can be attributed to the universal interest in the South American giants.

The enthusiasm about Patagonia also penetrated the schoolroom. In 1747 Emanuel Bowen's widely used geography of the world culled its information about South America from many volumes of travels, but nowhere did it mention giants. In 1771, however, at the crest of the wave of interest in the tall men, *A New System of Geography,* by Fenning and Collyer, had this to say in its section "Of Patagonia": [44] "There are here a people who are extremely remarkable on account of their bulk and stature." Reported first by Pigafetta, the article went on, "they were afterwards seen by other navigators, and their existence placed beyond doubt by the crews of Commodore Byron's ship the *Dolphin* . . . their middle stature seems to be about eight feet, their extreme nine feet and upwards."

In spite of the wide acceptance of the reports of giants, certain sophisticates of London were not so easily persuaded. On May 22, 1766, the month before he composed the satire urging that Englishwomen go to South America to investigate the size of the Patagonians, Horace Walpole wrote to Sir Horace Mann, "Oh, but we have discovered a race of giants! Captain Byron has found a nation of Brobdignags [*sic*] on the coast of Patagonia; the inhabitants on foot taller than he and his men on horseback. I don't indeed know how he and his sailors came to be riding in the South Seas. However, it is a terrible blow to the Irish, for I suppose all our Dowagers will be for marrying Patagonians." And beginning in November of the same year, Walpole's frequent letters to and from Mme du Deffand discussed the French book by the anonymous officer of the *Dolphin.* But by May 31,

1767, she was writing to complain that he would no longer talk about the matter.

Even more humorous were the scenes in the *Dolphin* comedy which involved two very important Frenchmen of the century, De Pauw and Voltaire, one because he was a prominent historian, the other because he had enemies and a wit. One of the first reactions among philosophers and men of science was that the existence of a nation of giants in South America disproved conclusively the famous theory of Buffon that the New World was peopled by races inferior in physical development to those of the Old World. De Pauw's part in our drama began with his two-volume *Recherches philosophiques sur les Américains,* which, unluckily for the immediate popularity of the book, supported the thesis of Buffon within months after the *Dolphin*'s report of giants in America. But De Pauw's ill luck was short lived, since his publishers turned defeat into victory by immediately issuing a new, three-volume edition, the third volume of which consisted of two parts, an adverse criticism of De Pauw's theories, written by a notorious anti-Buffonite named Dom Pernetty, and De Pauw's rebuttal, or "Defense." Dom Pernetty eagerly took over the Patagonian legend as developed by writers such as Harris and Debrosses, supplemented their facts, and produced over twenty-five pages to show that the giants existed. De Pauw's rebuttal is keen and cutting and funny. After claiming that up to that time no one had measured a live Patagonian or brought one back, he ended by drawing up a table to show that in their reports on the height of the giants Dom Pernetty's authorities varied from six to eleven feet. But best of all, he maliciously charged, Dom Pernetty took those figures and drew the conclusion that the Patagonians were twelve and one-half feet tall.[45]

Voltaire's part in the play should have been of minor importance and should have been restricted to the prologue, that part which took place before the *Dolphin* anchored in the Downs. But Voltaire was seldom permitted to play a minor role in anything with which he was connected, and so, near the end of the play, he was called back to the stage and for a brief scene stole the show. In 1752, while he was the guest of Frederick of Prussia, the great satirist had engaged in a feud with the academician, philosopher, and scientist Maupertuis, whom Voltaire correctly believed to be more honored than brilliant, whom he had personal reasons for disliking, and whose reputation he extinguished by making him the ridiculous hero of the *Diatribe du Dr. Akakia*. Two letters written by Voltaire in 1752 had made fun of Maupertuis' plan to send an expedition to Patagonia in order to study the "giant" intellects of the natives, an expedition which the Sage of Ferny thought would be even less profitable than had been Maupertuis' trip to the North Pole to measure the size of the earth. In 1773 these letters were brought to life, translated, and published by the *Gentleman's Magazine*,[46] which wanted simply to supply some humor to the many volumes of facts and surmises that had been published about the South American giants. But, as it turned out, Voltaire's wit helped to laugh away the legend, since that was the year of the formal closing of the show. This is the way Voltaire spoke of Maupertuis:

> I can only pity him; he has nothing more to be angry at. He is a man who pretends, that, in order to become better acquainted with the nature of the soul, we must go to the Southern hemisphere, to dissect some brains of giants, twelve feet high.

Then in a letter to Maupertuis himself, in answer to that injured scientist's threat of physical violence to the creator of Dr. Akakia, there occurs another reference to the Patagonians.

> I congratulate you on your good health, but I am not so strong as you: I have kept my bed for a fortnight, and I beg you to defer the little experiment in natural philosophy that you wish to make. You want, perhaps, to dissect me; but consider I am not a Patagonian, and my brain is so small that the discovery of its fibres will give you no new idea of the soul.

Voltaire's biting words would have been a fitting end to the play which had been so popular in Europe and America for seven years, but the final lines were to be more formal and less funny. They were provided by Dr. Hawkesworth's big, three-volume edition of the Admiralty's official collection called *An*

Account of the Voyages undertaken . . . by Commodore Byron, Captain Wallis, Captain Carteret, and Captain Cook. Since this publication was one of the most important in the history of exploration and discovery, it had many reasons for being popular; but undoubtedly the chief reason was the fact that seven years of evidence and discussion had provided so many versions of the heights of the Patagonians that the public was eager to read the official words of three trustworthy gentlemen who had conversed with the giants.

The lovers of the marvelous were to be disappointed, however, for the authenticated accounts failed to corroborate the witnesses that had been produced by Dr. Maty, Dom Pernetty, and all the others. It is true that Byron, in his section on Patagonia, used the terms "gigantic stature" and "enormous Goblins" and concluded that "these people may indeed more properly be called giants than tall men," since "the shortest were at least 6 feet 6 inches"; but he also said of the tallest Patagonian he saw, "I did not measure him, but if I may judge of his height by the proportion of his stature to my own, it could not be much less than seven feet." [47] These authorized figures did not agree very well with those which Thomas Pennant had attributed to Byron three years before; and to the European and American mind that had long been fed with images of nine- and ten-footers, a maximum of seven feet was a shocking disillusionment, hardly enough for a giant.

If the lover of the marvelous was not too disappointed by Byron's report, he might have turned quickly to the journals of Wallis and Carteret. But these were even more frustrating. Carteret agreed with Wallis, who after visiting the Patagonians twice had written, "As I had 2 measuring rods with me, we went round and measured those that appeared to be tallest among them. One of those was six feet, seven inches high, several more were six feet, and six feet six inches; but the stature of the greater part of them was from five feet ten to six feet." [48]

And so another "South Sea Bubble" was burst. Wallis and Carteret had measured the "giants," and Bougainville's men had measured them, and the measurements in no way agreed with the stories of the many eyewitnesses who had claimed eight, nine, and ten feet. Even the authorized estimates of Admiral Byron were only half a foot more than the measured heights. The newspapers and periodicals expended much space in reviewing the whole of Hawkesworth's collection of voyages, but particular attention was given to the brief sections on the Patagonians. Thereafter, public interest in the subject rapidly declined in England; and when the collection was almost immediately translated by Fréville and others and published in France, interest there subsided also. By 1790 the historian John Adams was able to choose circumspectly from the various accounts of the Patagonians, and he chose the story and the measurements of Wallis. But, ironically, the French translator of Adams' edition of travels failed to transpose the English measurements, and so the new generation in France read of a race that at least verged on gianthood.

While the Patagonian drama officially ended a few months following the publication of Hawkesworth's collection of voyages, the epilogue ran on well into the nineteenth century. After the great political events of the 1770's and 1780's had ceased to fill up the pages of the world's periodicals, editors again found space for this fascinating subject, especially for Thomas Pennant, least radical of the defenders of the myth.[49] And as late as 1815 the *North American Review* was one of those still puzzled by the wealth of witnesses who had seen the extraordinary people of Patagonia. "It is strange," the *Review* said, "that there should have been so much contradiction and even uncertainty. Nothing seems more incredible, and yet it is hard to account for the particular relations of so many persons of different nations, who in the course of one or two centuries, visited that country, and insisted upon having seen them, and been among them for days together."

During the nineteenth century, visitors to South America, intrigued by the legend of the giants, sometimes went among the Argentine natives in order to see for themselves. An Englishman, G. C. Musters, lived with the tallest tribe, the Tehuelches, for months, and in 1871 published a book called *At Home with the*

Patagonians, in which he asserted that the southern Tehuelches, somewhat taller than those of the north, had an average height of slightly over five feet, ten inches,[50] a figure that agreed with Wallis' measurement one century earlier. At about the same time, a Frenchman named D'Orbigny lived among the southern Argentinians for eight months and came away with measurements that ranged from five feet, eight inches, to six feet, three and one-half inches.[51] Ramon Lista, in 1879, reported a population of two to three thousand for the Tehuelches and gave the men of that tribe an average of six feet, two inches.[52] Modern researches largely ceased in that year, because in 1880 the Tehuelches were almost completely destroyed by the Rocca expedition seeking retaliation for native raids. Today anthropologists agree that the southern Argentinians came as close to being a race of giants as any ethnological group could, but no authority will now claim for them a height greater than that found by Wallis, Musters, or Lista.[53] Such a height, however, some three to five inches greater than for the average European, lent itself easily to exaggeration. One can understand Admiral Byron's claim that the shortest of the Patagonians was six feet and six inches, but it could not have been poor judgment alone that caused so many sailors on the *Dolphin,* and on other ships before it, to insist that they saw men eight, nine, and ten feet tall. Such exaggerations have motives behind them and may, therefore, be called lies, the motives being at least twofold: to startle the stay-at-homes with marvelous stories, as in the case of Charles Clarke in his letter to the Royal Society; and to sell a book, as in the case of that other, but anonymous, officer on the same ship who authored *A Voyage round the World, in his Majesty's ship the Dolphin.* The exaggerations of these gentlemen had as much influence on the course of eighteenth-century history as any other travel fabrication of which we know. Certainly its authors could not have anticipated the dramatic life of that lie as it went its way through the world of publishing, philosophy, science, education, religion, and journalism.

III

FALSE TOPOGRAPHY:
The Mississippi River
Region

So geographers, in Afric maps
With savage pictures fill their gaps,
And o'er unhabitable downs
Place elephants for want of towns.[1]

EARLY IN THE EIGHTEENTH CENTURY Joseph Addison, who knew very much about traveling, demonstrated also a keen knowledge of the nature of lying when he remarked that "there are many particular falsehoods suited to the particular climates and latitudes in which they are published, according as the situation of the place makes them less liable to discovery." In Addison's day it was not only true that the social climate of certain countries was more congenial for the publishing of some lies; it was even more true that the topography of certain places was better equipped for being lied about. The well-traveled and often-described regions of western Europe were too familiar for anyone there to divert the course of a river, invent a new water route between seas, or change the size of a waterfall; but there were other regions, discovered but not explored, that spawned many a geographical lie. One continent in particular lent itself to the production of such spurious offspring.

Until the end of the century the interior of Australia remained unknown and therefore relatively unfalsified. Africa was almost as dark, Egypt inspiring the greater portion of that continent's travel accounts and most of its few lies about topography. Parts of Asia—the Near East and India—were written about fancifully, but in general they seem to have been described accurately; other parts—China and Tibet—were left to the missionaries, who were more interested in converting souls and acquiring knowledge than in altering maps. European Russia may have been reported as a land where lions roamed the forests and czars rolled in wealth, but its geography usually remained untampered with; and Siberia, because of its geography, did not attract visitors. South America, on the other hand, was visited by many Europeans; but while they described its deposits of gold, exaggerated the size of the Patagonians, and, for the most part, lamented the Spanish occupation, they failed to alter the shape of the Andes or move the Amazon. Each of these parts of the world may have produced some sort of falsehood for the traveler to tell, but the continent that gave birth to the great majority of untruths about topography was North America, with its politically important Mississippi Basin and its elusive Northwest Passage.

Seeking new territories for trade under a farsighted minister Colbert and an industrious governor Frontenac, New France sent out the earliest of the men who explored the Mississippi Basin. Therefore, because they had first opportunity in a mysterious and desirable region, the travelers who told untruths about the Mississippi were Frenchmen. And the greatest of these was Father Louis Hennepin. Although he was not a Frenchman by birth, having been born in Belgium in 1640, he wrote and spoke in French as an abbé of the Récollet Society, a branch of the Franciscans strongly opposed to the Jesuits, who were firmly entrenched in Canada when Father Louis arrived in 1675. After some time in Quebec he went to the Great Lakes with La Salle and in the winter of 1679 was with the famous explorer at Fort Crèvecoeur on the Illinois River. On the last day of February in the leap year 1680, Hennepin and two companions climbed into their canoe, bade farewell to La Salle, and set off down the river on an exploring trip that was planned to take them to the junction with the Mississippi and then up that river into the great Northwest in search of water routes. Sometime in April and somewhere along the upper Mississippi, the three men were captured by a party of Sioux Indians, subjected to numerous indignities, and finally rescued by the fur-trading explorer Greysolon du Lhut, or Duluth, whose name was later bestowed on the lake city in Minnesota. The next year the Récollet was back in Paris, where in 1683 he published the story of his adventures, calling it the *Description de la Louisiane.* Afterwards, because of trouble with his religious superiors, he lived in Holland, England, and Italy. While in London in 1697 he almost succeeded in selling the English government his services as explorer in North America, and in the same year he did succeed in publishing another book, called *Nouvelle découverte d'un très grand pays,* or *New Discovery of a Great Country between New Mexico and the Frozen Sea.* This book brought him a fame that spread through Europe and that has lasted through two centuries and a half. But it was this book that made him the greatest of geographical liars.

There were both mercenary and political motives for the *New Discovery* to lie. Father Hennepin, as a renegade from the Récollet Society, was in search of money, and so he wrote a story that he hoped would sell. And because he had fled from France, where his accomplishments and pretensions were known in high places, he hoped by his claims to convince the English government that he was the best-qualified person to guide an expedition that would beat the French by ship to the mouth of the Mississippi. These political ambitions led him also to dedicate the *New Discovery* to the Protestant King William III of England, thus alienating even more the leaders of his religious order and his adopted homeland.

However, political ambition and the desire for money were not such strong motives for this man's lying as was his vanity, his desire to convince himself and others of his own importance or the importance of anything with which he was connected.

That egoism exhibited itself in an uncommon tendency to over-state and to brag. Not only do we have La Salle's testimony that "he will not fail to exaggerate everything . . . he speaks more in keeping with what he wishes than with what he knows," [2] but we have as well the evidence of Hennepin's own books, even the earliest, the 1683 *Description of Louisiana*. Here he frequently bragged of being the first priest to celebrate mass in the new areas in which he found himself.[3] He commiserated with a brother priest, poor La Motte, who "had to give up later and return to Fort Frontenac; he was unable to stand such an ardu-ous life." [4] Obviously Father Louis was equipped with the proper fortitude and stamina, for he himself tells us how "Sieur la Salle and I"—no others of the big party included—were sub-jected to hardships "which would perhaps seem incredible to those who have not made long voyages and new discoveries." [5] And, he said, "the more we suffered, the more it seemed that God gave me particular strength, for I often outpaddled the other canoes." [6] Nowhere did Father Louis inform his readers that Michel Accault, one of his two companions on the trip up the Mississippi, and not he himself, was the real leader of the little party. Furthermore, he insisted on placing a Récollet mis-sion far to the north of any that then existed, farther north even than he himself had been. According to Justin Winsor, "The placing of it there seems to have been a pretension . . . that his order had outstripped the venturesome Jesuits." [7] Perhaps his biggest exaggeration in that first book was the report that Niagara Falls was five hundred feet high, the first of many well-known magnifications of the size of that natural phenomenon which actually was not nearly two hundred feet tall. And in his later books, he increased the five hundred to six hundred, which to an Englishman or an American, with their different system of measurement, meant about six hundred and fifty.[8]

But all of the vanities and falsifications of 1683 were nothing compared with those that Hennepin placed in the *New Dis-covery* in 1697. Writing a safe ten years after the death of La Salle, the Récollet monk now claimed in his preface that modesty and fear of reprisal had earlier prevented him from

telling how he had descended the Mississippi to its mouth two
years before La Salle had made the trip. And the *New Discovery*
included a section that recounted the story of that fabulous
voyage which was supposed to have taken place between
February 29, 1780, when Hennepin and his companions left La
Salle at Fort Crèvecoeur, and the middle of April, when the
three men were captured by the Sioux. For it was in those some
forty days, the monk now related, that his speedy little canoe,
propelled by three oars, made the dash all the way down the
tortuous river to the Gulf of Mexico and all the way back,
against the strong muddy current, past the starting point, and
far up toward the headwaters. In order to steal honor from La
Salle, the audacious Hennepin was forced to fill his own account
with details lifted from the narrative of La Salle's expedition to
the Gulf in 1682 written by Father Membré, whose eyewitness
journal became part of a book about Canada put together by
Récollet Father Christian LeClercq and published in ample
time for his defected brother to rifle it. In order to get back to
Sioux country and be captured, mistreated, and rescued according to the schedule he had given in his earlier book, Hennepin
compressed the time for the trip south to about one-third, used
"we" or "I" wherever Father Membré had written the name of
La Salle, visited the same Indians La Salle met, saw the same
scenes in the same way, and observed Easter on the same day of
the month, even though he was claiming to have been two years
ahead of La Salle and should have celebrated it on quite a
different day.[9] "The records of literary piracy may be searched
in vain," Francis Parkman contended, "for an act of depredation
more recklessly impudent." [10]

The impudence of Hennepin's biggest lie has been matched
only by its success in bringing him both honor and notoriety.
Whereas the earlier *Description,* with its bragging and its comparatively minor exaggerations, produced only six quick editions
in five languages, the *New Discovery,* with its boast of beating
La Salle to the Gulf of Mexico, went through more than six
editions in French alone. Moreover, there were four complete

printings in Dutch, one in German, and two in English, with an abridgment published in Spain and another in America as late as 1820.[11] Furthermore, in 1698 the Récollet Father brought out another essay, called *The New Voyage,* which continued the hoax and was almost as popular, with at least nine different printings in four languages. All of this immediate success, from which Hennepin may have derived little financial benefit, was only the prelude to a lasting fame. His claims were certainly not accepted everywhere, however. In 1744, for example, the historian-traveler Charlevoix used Hennepin's books while calling them "anything but true"; and in 1750 the Swedish botanist Pehr Kalm discovered that in Canada Father Louis was known as *un grand menteur*—a big liar.[12] But the priest did not lack for defenders, especially in Belgium, the land of his birth. There the *Revue du Liège* ran an article praising him; and a book on Belgian travelers,[13] depending on that article and on one other source—the 1697 *New Discovery!*—eulogized the monk at some length for discovering the mouth of the Mississippi. La Salle, however, was generally credited with that honor, even though throughout the eighteenth century Hennepin remained an important source of information about North America, as in Emanuel Bowen's *A Complete System of Geography,* published in London in 1747.[14]

In the nineteenth century "the popular and political interest in Hennepin's books gave way . . . to scholarly interest," as one interested scholar has said. In spite of the early tradition concerning this traveler's mendacity, credit for exposing his methods and sources is generally given to Jared Sparks, historian-President of Harvard; however, before his *Life of La Salle* appeared in 1844 with the charges of plagiarism, a heated debate about the legitimacy of Hennepin's claims had been carried on between the *North American Review* and the *United States Magazine and Democratic Review.*[15] Sparks's charges paved the way for attacks by Parkman, Margry, Winsor, Thwaites, and others. Father Shea, most noted of nineteenth-century Catholic historians of America, began by doubting that Hennepin had even seen the upper Mississippi and ended with the theory that a ghost writer, a "literary jobber," had written the *New Discovery,* since no priest could be such a liar.

And the twentieth century has not lacked for either supporters or accusers of the Récollet. In the 1920's Father Goyens attempted to save some of the priest's honor and was attacked in turn by Abbé Scott. The most vigorous of recent clerical defenders has been Father LeMay, who wrote a number of articles in 1936–1938 for *Nos Cahiers* and died before completing a proposed three-volume work on Hennepin. But the support has not all been from the priesthood. One of the latest catalogues published by an outstanding dealer in travel books, although it tells of Hennepin's exaggeration of the size of Niagara Falls, is apparently unaware of the scholarship that has been done on him, describing the contents of his *New Discovery* and announcing it "as one of the most important volumes in the early history of the United States." [16] And the latest English translation of the *Description of Louisiana* contains an introduction that does not mention Hennepin's hoax until the last paragraph, which argues the worth of the *Description* and says defensively that *"mendacious* is an adjective sometimes applied to" its author "because in later books he claimed to have descended as well as ascended the Mississippi." [17] However, Jean Delanglez has recently shown that even this first book of Hennepin's is of little value, two-thirds of it having been taken from the *Relation des découvertes et des voyages du Sieur de la Salle,* once attributed to LeClercq but now thought to be written by Claude Bernou, and the other one-third containing so many errors of fact that it is unreliable.[18] This exposure may be the end of the story of Father Louis Hennepin's hopes, boasts, and plagiarisms; but his vain little soul must still swell with pride when it contemplates the pressure he has for centuries exerted on politics, geography, history, and scholarship.

There is no doubt that Hennepin's tale of beating La Salle to the Gulf of Mexico was a lie, but there is some doubt as to whether La Salle was a liar too. Although he had none of Hennepin's small vanity, he was proud and domineering, able to win the respect and fear of his followers but seldom their love. And he was a man of schemes as well as a man of vision. At first he sought a passage through the American Northwest to China and India; then turning his attention to the Mississippi, he decided that it emptied not into the Pacific, as many people thought, but into the Gulf of Mexico. Out of this decision came his first grand schemes. On his last trip to France before descending the Mississippi, he aroused the interest of Louis XIV, of Colbert, and of private businessmen by praising the potentialities of the great Midwest. He spoke of its fertility and its other natural resources. He urged that it was coveted by the English. He insisted that it was near enough to the gold and silver of New Spain to be the starting point for an invasion that would make France rich. And he described its natives as being tractable, friendly, much like Frenchmen, and ready to form the nucleus of an army that would plunder the Spanish mines. One can not be sure how much of all this La Salle himself believed, but his ardent pleading brought him the king's patent and thousands of *livres* from private citizens, including his own relatives, who after his death claimed that he had talked them out of half a million.[19]

Having successfully promoted his plan, La Salle returned to Canada and for three years underwent a life of extreme difficulty and disappointment before making the historic trip to the Gulf in 1682. But while his vision and his daring at last brought him this one great success of a lifetime, his schemes continued. Hardly was he back at Michilimackinac on the Lakes before he was sending a letter to Paris telling of his adventure and lauding the military value of the Mississippi water system. Five of the seven or eight big tributaries in that system, he said, come from the west, from "New Mexico, where the Spaniards have found such rich mines. From the Mississippi, one could harass and even completely ruin New Spain, for the Indians have . . . a natural hatred for the Spaniards, because the latter made them slaves." [20] In addition to this old story, retold in the light of new discoveries, he added important personal requests that proved him to have ambitions that were other than scientific or patriotic. Now he asked for valuable trade concessions: first, a monopoly of the Wabash; second, one that would include all of the east shore and run to a depth of ten leagues on the west shore of the Mississippi; and finally, one that would extend ten leagues on either side of the Arkansas River. The author of this letter was obviously hoping to keep interested a government that was anxiously seeking more money and power, and just as obviously he was doing it, at least in part, because he hoped for personal business and political benefits.

Even though his plans succeeded temporarily when he obtained leadership of a French expedition that attempted to discover the mouth of the Mississippi by way of the Gulf of Mexico, La Salle was killed before having the chance to strengthen his claims for trade concessions. And when he was dead, France lost much of its interest in attacking New Mexico by way of the rivers that flowed from the west. But his influence on geography was more lasting than was his influence on politics and business, and it affected more people. After writing the propagandistic letter of 1682, he had made notes on his discoveries and had drawn a rough map of the middle and western part of North America which is astoundingly inaccurate. It is true that in La Salle's lifetime it was impossible to determine longitude exactly, but even his latitudes were far off whenever he needed to make the cartography conform to the theory that his rivers led to New Mexico. And the worst of mapmakers did not, without having a thesis to defend, err so much in longitude. The outstanding peculiarity of this map is the fact that the Mississippi was made to bend far toward the Pacific Ocean, almost to the meridian of the Gulf of California, where at the westernmost point the Red River departed for the interior of New Spain and its reputedly rich mines.[21]

This rough drawing made by La Salle became quite important in France. It and the explorer's notes were turned over to the government and used as evidence for the geography of the New World, especially by Franquelin, the King's mapmaker in Canada. In 1683 his "Map of Louisiana or of the travels of Sieur de la Salle and of the country he discovered . . ." made all the important mistakes recorded on La Salle's own sketch, the Mississippi delta being much too far west and the longitudinal error between the mouth of the Red River and the mouth of the Illinois River being over 7°.[22] This official map and its distortions, placed in the *Archives scientifiques,* were much reproduced, both then and, more recently, by Winsor, Thwaites, and others, who recognized the false geography. Four years later, in another map,[23] Franquelin was still broadcasting these errors; but by 1699 he was changing his cartography to conform less with the then dead La Salle's drawings and more with traditional theories. And in later maps he continued, apparently with some reluctance, to move the Mississippi farther and farther east, where it belonged. However, it was not until after 1708 that he completely shook off the early La Salle influence, even though Iberville, Bienville, Le Sueur, and other explorers had with much exactness located the mouths of the Mississippi and its various tributaries, and even though other mapmakers, such as Delisle, had by 1700 begun to transfer those discoveries to widely disseminated maps, thus exposing the hoax.

The motives for La Salle's very influential distortions of fact —in the letter and on the map—have been defended, but the evidence is strong against him. One can try to clear the explorer completely by saying with his recent biographer, L. V. Jacks,[24] that while seeking to persuade Louis XIV in 1684, La Salle "evoked only the magic of words rooted in truth," that he and the king's minister Seignelay "shared" the "curious topographical blunder." Or one can point out, with Frances Gaither,[25] that although La Salle seems to have been motivated by a desire for personal ambition, his geographical "error" was perhaps based on a strong tradition concerning the proximity of New Mexico to the Mississippi region, a tradition fostered in La Salle's own lifetime by other explorers, like Marquette, who talked of western waterways to Spanish gold, and by people in authority, Colbert, for example, who four years before La Salle saw the mouth of the Mississippi had suggested to him that a port on the Gulf of Mexico would furnish a vantage point from which to harass the Spaniards. Or, with Jean Delanglez,[26] one can be completely convinced "that La Salle took liberties with the geography of the Mississippi in order to deceive Seignelay." And if one is so convinced, he can offer strong evidence [27] that by his distortions La Salle hoped to benefit both in power and money; that others had spoken only in vague terms of what the French might hope to do or find in the West, while he put definite statements in official reports and on a map; that his latitudes as well as his longitudes were much too far off to be mere errors; and that in La Salle's own day the Spanish ambassador to England wrote a letter to his superior in Madrid telling how the great explorer was trying to deceive the French government with a doctored map. Or, finally, one can be sure of La Salle's guilt but generously permit him to plead insanity, as Parkman did when he decided that either "the scheme of invading Mexico was thrown out as bait to the king, . . . or La Salle was mentally ill." [28] Of all these attitudes, the least tenable is that which offers total exoneration. But whether one defends La Salle's motives or whether one attacks them, the inevitable conclusion is that although this man's vast ambitions worked ultimately in the interest of France and civilization, the charge he leveled at Father Louis Hennepin, *"le grand menteur,"* can be applied also to him, that "he speaks more in keeping with what he wishes than with what he knows."

Exactly four months before the beginning of the year of Jubilee 1700, and two years after Father Hennepin had made his boast of beating La Salle, a young man in his thirties wrote a letter in which he accused the Récollet friar of filling his book with "trifling nonsense." This young man was Louis Armand Baron de Lahontan, and his letter was prefixed to a copy in his handwriting of the journal of Jean Cavelier, brother of La Salle and companion of the explorer both on the trip down the Mississippi and on the Gulf Coast voyage that ended with the death march in Texas. Ironically, the journal which Lahontan had transcribed also contained much nonsense, as numerous historians such as Parkman and De Villiers have shown.[29] But it is not the little lies of La Salle's brother that have affected history but rather the grand fabrications of the young man who transcribed them; for two years after sneering at Hennepin he published a book of travels that attempted to outdo the Father, not by inventing a voyage down a river but by inventing the river itself.

The Baron de Lahontan [30] was one of the notorious eighteenth-century "adventurers," in fact, perhaps the first of the great ones. His influence was so permanent, his autobiographical books were so popular, and his career was so exciting that he might have provided the beginning chapter for Peter Wilding's *Great Adventurers of the Eighteenth Century.* Born in 1666, the year called *annus mirabilis* by John Dryden, Lahontan early lost both his father and his lands; and at the age of seventeen he was in Canada serving as lieutenant in a detachment of marines sent to assist Governor la Barre in the Indian wars. In spite of the tradition, begun apparently by traveler Claude Le Beau, that the young marine never went much farther west than Quebec, he actually was more than once at Fort Michilimackinac, where three great lakes meet at the tip of northern Michigan; and in 1687 he accompanied Hennepin's rescuer, Duluth, and La Salle's most capable lieutenant, Tonty, to Fort Saint Joseph, near modern Detroit, where he was left in charge. He engaged in excursions against the Iroquois, burned his fort and retreated to Michilimackinac when he heard of a new Indian uprising, met and talked with Jean Cavelier and other survivors of La Salle's last expedition, and in the seven winter months of 1688–1689, excited by their stories and by a vivid imagination, made an exploring trip into the great Northwest in search perhaps of an El Dorado, perhaps of a passage to the Pacific, or perhaps of fame. He returned with none of these except fame, and that he carried about ignorantly for ten years, until Father Hennepin's "nonsense" taught him the value of his possession.

During that decade, and later, Lahontan led an even busier and more adventurous life. After becoming one of Frontenac's valued lieutenants in and around Montreal, even carrying the governor's dispatches across the Atlantic, he proposed a scheme for a Great Lakes navy and was sent with the proposal to Pontchartrain, the Minister in Paris. On his way he stopped off in

Newfoundland long enough to make a hero of himself in a battle with six English ships. In France the young soldier failed to get his navy but was given a company of one hundred men to lead back to Newfoundland, where he was to be second-in-command. But there he was unable to get along with the governor and deserted his post by taking a ship for Portugal. For nine years— 1694 to 1703—he skipped from one European country to another, escaping French arrest and offering unsuccessfully to spy on Spain for his native land. The refusal apparently snapped whatever tenuous lines still tied him to France, for while in England in 1696 the young Baron, his estate gone and his army pay curtailed, tried to purvey information to that country and succeeded in selling two documents to William III's Secretary of War.[31] But his success was only temporary, for the Treaty of Ryswick in 1697 not only made valueless his plans and drawings for capturing Quebec but ruined his hopes of military glory in the service of Britain, just as in the same year it ruined the schemes of Father Hennepin to lead English ships to the mouth of the Mississippi. Then, during the political pandering that immediately preceded the War of the Spanish Succession, the Baron de Lahontan again proffered France his services, this time in a plan to visit Spain for the purpose of spying out the strength of that country's forces and fortifications. Failing in France for the second time, he turned to the enemy Spain and offered her his copy of the journal of La Salle's brother. But again his schemes failed.

Rebuffed at every turn, the adventurer collected the "letters" he had written years before in Canada, added to them, and went to a publisher in Holland. And at last he was successful, for in 1703 two volumes by Lahontan appeared in The Hague, to be joined in the same year by an English translation, also in two volumes, in London.[32] Volume one of the French edition contained twenty-six letters said to have been written in the years that Lahontan spent in French America. Volume two supplied information about Canada and its natives, including an Indian vocabulary. The English translation reproduced all of the original work and added two sections, one a group of "Dialogues with an American Indian," and the other some letters about Portugal. The "Dialogues" were republished shortly in Holland as the third volume of the French edition; and then, in 1705, they were blown up to considerable proportions to become an important work in the history of radicalism. One other part of the earlier edition was increased in size in 1705, in fact, to more than twice the original length; that was "Letter Sixteen," which narrated the adventures of the 1688–1689 expedition into the country of the northern Mississippi. And it too became important in the history of ideas, in particular, false ideas about geography. For this was the letter that told of Lahontan's discovery of a great river that flowed from the northwest into the Mississippi, a discovery that for fourteen years was kept secret from the missionaries, the soldiers, the traders, the authorities of Canada, and—Gustave Lanctot adds—perhaps even from the discoverer himself.

No one has ever been able to find this *"rivière Longue."* It was much too big, too long, and too straight to be the Minnesota, and its junction with the Mississippi was much too far north for it to be the Missouri. In fact, Lahontan claimed in this same "Letter Sixteen" to have explored the Missouri also. But stranger than the appearance and geographical position of his river were the curious tribes of Indians who lived near its banks —the Essanapes, the Gnacsitares, and the Mozeemleks.

The Essanapes, a "very civil" nation of 20,000 warriors, exuded "sweetness and an air of humanity" and gave the party of Frenchmen a cordial welcome.[33] Before leaving them, Lahontan discovered that they were "Pythagoreans" when he observed thirty or forty newly married women running at full speed "to receive the soul of an old fellow that lay dying." But, he added, these Indians thought that "the soul of a man cannot enter into a fowl, or that of a fowl cannot be lodged in a quadruped, and so on." The most peculiar fact about the Essanapes was the position they accorded their "King." "When he walks," Lahontan said, "his way is strewed with leaves of trees, but commonly

he is carried by six slaves." Such practices, much more appropriate for an Eastern potentate, were of course unknown among
the red men of America.

Farther up the *"rivière Longue"* lived the Gnacsitares, enemies of the Essanapes. This tribe, Lahontan would have us
believe, knew and hated the Spanish even though it lived north
of the Missouri River. With them were some captive Mozeemleks, who looked like Spaniards and wore clothes. ". . . they
had a thick bushy beard, and their hair hung down under their
ears; their complexion was swarthy, their address was civil and
submissive, their mien grave, and their carriage engaging." They
told the young "discoverer" a wonderful tale. According to them
the *"rivière Longue"* took its origin in tall mountains to the
west, on the other side of which another river flowed down to a
great salt lake, three hundred leagues in circumference and
thirty wide, surrounded by six cities of stone and a hundred
towns. This was the land of the very gifted Tuhuglauk nation,
bearded Indians who wore garments reaching down to their
knees and boots reaching up to their knees. On their heads were
sharp pointed caps, and in their hands were sharp pointed canes.
They were artisans and made axes and other objects of copper.
One of the Mozeemleks who told this story had a copper model
suspended from his neck. ". . . from the figure," Lahontan
noted, "it appears to be Japanese." Just as the South Sea navigators who reported nine-foot giants in Patagonia had failed to
bring any of them back to Europe, Lahontan did not succeed
in persuading any bearded Mozeemleks to return to Canada
with him. No amount of money and presents would tempt these
Noble Savages, for, the author concluded sententiously, "nature
reduced to its just limits cares but little for riches."

Satisfied with his "discoveries," Lahontan took his party back
down the *"rivière Longue"* to the Mississippi; but before returning to the Great Lakes region, he spent almost a week exploring
the Missouri River, according to his account. The last part of
"Letter Sixteen" of *New Travels in North America* provided a
long list of the supplies and implements to be taken along into
Indian territory and enumerated the talents and abilities of the

leader of an expedition of discovery. Obviously believing that his book adequately displayed his own abilities, Lahontan concluded, modestly, "If I were possessed of all these qualities, I should esteem it my happiness to be employed upon such an enterprise both for the glory of His Majesty, and my own satisfaction."

The far-western geography which Lahontan described was not so curious as the appearance and manners of the Indians who were supposed to have reported it to him, nor was it so unbelievable as the *"rivière Longue,"* which he claimed to have seen with his own eyes. The mountains of the Mozeemleks, of course, might have been the Rockies, and the lake of the Tuhuglauks, the Great Salt Lake of Utah. However, while the northern Indians may have related such stories, Lahontan could also have gathered some like them from the companions of La Salle, for that explorer had seemed quite familiar with the movements and ambitions of the Spaniards in the region of the Rockies. And certainly for over one hundred and fifty years before La Salle and Lahontan, the Spanish children of Coronado had been searching for treasured cities of Cibola, as reported by Indians who lived by a river that, like Lahontan's, took its origin in tall mountains not far from a great salt lake.[34] Even the name that the Frenchman gave his river was similar to that of the 1,900-mile-long Spanish stream. One was the *"rivière Longue"*; the other—at least for part of its length—was the *"Rio Grande."* But whether the Baron de Lahontan manufactured a tale out of hints taken from the Spanish by way of La Salle, or whether he actually obtained his information from the Gnacsitares and the Mozeemleks, Indian tribes no one else has seen, it is obvious that he mixed fiction with whatever truth he used.

Lahontan's river and his far-western salt lake were his most important inventions, but they were not his only ones. Nor were all of his inventions of geographical interest alone. Elsewhere in his writings he provided an Indian vocabulary that, while on the whole comparing favorably with other such vocabularies of the time—the one by the trader John Long, for example [35]—is sometimes quite fanciful. In it he gave the twelve months such poetic names as "the Moon of Swallows," for May, and insisted that every thirty months the Hurons added a "Lost Moon." Almost a hundred years later these pretty names were to be stolen by Jonathan Carver, who was to pass them on to such writers as Crèvecoeur, the "American Farmer." [36] But more influential than his Indian vocabulary, more obviously false, and more a geographical lie, was Lahontan's estimate of the height of Niagara Falls. While Father Hennepin had given them five hundred feet—later increased to six hundred—the Baron, who had cried nonsense at his predecessor, now gave them "seven or eight hundred" feet.[37]

Lahontan's books were so popular that they went through thirteen editions in fourteen years, and since his own time other editions have been made, totaling over thirty in at least five languages.[38] He was lionized in Europe, visiting courts in several countries, and became a close friend of the philosopher Leibnitz, who propagandized the works and the talents of the traveler from America. His success as a socialite enhanced Lahontan's prestige as a writer, and he had considerable influence on many eighteenth-century ideas, much of that influence being in what people thought about the shape of the earth's surface. His description of Niagara Falls, giving it five times its real height, can be found almost verbatim in the 1747 *Complete System of Geography*. And, although Fenning and Collyer's [39] geography of 1771 avoided this particular false report, others used it. For in 1822, exactly one hundred years after Charlevoix and a government surveying party had settled on 140–150 feet as the correct altitude of Niagara, the *North American Review* complained, "Whether these accounts were not believed, or that people prefer falsehood to truth, we are not able to say; but certain it is, that the old fictions of Hennepin and La Hontan continued to find a place in the geographies of Bowen and Middleton and others very nearly to the end of the last century." [40]

The *"rivière Longue,"* with its related geography, was almost as tenacious and even more influential, muddying up the maps of many eighteenth-century cartographers.[41] The best-known mapmaker in Lahontan's day, the French Guillaume Delisle, seemed to have some doubts about the "discoveries" recorded in the Baron's first Dutch edition; but he used them nevertheless. On his *"Carte du Canada,"* which came out only months after that first edition, Delisle drew in a "Western Sea," the great salt lake reported by Lahontan's Mozeemleks, and reproduced the *"rivière Longue"* exactly as the Baron had given it, carefully acknowledging his source in an inscription on the map. As late as 1718 the Jesuit Father Bobo, one of the first to see through Lahontan's hoax, was writing to Delisle urging the geographer to remove the river from his maps because it was unknown by "all Canadians, and even the governor of Canada." But Father Bobo apparently had no influence. At least, French travel books continued to reproduce Lahontan's fanciful topography, for example, Père Labat and François Coreal in 1722. In England Herman Moll was only the outstanding of many victims of the Baron's mendacity, including the "Long River" on his map of the world found in such books as the 1712 edition of Woodes Rogers' *A Cruising Voyage Round the World.* During the mid-century revival of the search for a Northwest Passage, Arthur Dobbs and Henry Ellis published books to promote or report expeditions to Hudson Bay and included prejudiced maps, part of the fancifulness of which can be traced to the *"rivière Longue"* and the Sea of the West. Still later, in 1765, Samuel Engel brought out a map that showed the western part of North America much as eighteenth-century cartographers, thinkers, and readers envisioned that yet unexplored land. Wherever possible Engel had made use of Lahontan.

While the *"rivière Longue"* itself was found on many maps, some of its defenders and users began very early to call it by some other name—usually the Missouri or the Minnesota, in spite of Lahontan's own statement that he had explored the Missouri too. As late as 1816, for example, one reviewer of Lahontan's *New Travels in North America,* announcing confidently that book's authenticity, said of its author, "He undertook an expedition of discovery and penetrated high up the Missouri." [42] In 1900 François de Nion, in his edition of the travels, presented a lengthy defense of Lahontan's veracity, concluding that the *"rivière Longue"* was either the Minnesota or the Saint Peter; and in 1932 Stephen Leacock joined the ranks of the supporters with his *Lahontan's Voyages*.[43]

But these editors are the only modern writers who have sought to whitewash the Baron completely. Justin Winsor, Francis Parkman, Nellis Crouse, and Gilbert Chinard represent the consensus when they say that Lahontan is necessary to the historians but that he must be handled with caution. His "account of the Long River," Winsor pointed out, "is a sheer fabrication; but he did not, like Hennepin, add slander and plagiarism to mendacity." [44] And, Parkman added, in a statement that would fit more than one famous traveler, Lahontan was "a man in advance of his time. . . . He usually told the truth, when he had no motive to do otherwise, and yet was capable at times of prodigious mendacity." [45]

One important bit of evidence that Lahontan's *"rivière Longue"* owed something to the Spanish Rio Grande is the story of Jean Couture, who handled geography even more grandly but with less influence than his contemporary did. With another Frenchman this *coureur de bois* had been sent to maintain a post on the Arkansas River; and there in 1687 the two men were found by Cavelier, Douay, and Joutel, the remnants of La Salle's last party of exploration, who were on their way north to Canada. Cavelier and his companions told the story of their adventures, including the murder of La Salle, to the Arkansas River sentinels and then went on to report to Tonty in the Illinois country. But to him they told half-truths and lies, leaving the impression that La Salle was still alive. However, after their departure for France, Couture arrived at Tonty's headquarters and repeated the true story given him many months before. Sent on a new mission down the Mississippi, Couture went about 250 miles to the Illinois River, wrecked his canoe, and returned. This little junket, magnified thirty- or fortyfold, became "one of the most fantastic in all the literature of mythical travels." [46]

Couture claimed that alone and in a tiny, frail canoe he had paddled all the way to the mouth of the Mississippi, taking time out for side excursions up the Arkansas, the Missouri, and other rivers. On the Gulf of Mexico, still in his canoe, he had paddled along the coast eastward to Mobile Bay and then westward to the mouth of the Rio Grande. But the intrepid *voyageur* did not stop there. Turning his back on the tall waves of the Gulf, which would have capsized a man of less balance, he headed up the Rio Grande, following that river nearly 2,000 miles to the Rockies, where he finally left his hardiest of canoes. Then he crossed the mountains, went down a river he called the *"Saint François,"* and paddled another canoe over the salt *"Baja"* to the "Island of California." At this point, either tired or lonely, Couture reversed his tracks—and his canoe—and in short order was back in Canada.[47]

This fictitious trip is too much like the voyages of Hennepin and Lahontan to divert us very long, but it was of considerable importance in the eighteenth century. In the first place, it may have provided suggestions for Lahontan's imaginary river that flowed from the Rockies, on the opposite side of which was another river, like the *"Saint François,"* that led to a salt lake. In the second place, Couture's claims were accepted by geographers, for at least one of them, on a map still to be seen in the Bibliothèque Nationale, recorded every detail of the supposed voyage; and in the nineteenth century, G. Marcel in his *Cartographie de la Nouvelle France* seems to have believed the fiction.[48] Finally, this and other tales by Couture made him a legend among the English in Carolina, who accepted both his pretended and his very real knowledge of the Mississippi region when he became a renegade from the French, appointed him to lead important exploring and trading expeditions—inspired in part by his stories of gold and pearls—and maintained the opinion that he was "the greatest trader and traveller amongst the Indians for more than Twenty years." [49]

CHAPTER

IV

MORE FALSE TOPOGRAPHY:
The Northwest Passage

"Falsehood flies and truth comes limping after it." [1]

NORTH AMERICA contained the Mississippi River, with its
overly discovered mouth, its movable course, and its too numerous tributaries, and it also contained the great expanse of unexplored arctic reaches that were supposed to provide a usable
Northwest Passage between the Atlantic and Pacific oceans. The
body of eighteenth-century literature dealing with this hoped-
for route is immense, and much of it consists of travel lies told
by writers most of whom voyaged only in their imagination, or
of books, articles, and maps that made use of the lies.

In the eighteenth century the first, and perhaps the most, influential fabrication about a Northwest Passage was the "Letter
from Admiral Bartholomew de Fonte," which purported to tell
of a voyage from the Pacific to the Atlantic Ocean made entirely
by water in 1640. This "Letter" first appeared in London in the
Monthly Miscellany of 1708 and has often been reprinted, most
recently by Henry R. Wagner in "Apocryphal Voyages to the
North-West Coast of America." [2] According to the dozen pages
of de Fonte's journal, the supposed "Admiral of New Spain, and
now Prince of Chili," sailed from Lima April 3, 1640, with four
ships, commanded by himself, "Vice-Admiral Don Diego Pennelossa," Pedro de Bonarda, and Philip de Ronquillo. The

group went up the coast of South America, stopped long enough to assign "Vice-Admiral Pennelossa" the task of investigating the question of whether California was an island, and with three ships continued to 53° North Latitude. There de Fonte found a large river up which he sailed to a lake he named *Belle*. Dispatching Captain Bonarda by ship and boat northwards to explore other lakes and rivers, he left his remaining two ships in Lake Belle and went by boat down a river with eight falls that lowered him thirty-two feet into another lake he named *de Fonte*. From here he passed through a strait, entered an arm of the Atlantic Ocean, and found a ship from Boston with Captain Shapley and owner Major General Gibbons aboard. After exchanging presents with the Americans, de Fonte manned his boats, returned to Lake Belle, picked up Captain Bonarda, who had explored the far North to 79° latitude, all the way from the Pacific to Davis Strait, and then came home, having concluded "that there was no Passage into the South Sea by that they call the North West Passage."

The motive behind the creation of de Fonte is still unknown, but his voyage has long been discredited. It belongs with the spurious travels of Couture, with the trip down the Mississippi that Louis Hennepin never took, and with the adventures of the many creations of Defoe. In fact, Defoe has been suggested as the author of the de Fonte "letter." The more generally accepted theory, however, is that it came from the pen of James Petiver, who was writing for the *Monthly Miscellany* at the time that magazine published the piece. But whoever wrote the "letter," its geography has been condemned as impossible by all professionals who have studied it since the opening up of northern North America at the end of the eighteenth century, among them Burney, Winsor, Crouse, Wagner, and Wroth, who agree that no system of rivers and lakes, even remotely resembling that described in the journal, can be found which will permit one to go entirely by water from the Atlantic to the Pacific, especially at the latitudes named.[3]

Even in the eighteenth century the journal was sometimes thought to be a fake, and now its suspicious features are easily recognized. In the first place, the Spanish original was never found, while the Spaniard de Fonte measured time from the beginning of the reign of Charles I of England. And not only did William Dampier's *New Voyage* of 1697 apparently supply hints for the author of the spurious letter of 1640; the place names employed in reporting the first part of the voyage were not used until forty-five years after de Fonte's supposed time, when they first appeared on maps in William Hack's famous *Buccaneer's Atlas*. Furthermore, only one of the four ship captains named has ever been identified, and that one, "Vice-Admiral" Peñalosa, would have been sixteen at the time of the episode credited to him. He was in reality an adventurer well known in England because of his own fabricated journal telling about the fabulous city of Quivira, a journal he failed to exploit in London in 1671–1673 before taking it successfully to La Salle and the French government.[4] And finally, all of the supposed letter's details—lakes, rivers, trees, fish, natives—are the kind that could be easily borrowed by a student of geography such as Defoe or James Petiver. Even Captain Shapley and Major General Gibbons, two actual New Englanders whom de Fonte met in Hudson Bay, could have been taken from a book; the most convincing writers of such hoaxes knew the value of mixing real people and places with apocryphal people and places, but the real people— as in this case—were nearly always dead and unable to defend themselves.

For a long generation the de Fonte letter lay apparently unnoticed in the yellowing pages of the *Monthly Miscellany*, but it was to be made the starting point of the eighteenth-century interest in the Northwest Passage, even though the arousing of that interest was aided by a tradition that dated back two hundred years.[5] In the sixteenth century the Italian Verrazano saw Chesapeake Bay across a strip of land—or Pamlico Sound across a barrier island [6]—and returned to Europe claiming to have sighted the Pacific Ocean. And mapmakers of the same century, with no actual evidence to go on, filled up the top of North America with imaginary geography, which by the 1560's began to include in the arctic regions a mythical Strait of Anian that joined the Atlantic to the Pacific. This early strait was too far north to be of much benefit to trade, but geographers, sailors, and ambitious businessmen quickly combined to make it usable by moving it farther south. Many stories were told of ships that navigated this body of water,[7] but always the storytellers were too interested, too ready to make eyes open and palms itch for gold, or too willing to accept command of expeditions. Although all such voyages are now known to have been manufactured out of whole cloth, the projectors of the eighteenth century, lacking the Panama and Suez canals, were inclined to accept any evidence in their haste to find a natural waterway across North America. And so, when de Fonte's letter was pulled out of the files of the *Monthly Miscellany* and exploited by the interested Arthur Dobbs, the European public was conditioned to accept it, just as two decades later the same public was willing to adopt the story of the Patagonian giants because of the long, though dormant, tradition behind it.

Arthur Dobbs was engineer-in-chief and surveyor-general of Ireland under Robert Walpole and an energetic man who wished to arouse the Hudson Bay Company to greater trade and broader discoveries. By means of published articles Dobbs accused the company of not wanting to find a northern short cut to Asia, and soon the public was on his side against the powerful trade monopoly. In 1741 he hired Captain Christopher Middleton to make a voyage, the object of which was to explore all the inlets of Hudson Bay in an attempt to locate the fabled and much-desired water route. The voyage failed to find anything, but Dobbs was not discouraged. In 1744 he published a book called *An Account of the countries adjoining to Hudson's Bay* and inserted an abstract of the 1708 de Fonte journal, most of which he said he believed. Furthermore, he accused Captain Middleton of having been derelict in his searches, using as evidence a private letter from one of the lieutenants on the voyage. Not only was Dobbs able to convince many English readers; his arguments impressed the government so much that a new expedition of two ships was sent out in 1746 to make a more thorough search of Hudson Bay. Again the voyage was a

failure. But again interest was not killed, this time because two
accounts of the expedition were published in 1748, by Henry
Ellis and Charles Swaine, both of whom had gone along and
both of whom were enthusiastic about a possible Northwest Passage. Swaine, who had been clerk on the *California,* followed
Dobbs very closely in exploiting and defending de Fonte and
provided a "Chart for the better understanding De Fonte's
Letter." The next year Arthur Dobbs was still urging the like-
lihood of a Northwest Passage, this time trying to do an even
more impossible task by reconciling de Fonte's version with the
quite different one given in the sixteenth century by Juan de
Fuca. A few months later, however, when more ships returned
with more stories of failure, Dobbs lost interest and abandoned
his project—at least for the time being—of needling the government and the Hudson Bay Company.[8]

But while the most important English supporter of the short
cut to the East lost interest in the project and in de Fonte, the
furor he raised lived on. At the peak of the excitement, in 1747,
Emanuel Bowen's popular geography was first published. In it
was a long account [9] of all the efforts to find such a passage and
a summary of the "several arguments urged to prove not only the
Probability, but even the Reality, of a North West Passage into
the South Seas." There were frequent references to Dobbs and his
theories and to the false accounts on which they were based. Although this geography included some arguments against the
possibility of a Northwest Passage, it very carefully answered
them all. Many of Bowen's facts came from John Harris' collection of voyages, which had been published early in the century
but which, perhaps because its information tended to support
the newly aroused public opinion, was revised, enlarged, and
republished between the years 1744 and 1748, at the height of
the commotion created by Dobbs's resuscitation of the *Monthly
Miscellany's* letter by Admiral de Fonte.

Geography books and collections of travels were affected by
the enthusiasm of the 1740's, but perhaps its greatest historical
influence was exerted through the cartographers; for, someone
has observed, "There is nothing that has such an air of veri-

similitude as a map." [10] From times long before Ptolemy to the end of the eighteenth century—hundreds of years without instruments to provide exact locations—mapmakers were called upon to use reason, ingenuity, and imagination in deciphering known facts about the surface of the earth. But often they employed more imagination than reason or were too quick to accept new reports. Sometimes they filled in unexplored lands with pictures of sheep, horses, and humpbacked cattle, as on the Hondius globe of 1600, or, more boldly, with invented rivers or mountains, as on the Plancius Planisphere of 1592. Sometimes they sprinkled uncharted seas with nonexistent islands, as on the Henry Briggs map of North America that appeared in the third volume of Samuel Purchas' *Pilgrimes* in 1625. Sometimes, having no facts, but impelled by weighty motives, they devised theories as whimsical as the lies of some of the travelers they depended on.[11] In general, the mapmaker with the greatest reputation was most successful in getting the public to accept his theories. Such an explanation may account for much of the success with which, in the 1750's, the de Fonte fabrication was treated on the fantastic maps of Joseph Nicholas Delisle and Philippe Buache; for one was the brother and the other the brother-in-law of the most respected French cartographer of the century, Guillaume Delisle, who had died long before but whose name added prestige to the fantasies of his family.

In the second decade of the century, attracted by Russia's new interest in science and the arts, Guillaume Delisle's two brothers, Joseph Nicholas and Louis, had gone to that country as geographers. Louis accompanied Chirikoff, a commander who after making notable discoveries on the second Bering expedition died of scurvy at the end of the voyage. Joseph drew the map which was used on that expedition. As he was preparing it in 1740, a manuscript came to him from England, containing a copy of the de Fonte letter. To the false information given in this fabricated narrative, he added the real information derived from Bering's first voyage of discovery and filled up a chart of the arctic lands and waters that was so erroneous, one contemporary claimed, it did the Russian mariners "more harm than good." [12] In 1747 Joseph Delisle returned to Paris and three years later appeared before the Academy of Sciences to report on the Russian findings in the North Pacific, to read a French translation of de Fonte's letter, and to show a map which he and his brother-in-law Philippe Buache had prepared to make clear the discoveries of the supposed Spanish admiral. To add irony to irony, the mapmakers had with great difficulty and ingenuity correlated the de Fonte story with two other imaginative reports, those given by the Baron de Lahontan and Juan de Fuca, and with the real and more recent discoveries of the Russians in the Bering Sea area. This chart, "as adventurous a piece of geography as was ever published," [13] was reproduced over and over by Delisle and Buache and by the many attackers and defenders it inspired.

The debate over the merits of this "piece of geography" continued to the end of the century. The Academy received Delisle's report "with laudable circumspection," one Spanish writer of the day said in claiming that his country had never produced an Admiral de Fonte.[14] Actually the memoirs of the Academy show that it expressed approval of the plan submitted by the brothers-in-law to investigate the northwest coast of America but at the same time it hoped for more evidence before doing anything.[15] Although the leading French cartographer of the day, Jacques Nicholas Bellin, refused to honor the fantasy, it was at times accepted in France, for example, by a reviewer in the *Journal des Sçavans* in 1766.[16] What success Delisle and Buache had in their own country can in great part be attributed to their close relationship with the highly respected Guillaume Delisle.

In England, where there was a long record of interest in the Northwest Passage, an interest revived shortly before by Arthur Dobb's use of de Fonte, the imaginary cartography of the two brothers-in-law had a much more considerable vogue. In 1754, for example, the *Gentleman's Magazine* devoted space in two numbers to "Some Account of a Chart lately published at Paris by M. de l'Isle, with the different Conjectures and Opinions it has produced." [17] The second of these, the April issue, printed an adverse criticism of the French map and included seven reasons why the "le Fonte" narrative was a "forgery," obtaining the reasons largely from a bitter attack published in London the year before by John Green, perhaps the most outspoken critic of the French mapmakers.[18] Nevertheless, the editors of the *Gentleman's Magazine* permitted the defense to have the last word, for their article closed with a strong rebuttal by an old friend and popularizer of the de Fonte geography—"Arthur Dobbs, esq., governor of North Carolina." Dobbs, preparing to leave for his newly assigned post in America, still believed in the existence of, and the voyage by, de Fonte; but he was no friend of the French mapmakers, accusing them of using the Spanish admiral's geography in order to dissuade any further attempts to find a northwest water route from Hudson Bay because the land and trade around the Bay had been given to Britain. Dobbs's charge must have seemed well founded, for before the year was out the *Evening Advertiser* was urging that the £20,000 reward being offered for discovery of a route from the east be increased to £50,000 so that ships would be enticed to make the approach from the much more distant California side,[19] that is, the side into which de Fonte had purportedly sailed.

Arthur Dobbs's reappearance in the *Gentleman's Magazine* in 1754 may have had some connection with Benjamin Franklin's interest in de Fonte and a northern waterway to the Pacific. Ten years earlier Franklin had read Dobbs's arguments with approval and had favored him in the controversy with Captain Middleton. Then Charles Swaine,[20] the clerk on Dobbs's *California* in 1746 and author of a book defending both the alleged admiral and a Northwest Passage, came to America in 1750. There he persuaded Franklin and others to back him in a search for the much-sought-after Passage; and at the height of the debate over the Delisle-Buache fantasy, in 1753 and 1754, Franklin actually sponsored two sailings of the *Argo* from Philadelphia to Hudson Bay, both times under the command of Dobbs's former protégé Swaine. Although these expeditions failed in their primary objective, Franklin seemed never to lose hope. As late as 1772 he was wishing the French success in their projected voyage to the North Pole and in finding "a Passage round the North of America." [21] During some three decades of the busiest part of his life, Franklin's interest in a water route between oceans was kept alive by Dobbs and Swaine and particularly by their arguments concerning de Fonte, as the recent publication of a formerly unpublished letter reveals.[22]

This letter, which Franklin wrote in 1762 to Dr. John Pringle, his close friend and a fellow member of the Royal Society, is a long apology for the de Fonte hoax. As a defense it shows ingenuity and knowledge, but it also displays more bias and faulty reasoning than are usually discovered in the writings of the reasonable, scientific Dr. Franklin. For example, he made certain hurried assumptions about the journal. "If a fiction it is plainly not an English fiction," he claimed. Yet it is much more nearly an English than a Spanish fiction because only an English manuscript ever turned up, its dates are related only to English kings, and except for a Dutch book of 1705, its possible sources are all English. "The country is not described to be wealthy," Franklin argued. But while it offers no gold mines, the journal tells of "very excellent timber," bountiful supplies of strawberries and other fruits, and an abundance of fowl and fish, the "Mullets," for example, being "much delicater than are to be found . . . in any part of the world."

In his letter to Dr. Pringle, Franklin was also guilty of an error in science. As an eighteenth-century authority on meteorology and hydrostatics, he expounded an ingenious theory that the level of the Atlantic Ocean at Hudson Bay could be thirty-two feet lower than that of the Pacific, as the alleged journal apparently said. The Atlantic was lower because of the strong northwest winds, Franklin reasoned, not having the exact information of the twentieth century, which says that all ocean levels are approximately the same and that winds cannot affect them more than a few inches.

Franklin's bias not only forced false assumptions and errors; it made him zealous in following up the journal's reference to

Shapley and Gibbons. He wrote letters to Massachusetts asking the help of Thomas Prince, the antiquarian, who proved that the men actually lived and sailed; and he uncovered in Increase Mather's *An Essay for the Recording of Illustrious Providences* (1684) an account of how Major General Gibbons and his crew, of Boston, were once saved by a French pirate whom the General had formerly befriended. But the use to which Franklin put his discoveries again demonstrates his prejudice, for it is now agreed that the attempt to reconcile the events of the de Fonte story with those in Increase Mather are —even allowing for our superior knowledge—far from convincing. One can only conclude that the author of the 1708 hoax might have borrowed the name of his Major General Gibbons from the 1684 *Illustrious Providences,* or, better still, from Cotton Mather's *Magnalia Christi Americana,* which contains the same story and which was published in London only six years before de Fonte was invented.[23] Although Franklin's researches uncovered some real names in the false journal, they did not reveal to him that at least three different publications had already divulged the fact that a Shapley had lived in Massachusetts.[24] Furthermore, his zeal for information did not drive him in directions that might disprove his thesis, since he argued that the Spanish themselves denied de Fonte "but faintly." Actually the best contemporaneous exposé of the supposed voyage was probably that written by a Spaniard, Father Burriel, in *Noticia de la California,* and published five years before Franklin wrote his letter.

With the letter of 1762 Franklin included a chart of northern North America, the logic behind which was more prejudiced than his own. Of it he said to Dr. Pringle, "I intended to sketch a little map, expressing my idea of De Fonte's Voyage, as you desired. But I find one done to my Hand." The map which Franklin sent, with several very minor changes, was that presented the Academy of Sciences by Delisle and Buache, attacked successfully in Franklin's own day, shown by the end of the century to be impossible, and now called a "fantasy." Franklin's reading of Dobbs, his meeting with Swaine, his investment of huge sums in the ventures of the *Argo,* and his association with scientists in the Royal Society and the French Academy of Sciences, both of which had long pursued the Northwest Passage—all these reasons caused Franklin, himself the contriver of many literary hoaxes, to succumb more and more to one of the most influential travel fabrications of the century and, finally, to defend it with enthusiasm.

Franklin, Dobbs, and Swaine were the last important defenders of de Fonte, but the hope of a Northwest Passage caused such hoaxes to receive a ready hearing always; and hardly had the fictitious Spanish admiral lost favor, when another influential travel lie of the same sort was presented to the world. Although its birth is shrouded in mystery too, this lie may have been born early in the seventeenth century, the reputed father being another Spaniard, Lorenzo Ferrer Maldonado. But its christening took place late in the eighteenth century before the distinguished members of the Academy of Sciences in Paris. The godfather who officiated at the ceremony was Philippe Buache de la Neuville, a geographer-nephew of that other Buache who, before the same distinguished audience, helped to perform a similar service for the illegitimate offspring of the *Monthly Miscellany.*

In 1790 the younger Buache read a memorial before the Academy, defending the existence of a Northwest Passage and reviewing the evidence offered by many navigators, but failing to mention the then generally discredited de Fonte. Instead he relied chiefly on Captain Maldonado, the account of whose voyage Buache summarized at great length, telling how in 1588 the Spaniard sailed his ship into the east side of North America at about 70° North Latitude, descended gradually south as he went west, and at 60° discovered the Strait of Anian, going on to Japan and China before retracing his route. Maldonado's voyage, reported before such a distinguished group, created an excitement among statesmen, geographers, and historians that lasted for two decades; and, as a result, even though it has been proved impossible, it is historically of much interest.[25]

While de Fonte apparently never existed, Lorenzo Ferrer

Maldonado was a real person. In 1618 Don Garcia de Silva y Figueroa, one of the better known writers of the day, told how in 1609 he met a man whose name he forgot but who was prominent then for being a projector of flamboyant schemes.[26] In particular, Don Garcia said, the man was presenting memorials to the Council of State, accompanied by bad drawings, in which he claimed to have gone through the Strait of Anian to the South Sea. Although Don Garcia reported latitudes and longitudes and times of the year that do not always agree with those in the document quoted by Buache, the projector of 1609 was almost certainly Maldonado; for in 1672 Don Nicholas Antonio in his bibliography of writers [27] included Maldonado as the author of two works, one of which was entitled *Imagen del Mundo,* or *A Picture of the World,* and the other of which he had seen in manuscript in the possession of the Bishop of Segovia. According to Don Nicholas, this manuscript, called *Relacion del Descubrimiento del Estrecho de Anian,* gave an account of its author's discovery of the Strait of Anian in 1588. Then the bibliographer appended a little statement to the effect that Maldonado was said to have tried unsuccessfully to construct a compass without variation, an activity which Don Garcia had attributed to his anonymous mariner of 1609. And we know that about four years after Maldonado is said to have presented the Council with his *Relation,* Quiros wrote a letter to that same Council outlining plans for a voyage to the South Sea and indicating that Lorenzo Ferrer Maldonado was willing to accompany him as one of three captains.[28] So the man existed and actually wrote something about a supposed trip through the mythical far-northern Strait.

In 1781 a manuscript of Maldonado's *Relation,* accompanied by three drawings and two small maps, turned up in the library of the Duke of Infantado, whose ancestor had been one of the most important members of the Council of State during the torrid summer months of 1609 when Quiros was fighting for well-deserved recognition and Maldonado was attempting to sell a scheme.[29] Copies of the manuscript were made by the geographer Don Juan B. Munoz [30] and given to several people in and out of the government. One Spanish book of 1788 described the voyage,[31] with Maldonado's plans for fortifying the Strait, and presented arguments for and against its authenticity but on the whole accepted it. Then in 1790 Buache read his memorial, depending heavily on one of the copies of the *Relation* made by Munoz. This recognition caused the government of Spain to send orders to Captain Malaspina, at Acapulco on the Pacific coast of America, to take his ships and locate the strait that Maldonado claimed to have discovered in 1588. Malaspina spent weeks in a vain search and then continued with his scientific voyage around the world. On his return to Spain, one of his lieutenants named Ciriaco de Zevallos wrote an article [32] exposing Maldonado's fictitious voyage by demonstrating the falseness of its geography and the ignorance of its author in the ways of the sea. Others joined the attack, Malaspina himself, for example, and Baron Humboldt, the famed world traveler and scientist.

However, the affair was not ended. About 1810 Carlo Amoretti, librarian of the Ambrosian Library of Milan, discovered another Spanish manuscript of the *Relation*. Having become well known for finding and publishing Pigafetta's account of Magellan's circumnavigation, Amoretti saw an opportunity to repeat his success; so he translated the account and published it in Italian and then in French, adding a long defense of its authenticity.[33] But the defense was not at all convincing to a world that had read so many recent reports, such as those of Captain Cook, that told of far more land and ice to the north than Maldonado had found. In his great collection of voyages published in 1817, James Burney summarized the *Relation* and dismissed it as a fabricated piece of propaganda; and the next year Sir John Barrow's volume of voyages to the Arctic likewise dismissed it.[34] However, because so many people had wondered whether it was spurious or not, Barrow translated every word of the original Spanish document in order, he said, that the public might judge for itself. Maldonado has continued to be of interest to geographers and readers of travel literature, and since Barrow's time at least three writers have treated the Spanish ad-

venturer at great length.[35] Like de Fuca's story of a voyage
through North America from the west side, Maldonado's is a
geographic hoax of the late sixteenth century, but unlike de
Fuca's supposed voyage this one remained secret for two hundred years until the second strong eighteenth-century revival of
interest in the Northwest Passage made it famous.

Some of those who read the *Relation* have preferred to
class its author not with de Fuca but with the *Monthly Miscellany's* inventor of de Fonte, believing that Maldonado was not
really the author of the manuscript which Munoz said he discovered and copied in 1781. Burney, for example, followed by
Barrow, believed it to have been written not by a Spaniard but
by someone from the continental shores of the North Sea, since
all the distances reported in the *Relation* are worked out in
German, rather than Spanish, leagues. But Don Garcia had carefully stated that the 1609 mariner had lived in the Hanseatic
cities of the north, a fact that would give him a knowledge of
German. However, apparently no one but Munoz has ever seen
that original manuscript found in Spain, and no one but Carlo
Amoretti has seen the one at Milan. The historian Navarrete
described the copy in the library of the Duke of Infantado without claiming to have seen it, but his description could have
been taken from Amoretti,[36] who long before had stated unequivocally that his document, well preserved and clear, was
written in a late fifteenth- or early sixteenth-century hand.
Not knowing how well qualified the biased Italian Amoretti was
to determine so exactly the date of a Spanish document by its
calligraphy, one might wonder if his copy was not one of those
made twenty years before by Munoz, for Amoretti did not know
when or how his library acquired the manuscript. The most suspicious fact about the entire incident is that the *Relation* was
first discovered within a year of the time that Don Garcia's account of Maldonado was published.

There are other suspicious facts. In the first place, the map
of the Northern Hemisphere attributed to Maldonado seems
to be like those of Zaltieri, a type long out of date by 1609,
Japan, for example, being placed very incorrectly when its posi-

tion was quite well known by the beginning of the seventeenth century, when the manuscript was supposed to have been written. Maldonado would have been less likely to make that mistake than an eighteenth-century hoaxer, who could have depended on a map half a century too old. Second, the *Relation* claims that Maldonado met a Hanseatic ship from St. Michael, now Archangel, while he was in his Strait, and that this ship was returning from China with a load of silks; but it was the eighteenth century that made the Russians famous for exploits in the Pacific Ocean and the Bering Strait. And finally, the *Relation* has much to say about the feasibility of sailing in Arctic waters, asserting that there was much less ice there than some people thought; by a sort of coincidence, shortly before copies of the document became public property, Daines Barrington and others who believed in an Arctic passage to the Bering Sea collected and published numerous reports of mariners who told of having sailed in unobstructed waters as far as 83° North Latitude, one even claiming to have gone to 89½°, where he found an active volcano.[37] Other arguments could be advanced to show the strong possibility that the *Relation* of Maldonado's discovery of the Strait of Anian was simply a late eighteenth-century forgery composed by an overardent defender of the Northwest Passage tradition who read Don Garcia's description of Maldonado's manuscript and then wrote an invention of an invention.

However, any one of these arguments can be countered with a defense. And there is always the fact that Maldonado did write a paper about a supposed voyage and one bibliographer saw it over fifty years later. But what is important is not the antiquity of the manuscript but the fact that Buache and Munoz, actually two of the most important geographers in Europe, believed it, that a leading librarian published and defended it, that scientists listened to it, that Spanish statesmen took a chance on it, that shiploads of men sailed hundreds of miles and spent weeks testing it, and that dozens of writers have translated it, studied it, and made it famous. Truly Jonathan Swift was right when he said that "if a lie be believed only for an hour it has done its work . . . Falsehood flies and truth comes limping after it, so that when men come to be undeceived, it is too late; the jest is over and the tale has had its effect." [38]

Maldonado's was the last of the great hoaxes that affected the geography of northern North America. After the voyages of such mariners as Cook and Amundsen, a Northwest Passage was satisfactorily proved nonexistent, at least at the latitudes reported in the spurious voyages of de Fonte and Maldonado. Although neither of these two men lived in the eighteenth century, both enjoyed their greatest notoriety then. One existed only after being created in 1708; the other was real but exerted no lasting influence until his manuscript, or at least his name, was rediscovered near the end of the period. Since neither of the voyages attributed to them could possibly have been made, their completely fake manuscripts might both have been considered among the fireside travels of the school of Defoe. But then, as we shall see, almost every kind of travel falsification in the century involved geography in some fashion, Defoe's perhaps most of all.

CHAPTER
V

FIRESIDE TRAVELERS,
Before Defoe

". . . may go round the world with Dampier and Rogers, and kno' a thousand times more in doing it than all those illiterate sailors." [1]

IN A WAY, all travelers who tell falsehoods of any sort are fireside travelers. If one of them actually makes a voyage and then waits to write about it when he is comfortably seated in his warm study at home, he may add to or alter certain circumstances of the trip and thus be guilty of a kind of falsification, of grafting a domestic, hothouse product on an exotic plant. Or the innocent traveler may be the victim of a fireside editor or translator, either contemporaneous or of a later period, who feels that the original journal must be made more attractive to the public or must be tailored to fit the needs of what is considered to be a more sophisticated or a more robust time. But the most obvious kind of fireside traveler—if not the most common—is the one who never leaves his home, the one who sits cozily at his desk by the fire and journeys wholly by imagination, meanwhile letting his pen fill up an entire book with the mental wanderings. Because they knew so well the techniques and materials of the authentic voyage literature, such writers have frequently been successful in getting their imitations accepted as real. The eighteenth century is unique in the wholesale production of this variety of fictitious travel literature,[2] the kind that because it was designed to be believed should be separated completely from that other prolific variety of the period, the imaginary travel accounts, such as the fantastic, the utopian, the lunar literature, which were not intended to fool the general reader.

SOME TRUTH, SOME FICTION

One fireside traveler who actually went somewhere was the German Karl Ludwig Freiherr von Pöllnitz. In his own words he was "a cavalier of wit and distinction, but an adventurer of the first rank; a regular Proteus: courtier, gambler, author, scandalmonger, Protestant, Catholic, canon, and what not." [3] Very much like his older contemporary, the Baron Lahontan, Pöllnitz served in three armies, changed his religion six times, wandered all over Europe as a political spy, became a confidant of Frederick William I and Frederick the Great of Prussia, was always in need of money, and was always trying to get it. His *Mémoires* of 1734 went through many editions and translations and were as successful as his historical novel of the same year, *La Saxe galante*. These *Mémoires* pretend to cover Pöllnitz's life during the period 1729 to 1733 but in reality are entirely imaginary, except that they are cunningly based on the German's real travels from 1710 to 1723, which he described "more or less faithfully" in his last book, the *Nouveaux mémoires* of 1737.[4] He changed the events of his life to suit a fictitious chronology, invented others, and borrowed facts from more honorable travel writers, as in his own two "letters" on England where he relied, without saying so, on Béat de Muralt's *Lettres sur les anglois*.

An even more notorious adventurer, this one from Hungary, was Count Benyowski, who died in 1786 in an abortive attempt to colonize Madagascar for the French. His backer, a descendant of the circumnavigator Magellan, desiring to recoup his financial losses, prepared an edition of Benyowski's journals for publication; but when he died also, the book was brought out in London in 1790 by a fellow member of the Royal Society named Nicholson, who wrote an introduction that was highly eulogistic of Benyowski.[5] The book, called *The Memoirs and Travels of Mauritius Augustus, Count de Benyowsky, in Siberia, Kamchatka, . . . and Formosa,* recounted the author's experiences between 1770 and 1772 and became one of the most popular of travel relations, going through at least ten editions in German and Polish alone. In his journal Benyowski made himself the center of attraction and included a sentimental story of an affair with the young daughter of the Governor of Kamchatka, whom he could not marry because, like Odysseus in the story of Nausicaä, he already had a wife. The adoring girl nursed him through an illness and then started back with him to Europe as his "daughter," only to die pathetically on the way. Benyowski's vanity relates him to such travelers as Hennepin; his sentimentality places him in the tradition of Laurence Sterne.

When the *Memoirs* first appeared, it received much attention in the press. The *Critical Review* found it "wonderful, interesting, animated, and sanguine in the events, circumstances, and manner of relating." [6] However, the reviewer doubted the story of the governor's daughter and asserted that Benyowski certainly did not go on at least one of the voyages he claimed to have taken. The *Gentleman's Magazine,* which subjected all travel books to close scrutiny, was more condemnatory, pointing out that a number of the prints in the *Memoirs* were taken from at least two of the well-known, eighteenth-century collections of voyages and concluding that Benyowski's own pen "represents him as little influenced by a regard to truth, . . . his accounts savour much of romantic embellishment and exaggeration." [7] Yet the *Gentleman's Magazine,* relying on the book being reviewed, did give a complete summary of the author's life, speaking sarcastically all the while but helping to perpetuate a number of untruths which Benyowski told but which were not revealed until over a century later. For example, he claimed to have been born in 1741 and to have engaged as a colonel in three famous battles of 1756, 1757, and 1758, when he would have been fourteen, fifteen, and sixteen years old. Then, in the period when he was attempting to get government backing for the Madagascar venture, he gave his rank in those battles as general.

The truth is, as Captain Pasfield Oliver showed in 1890,[8] birth records in Verbowa, Poland, prove that he was born not in 1741 but in 1746, a date that would make him actually ten, eleven, and twelve at the time of the battles, hardly an age for even a Benyowski to be a colonel or a general.

But the disclosures made by the *Gentleman's Magazine* and Captain Oliver have not completely destroyed the effects of Benyowski's mishandling of the truth. For example, in its biography of the traveler *La Grande encyclopédie* depended as far as possible on his own *Memoirs* and then followed other sources, with never any suspicion that he was a liar. And the much later *Larousse du XX*[e] *siècle* is just as trusting. Perhaps even worse, the English and American encyclopedias ignore him completely, thus helping to keep the falsehoods alive. Benyowski lives most, however, in the literature inspired by his colorful life.[9] A Polish poet made him the hero of a poem; one novelist put him in her novel: another, the Hungarian Jokai, trusting him implicitly, brought out a huge edition of the *Memoirs;* a Frenchman, Alexandre Duval, composed an *opéra comique* entitled *Benyowski ou les exiles du Kamchatka;* and most impressive of all, the German Kotzebue, who often turned to travelers for subject matter, wrote a drama about the adventurer and called it *Die Verschworung in Kamchatka.* Such honors would hardly have come to the Hungarian Benyowski if he had not lied so successfully.

Europeans who went to America in the eighteenth century were especially addicted to padding their accounts or altering the facts. The most widely read and yet, finally, the most notorious of these, at least among Englishmen, was Jonathan Carver. In spite of his some twelve years in the Great Lakes region with Major Robert Rogers, Carver was not at all a dependable reporter, even though he was one of the most popular sources for other travelers who, like Chateaubriand and Crèvecoeur, at times felt the need of a crutch, and for romantic poets like Schiller, who borrowed an Indian death song from him. In his *Travels,* which enjoyed many reprintings and several translations after the first London edition of 1778, Carver boasted of his experience and his originality: "I am able to give a more just account of the customs and manners of the Indians, in their ancient purity, than any that has been hitherto published. I have made observations on thirty nations and though most of these have differed in their languages, there has appeared a great similarity in their manners, and from these have I endeavoured to extract the following remarks." [10] And then for all of his chapters on Indians he drew heavily upon other travel books. In one breath he maligned Lahontan, Hennepin, Adair, and Charlevoix and in the next breath took here a chapter on Indian marriage ceremonies from Lahontan, there a passage on war from Charlevoix, here a description of Indian lacrosse from Adair, and there "a short Vocabulary of the Chipeway Language" from "La Hontan's Dictionary of the Algonquion Language." Even the famous funeral speech which Schiller rewrote from Carver as the universally admired *Nadowessiers Todtenlied* was itself a rewriting of one in Lahontan.[11]

The only ardent defender [12] of Carver has advanced the claim that plagiarism was an eighteenth-century practice and therefore forgivable, but the less culpable plagiarists did not, as Carver did, insist so strenuously on their own originality. And even the defender has admitted that Carver lied in two ways: A lie of omission was his failure to give any credit whatsoever to Major Rogers' scheme to find a Northwest Passage, the scheme that Carver said drew him to the Great Lakes region and gave him something to write about and which he claimed as his own. A lie of commission was his attempt to avoid implication in Major Rogers' supposed treason by changing the date of his return to Fort Michilimackinac, thereby claiming not to have been present at the time the trouble began.

Carver's *Travels* has been much admired and referred to, Moses Coit Tyler, the dean of scholars of early American literature, praising it thus: "Besides its worth for instruction, is its worth for delight; we have no other 'Indian book' more captivating than this. Here is the charm of a sincere, powerful, and gentle personality—the charm of novel and significant facts, of noble ideas, of humane sentiments all uttered in English well-ordered and pure." [13] But over half a century before Professor Tyler's praise was written, Schoolcraft and other Indian authorities had already begun to expose Carver's volume as being largely a fake. And still in spite of, or perhaps because of, its false claims and its spurious origins, it is enjoyable reading, a necessity for the student of Americana, and a collector's item.

Even more has been written about the great French literary figure Chateaubriand and his visit to North America made between July and December of 1791. In several of his works, the *Essai historique* of 1794, the preface to *Atala* of a few years later, and the *Voyage en Amérique* published in 1827, Chateaubriand claimed to have traveled through New England and New York, to have visited George Washington, to have seen the Great Lakes and Niagara Falls, to have descended the Ohio and the Mississippi during a period of trouble with the Indians and the Spanish, and to have returned overland to Philadelphia—all in six months' time. Not until the very end of the nineteenth century were Chateaubriand's claims seriously doubted. Then someone showed how impossible it would have been for even this energetic young Frenchman to carry out such an itinerary in so limited a time.[14]

Although admirers of Chateaubriand rose to defend the veracity of one of France's outstanding literary figures, most of them had to be content with the theory that he went everywhere he claimed except down the Mississippi and perhaps the Ohio. From time to time other readers discovered that here and there Chateaubriand's details seemed remarkably like those of certain travel writers who preceded him in print. Finally, in 1915 Gilbert Chinard demonstrated conclusively [15] that the passages in the *Voyage en Amérique* which describe the Great Lakes area, the Ohio region, and the southern part of what is now the United States were rewritten from other travel books, notably those of William Bartram, Gilbert Imlay, and Jonathan Carver, the last two of whom had also been good models for his methods, since like him, they had used a few of their own experiences and many that were not their own. But none of the accusations, whether harsh or gentle, has been able to hurt the reputation of François Marie René de Chateaubriand, the friend of Madame Récamier, the popular literary arbiter of France, and the author of such well-known and widely read works as *Atala* and *René*.

These travelers who did go somewhere but who came home to embellish their adventures were so numerous that an account of them must be content to show how many nations they represented and to provide only the best-known and the typical examples.[16] However, many other writers of this type are treated elsewhere in the present book, among them Hennepin, in the chapter on "False Topography," or Samuel Jenner, a "Peculiar Plagiarizer." Some of the group may have been willing victims of ambitious editors who knew the financial benefits to be derived from finding someone just back from distant places. Whether the far wanderer had a manuscript journal or not did not always matter. A hack writer could be found to give him one. For example, Carver's *Travels* has been credited, with good reason, to his friend, benefactor, and publisher, Dr. John Lettsom; and much of the political philosophy found in Lahontan has been attributed to the geographer Nicholas Gueudeville.

EDITED TRAVELS

In fact, eighteenth-century editors and translators often caused travel books to say something their authors had not intended to say, sometimes with the apparent approval of the author, sometimes obviously without it. One notorious example, early in the period, is that of the "barefaced doctoring" of Basil Ringrose.[17] Before Ringrose, like Lionel Wafer one of the more "gentlemanly" buccaneers of the Spanish Main, went out on his last and fatal expedition, he left his manuscript of *The Dangerous Voyage and Bold Attempts of Captain Bartholomew Sharp, and others,* which became the second volume of Exquemelin's famous *Bucaniers of America*. Before the two volumes appeared in 1784–1785, someone, perhaps Captain William Hacke, who had stayed behind to publish his own books, obtained access to Ringrose's manuscript and altered it whenever he found an opportunity to enhance the prestige of his friend Captain Sharp, whose *Voyages and Adventures* was going through the press at the same time. For example, where Ringrose thought the pirate Sawkins "as valiant as any could be," the unknown hand added, "next to Captain Sharp." After Sharp had been replaced as commander of an expedition, the new leader ordered an old Spanish captive to be killed. At this point, obviously with the intent of making his friend more appealing, the editor inserted a touching scene in which Sharp called for a bowl of water and dramatically washed his hands before the crew, saying, "Gentlemen, I am clean of the blood of this old man." Entirely different motives—prudishness and the fear of hurting people still alive —caused John Fielding in the middle of the century to change the text of *A Voyage to Lisbon,* written by his famous novelist-brother Henry, who had died before being able to publish the work himself.

Prudishness also caused an Englishwoman translator of Le Vaillant's 1790 *Voyage . . . dans l'intérieur de l'Afrique* to adopt this practice: "I have likewise softened (if I may be allowed the expression) a few passages that possibly might be accounted mere effusions of fancy and vivacity in a French author, but which would ill accord with the temper and genius of English readers." [18] The "softened" passages usually have to do with sex. A thirty-five-word frank treatment of a native warrior's loin cloth and its deficiencies as a *"couverture"* became simply a statement that the warriors wore cloths that "hang from their girdles." When Le Vaillant said that the native women were "more coquettish than the males," the woman translator defended her sex by omitting the damaging statement altogether.[19] Even the pictures in the two editions are sometimes different. When Le Vaillant's original plate showed a Hottentot woman with a splendid coat thrown over her back but with her front entirely naked—the object being to give an example of the extraordinary custom of growing "des grandes lèvres des parties de la femme"—the translation reproduced her not only with the coat but with an apron in front that both prevented embarrassment and completely destroyed the reason for having a picture. A Kaffir warrior was also pictured as being less exposed than in the original, but for compensation he became very noticeably more handsome, with a much nicer face, broader shoulders, and a better-developed chest.

Friendship, an overly developed sense of modesty, even politics or a desire to create marvels,[20] could motivate the changes made by those people who saw travel books through the press; but the most common type of editorial influence was that illustrated perhaps by Carver's case and undoubtedly by the case of Benoît de Maillet, who was in lower Egypt in the early eighteenth century. His editor at home, the Abbé Le Mascrier, collated the works of a number of other travelers and inserted a description of upper Egypt, thus making it appear that Maillet had been there too. The result was that the spurious section contains a number of errors in geography, partly because the editor had not been in Africa and partly because one of his sources was Paul Lucas, the least reliable, the most inclined to falsehood, and the most popular of French travelers to Egypt.[21]

The chief reason why editors could influence travel accounts so much in the eighteenth century is that it was a period in which collections of voyages were very popular. From 1660 to 1800 over a hundred such collections were made, many in several editions, many translated into more than one language, and some that included twenty, thirty, even one hundred volumes. Early in the century their editors, following the practice of Ramusio, Hakluyt, and Purchas, were inclined to reproduce the original voyages, but by 1750 the method had been almost universally adopted of summarizing, combining, rearranging, and rewriting the books selected.

One of the best known of these editors was Tobias Smollett, who between 1756 and 1770 worked on at least three compilations, including a seven-volume *Compendium of Authentic and Entertaining Voyages,* and wrote his own *Travels through France and Italy.* Smollett's methods were typical, one of the most common being illustrated in the *Compendium.* Here he attributed a section on Ceylon, Coromandel, and Malabar entirely to Philip Baldaeus' 1672 account when some twenty pages of the section were extracted from other sources.[22] And he was liable to prune away anything he did not like or believe, as when he removed nearly all the enlivening anecdotes and the Roman Catholic "fanaticism" in Gemelli Careri's *Giro del Mondo,* because that favorite Italian traveler was "too apt to believe some ridiculous reports of Knavish or credulous priests and missionaries." [23] All this might have been expected, because in the preface to the *Compendium* Smollett announced that in handling his voyages he would "polish the stile, strengthen the connexion of incidents, and animate the narration, wherever it seemed to languish." But even this very liberal aim did not allow for some of Smollett's acts, such as his references to writers he did not use or, in one case at least, to a traveler who never existed.[24] That an editor who followed such policies was not unusual is proved when one learns that the *Compendium* itself was plundered by at least seven other compilers within a dozen years after its appearance.

Smollett's background as a free-handed collector of voyages prepared him well for the writing late in life of the *Travels through France and Italy,* a book of letters long thought to have been "actually written (at the places and dates prefixed to each epistle) and sent to personal friends for their private edification and amusement." [25] But while there were authentic travel letters in the eighteenth century, although not usually designed for publication, such as Boswell's from the home of Voltaire, most epistolary travel accounts were edited as much as were the journal or narrative types; and Smollett's volume is no exception. Much of it was written after his return to England, and in it he left the impression—to last for 150 years —that the knowledge and learning he displayed were original with him. In his account of Rome, for example, he insisted that "the remarks are all my own." Then he immediately worked into his own authentic observations some thirteen pages from a newly published guidebook called *Roma Antica, e Moderna* and for other supplementary facts, even many of his highly praised classical references, went to previous travelers such as Keyssler, Büsching, and Montfaucon. His only important sin in the *Travels,* however, even when judged by more exacting times, was to take from the already-referred-to guidebook an extended passage on Roman festivals and put it in what must have seemed to him a thin section on Nice. When all of these tamperings with reality are revealed, the only defense of Smollett to be offered is that his methods, both in editing the voyages of other writers and in writing his own, were not at all unusual in his day. What is true of him is true of Jonathan Carver—or Carver's editor. More important than any defense, however, is to remember that although Smollett was once known as much for his work with travel literature, today he is thought of primarily as the author of travel novels such as *Roderick Random* and *Humphrey Clinker.*

THE PRECURSORS OF DEFOE

While voyagers who mixed some fictitious elements with their own observations constituted the most common kind of travel falsifier in the eighteenth century, and while free-handed editors and translators were numerous and effective, the term "fireside traveler" is most correctly applied to the third type suggested, that best represented by Daniel Defoe, not in his one authentic travel book, *A Tour thro' the Whole Island of Great Britain,* but rather in his many pretended, sometimes just as excellent, accounts of visits to other lands. Seldom is it true, however, that the great representative is also the progenitor; and in the production of wholly fictitious books of travel, Defoe was preceded by a host of writers in his own day, most of whom were Frenchmen.

Three [26] of these belong together as late seventeenth-century authors of romances of adventure, shipwreck, and utopian life among strange people in the then unknown, but imagined, Austral continent. Gabriel Foigny's *Les Avantures de Jacques Sadeur,* published first in 1676 and then in five other editions by 1732, has, unlike the many travel books of Defoe, much that is incredible—for example, there are giant birds like those in *Sinbad* and the second book of *Gulliver,* but, as in Defoe, there are many details of ships and geography that are realistic, Jacques Sadeur even pointing out errors which he claims that the geographers have made. This book is most like Defoe in its dependence upon real travelers, such as Quiros, in its concern with colonizing southern lands, in its presentation of a "biography" extracted from the invented Sadeur's journal, to which is added a poignant tale of the narrator's last days, and in the "editor's" claims that he talked with Sadeur at the time of the voyager's arrival in Livorno. It is most unlike Defoe's narratives in its too obvious propaganda for deism and community rearing of children.

Denis Vairasse's popular *History of the Sevarites* (1675) foreshadowed Defoe even more than did the adventures of Sadeur. In the first place, it used more of the authentic voyages, like those of Tavernier, and the histories, such as Garcilaso's account of the Incas. In the second place, Vairasse's Captain Siden, who lived fifteen years in his southern Utopia only to be killed by pirates as he came within sight of his home port, like Sadeur and certain of Defoe's characters left a manuscript journal which the "editor" did no more than arrange. And finally, Vairasse not only omitted anything incredible but his attempts at verisimilitude were even better than those of Foigny, his preface containing an authenticating, signed letter and a testimonial about the exact sailing date and the shipwreck of Captain Siden's vessel. So clever were all these devices that a reviewer in the *Journal des Sçavans* failed to realize that the voyage, the captain, and the Sevarites were all apocryphal.

Les Voyages et avantures de Jacques Massé (1710), by Simon Tyssot de Patot, is perhaps the best and most believable of the three romances. It too was propaganda, creating a Utopia and attacking Christianity in general and Roman Catholicism in particular. But more important for the history of fireside travels, it too had sources in voyage literature and gave precise details about sailing, medicine, science, geography, and biography.

Defoe might have learned much from this book, but he would have had to use it in French since it was not translated into English until the year after his death.

Gatien de Courtilz [27] was quite different from these three romancers in that only one of them wrote as many as two such pieces of fiction while he produced them wholesale. Furthermore, most of his counterfeit biographies avoided oceans and uncertain geography, were called *Memoirs of* ———, and told of the intrigues and the travels through Europe of soldiers, courtesans, or courtiers. A most successful and facile writer, he was often accused in print of being a fabricator, but he never seemed perturbed by the charges. When in 1685 he published the *Vie du Vicomte de Turenne, par le Capitaine du Buisson, du Régiment de Verdelin,* writers hastened to prove that no such captain existed. Undismayed, Courtilz not only republished the volume but added a second "manuscript" left by the "Capitaine," which, he said, was the more complete. Courtilz's usual practice was not to claim his works but, like Defoe later, to attribute them to others, an old soldier perhaps, or a woman who knew court life thoroughly. As a result, his bibliography is in a greater state of confusion than is Defoe's. Because of such methods, even though they drew charges of lying from his contemporaries, Courtilz is now ranked high in the development of fiction. In fact, one of the most respected treatments of the English novel says that "Courtilz and Defoe are the founders of historical fiction . . . in that they passed off what they wrote as history and not as fiction." [28]

The contrivers of geographical romances and the authors of historical memoirs employed nearly every technique later to be thought of as belonging to Defoe, but none of the four men already discussed was so successful as the master, either in remaining anonymous or in producing hoaxes that would endure. There were contemporaries of Defoe who did rival him in those respects, however, each producing a travel book which, like many of his, was so expertly put together that it passed as being authentic; and although one of the hoaxes was exposed while its author was still alive, the others almost passed the test of time.

George Psalmanazar,[29] whose real name has never been known but who was probably a native of France, wrote *An Historical and Geographical Description of Formosa* in 1704 and a volume of *Memoirs,* published in 1765, two years after his death. Between those dates he was a very busy hack writer, working on the great collections of geography, history and travel, and writing even more than Smollett of *The Modern Part of an Universal History.* His *Memoirs* have always been considered truthful, but his book on Formosa was a blatant fraud. By depending most on his posthumous "confessions," which may have inspired Rousseau to begin his somewhat similar ones the next year, scholars have put together an almost unbelievable record.

Psalmanazar lived most of his early life in southern France, being shunted about very much because his parents were far apart and because of his schooling at the hands of both Dominican and Jesuit monks. He was a brilliant boy, argued with his teachers, learned Latin and Greek, studied philosophy, and set out on his own at about the age of sixteen. He told of once losing a job because he preferred to keep his chastity and of being horrified at the evils of men, especially after enlisting in the army of the Duke of Mecklenburg. During his some six years of wandering, he formed and executed the plan of pretending to be from Formosa, since his studies informed him that all Europeans were ignorant of that island. He invented a false language for his adopted country and studied and practiced it in order not to be trapped by suspicious strangers. Then a Scots army chaplain named George Innes found him, "converted" him from Formosan paganism to Christianity, took him to London, and brought him before Bishop Compton, who, accepting his story and his language, sent him to Oxford to teach Formosan to future missionaries. Psalmanazar, because of his wit, his languages, his knowledge of people, and his aggressive personality, became a popular figure socially. The booksellers, aided by the clever Innes, who had apparently seen through his protégé from the first, played on the vanity of the young adventurer and persuaded him to write a book about Formosa.

The preface of that book told why Psalmanazar felt obligated to publish it. He did not want the English people "to remain in Ignorance" or be "deceiv'd by Misrepresentations" in the "many Romantic Stories" which they read of the East; his "truth ought to dispel these Clouds of Fabulous Reports." The people most guilty of giving the false picture of the Orient, he said, appealing to Protestant England's prejudices, were the Jesuits. "I thought therefore it would not be unacceptable if I publish'd a short Description of the Island of Formosa, and told the Reasons why this wicked Society, and at last all that profess'd Christianity, were, with them, expell'd that Country." The bold young author pointed out errors in the books of former travelers to the East; he begged the indulgence of his readers because he had been only nineteen on leaving Formosa and was therefore unqualified to discuss certain very mature questions about it; and he told how the Jesuits—Father Fountenoy in particular—had heard of his manuscript and were vainly trying to convince people that he was a fraud.

The book contains sections on the history, the laws, the religion, the schools, the festivals, the agriculture, and the language of Formosa. The island was in some ways depicted as a paradise, with fruit trees bearing twice a year and producing fruit better than any in Europe. The natives sometimes roasted their meat, but "they commonly eat the Flesh of Venison and of Fowls raw." Such a statement had long been prepared for by its author, who had accustomed himself when in public to eat his meat uncooked. The language of Formosa, displayed in the usual travel-book fashion [30] in translations of the Lord's Prayer, the Ten Commandments, and the Apostles' Creed, was strikingly like Latin and Greek, the "articles" being *oi hic, ey haec,* and *ay hoc.* The religion of the Formosans was a blend of eighteenth-century rationalism—"men by degrees corrupted themselves"— the Hebrew rites of the Old Testament, and the transmigration of the soul theory found so often in fireside travels just before

Psalmanazar, for example, in Lahontan's Indians and Vairasse's Sevarites. All of these facts, and many others, were believable.

But there were passages in the *Description of Formosa* that caused some of the author's followers to forsake him. The Earl of Pembroke was one of these. Reading that classical Greek was taught in the colleges of Formosa, he declared Psalmanazar a fake and would have nothing more to do with him. The most difficult part to accept told how, through his ancient prophet Psalmanazaar [sic],[31] God ordered that each New Year's Day his wicked people of the little island must sacrifice 18,000 boys under nine years of age—which the people did. The wits of England made merry over this claim, especially when they rather unfairly coupled it with the religious ceremony in which the Formosans, much like the ancient Hebrews, were described as being fed pieces of the sacrificial meat of animals. At least, the following notice appeared at the end of *Spectator* No. 14, on Friday, March 16, 1711: "On the first of April will be performed at the Play-house in the Hay-market an opera call'd *The Cruelty of Atreus*. N.B. The Scene wherein Thyestes eats his own children is to be performed by the famous Mr. Psalmanazar lately arrived from Formosa: The whole Supper being set to Kettle-drums." [32] Years later, in "The Modest Proposal," Jonathan Swift was still keeping the fun alive by referring to his "friend" from Formosa who was an authority on the subject of eating children. But while Psalmanazar's bloody ritual repulsed some readers and made others smile, its inventor had ample precedent in the history of Spanish America. For example, a popular English geography at this time, John Ogilby's *America*, reported that once the Mexican town of Chulula sacrificed 6,000 children yearly; and only four years before the *History of Formosa*, Gemelli Careri had told of 20,000 human sacrifices a year in Mexico and of Peruvian priests who offered up children six to ten years of age.[33]

Psalmanazar's book went through an immediate second edition, was translated into French and German, and caused "pamphlets innumerable to be written for and against the author." [34] The title of one of these, by an anonymous writer, reveals the extent of the controversy: "An Enquiry into the objections against George Psalmanazaar of Formosa. In which the Accounts of the People, and Language by Candidius, and other European Authors, and the Letters from Geneva, and from Suffolk about Psalmanazaar, are proved not to contradict his accounts. To which is added George Psalmanazaar's Answer to Monsieur D'Almavy of Sluice [Sluys]." [35] The sort of protests which this pamphlet was answering seemed to be strong enough for the world of letters to become wary of accepting Psalmanazar completely, for his account of Formosa was never used by geographers and historians during the eighteenth century, even though they often succumbed to other such forgeries. In fact, the author admitted, in his posthumous and more reliable *Memoirs,* that in spite of an ardent defense by his protectors the "fabulous account was as much discredited by the greatest part of the world as ever."

However, before time ran out on the schemers completely, Psalmanazar's sponsor, George Innes, profited from his fraudulent investment by receiving an appointment as Chaplain General to the army being sent to Portugal. Nor was it the last time he was to receive rewards because of a literary hoax, since in 1728 he published as his own the Reverend Dr. Campbell's "An Enquiry into the Origin of Moral Virtue," getting away with his crime for two years and thereby receiving a promotion in the church.[36] The cause of all the excitement remained popular and socially acceptable, and that in spite of such incidents as the one in which the astronomer Halley, to his own satisfaction at least, showed how little the pretender knew about the sun's declination in Formosa. Gradually the world forgot Psalmanazar and he existed as a tutor, as a mess secretary for soldiers, and finally, as a translator and hack writer. Sometime in middle life, according to his *Memoirs,* he underwent a "conversion," chiefly because of reading William Law's *Serious Call to a Devout and Holy Life,* a book that affected eighteenth-century readers even more famous—John Wesley, for one. The result of the conversion was that Psalmanazar retired to a dreary part of London, immersed himself in his work,[37] and tried to make amends for what he called his "base and shameful imposture" by exposing it himself in a section on Asia which he wrote for Emanuel Bowen's *A Complete System of Geography* in 1747 [38] and by trying to live an exemplary life. He apparently succeeded because Dr. Johnson, who often dined with him in Old Street, not only hoped to pattern his own last days after those of Psalmanazar, whose company he sought more than that of anyone else, but insisted that he would "as soon think of contradicting a bishop" [39] as the man who confessed to writing a "fictional account" of his own travels and conversion, "all or most of it hatched in my own brain without regard to truth or honesty." [40]

It may be that Horace Walpole was right in believing that as a literary liar "Psalmanazar alone seems to have surpassed the genius of Chatterton," [41] but Walpole did not know of the many travel forgeries of the late seventeenth and early eighteenth centuries that have been exposed since his time. One of these was a book of "Ingenious and Diverting Letters" called *Relation du Voyage d'Espagne* (1691), written by Marie-Catherine de la Motte, baronne d'Aulnoy, as a sort of sequel to her *Mémoires de la Cour d'Espagne* (1690). Mme d'Aulnoy's fairy tales for children would alone make her important in the history of literature; but in her own day she was widely known, not only as the author of biography, romance, and lively, fictitious memoirs of English court life, but for her books on Spain, which had "an instant and very great success." [42] Both the *Memoirs of the Court of Spain* and the *Travels* were immediately translated into other languages—many times into English—and were rifled by subsequent travelers and historians, either with or without acknowledgment. In the nineteenth century they were admired by Sainte-Beuve and Ticknor and given unbounded praise by Taine.

Almost from the first, however, there were readers who were ready to question the reliability of Mme d'Aulnoy's reports on Spain. A dozen years after her death in 1705, the Abbé de Veyrac called her *Memoirs* and *Travels* "a chain of fabulous tales or piquant mockery to throw ridicule upon Spaniards." [43] Some readers noted that she mixed romance with history; others warned against her vivid imagination. By 1865 bibliographers knew that the *Memoirs* were based largely on the work of someone else, and by 1911 Martin Hume was able to express the doubt that Mme d'Aulnoy had even been to Spain, since, he said, "much of her information is easily traceable to other books." [44]

Nevertheless, it was not until 1926, in the age of "exposure," that Professor Foulché-Delbosc, a scholar-detective who knew the eighteenth century, travel literature, and Spain, proved conclusively that, like her *Memoirs,* Mme d'Aulnoy's entertaining *Travels* was a fraud. [45] In spite of the avowal, in her foreword "To the Reader," "I cite no feigned names, no persons whose death may give me liberty of attributing what I please to them," she invented the people encountered on her alleged journey to Madrid in 1679, and she not only assigned adventures to people dead and unable to defend themselves, but she moved dead people around in times when they could not have been alive. In spite of her promise to give only "an exact and true account of what I met with in my travels," she retold—often in the words of the original—facts and incidents which she read in French periodicals, letters from Spain, and—most of all—books of real travelers. For example, the Duchess of Medina Celi's lawsuit came word for word from a letter that appeared in 1678 in the *Gazette,* a favorite source for Mme d'Aulnoy. A bullfight, which could not have taken place on the date given, was lifted from Carel de Sainte-Garde's *Mémoires* of 1665. And half a dozen other books, even other people's then unpublished journals, were ransacked in the same fashion. After studying Mme d'Aulnoy's life and discovering exact sources for all her *Memoirs* and one-half her book of *Travels,* M. Foulché-Delbosc concluded that she "never went to Spain" and that her two works on that country are "mere compilations" put together "intelligently and adroitly." How intelligently and adroitly are revealed in the unbelievable success of her hoax and in the extent of the scholarship demanded in finally unmasking her.

But the acceptance of the exposure of Mme d'Aulnoy has been considerably delayed by an article written in 1928 by Mme

Jeanne Mazon.[46] This defense was willing to believe those contemporaneous witnesses who said that Mme d'Aulnoy had been in Spain, all of whom—M. Foulché-Delbosc proposed—could have been depending on the published words of the lady being charged with deceit. Mme Mazon insisted that it is not enough to show that one-half of the *Travels* was unoriginal; the prosecution must prove that every fact and incident in the volume be traced to some outside source. It was natural, she thought, that Mme d'Aulnoy resort to news reports and to other travel writers in order to refresh her memory about the geography and life of Spain, since she had waited ten years to tell about her trip and would have forgotten much. Furthermore, the defense said, the parts of the *Travels* still unidentified as belonging to someone else contain observations that could be personal and not borrowed. The prosecution had contended that these unidentified portions were the product of Mme d'Aulnoy's invention, a faculty she displayed well in her novels, her fairy tales, and her entirely fabricated *Memoirs of the Court of England* (1695). Mme Mazon's spirited fight has correctly persuaded people not to insist dogmatically that Mme d'Aulnoy never went to Spain, but it has had the further effect of obscuring the real issue.

The real issue is the fireside nature of Mme d'Aulnoy's books on Spain. It is not surprising that certain standard reference works published before M. Foulché-Delbosc's disclosure ignore the question entirely or imply that the books are genuine. It is surprising, however, that later ones make the same mistake or that the *Encyclopædia Britannica* (1959), believing that Mme d'Aulnoy provided "vivid descriptions of contemporary manners," is completely unaware of what the twentieth century has revealed about those descriptions of manners. And when a standard reference book is unaware of the latest scholarship, it may not classify the *Memoirs* and *Travels in Spain* quite so correctly as they should be classified. The *Dictionnaire des Lettres Françaises* (1954), for example, has much the best brief account of Mme d'Aulnoy; but, influenced by Mme Mazon's article, it concludes—much too weakly—that the borrowings and imitations in the books "have divided the critics into two camps. Some would have it that they contain only thefts and plagiarisms. Others see in those accounts a picaresque spirit that already foreshadows Le Sage and Beaumarchais. The truth is without doubt, as always, between these extreme opinions." [47] The truth is, of course, that if Mme d'Aulnoy went to Spain she gave very few, if any, original impressions of her stay there and that she was such a wide reader and careful workman that she has for an astoundingly long time been able to convince readers of her originality. But while her duplicity was such a well-guarded secret that her *Memoirs* lived as fact for one hundred and seventy-five years and her *Travels* lasted more than a half-century longer than that, Mme d'Aulnoy's methods of making a travel book were known in her own day by writers other than herself.[48]

Among them was the author of the *Voyage et avantures de François Leguat,* which appeared first in London in 1707, two years after the death of Mme d'Aulnoy, and then often in French, English, Dutch, and German.[49] This book tells how Leguat, a French Protestant, and eight other men from England shipped as colonists for the island of Bourbon in the Indian Ocean but ended up instead on Rodriguez. Leguat, older than his companions, wandered over the little island, studied the flora and fauna, and philosophized about the superiority of a state of nature over a corrupt city life. The other settlers becoming weary of their bachelorhood, they all built a boat and set out for Mauritius but were forced to return because of a leak. Although a second attempt was successful, they were imprisoned by the Dutch after one of them innocently tried to sell a piece of ambergris, on which the Dutch East India Company had a monopoly. They were sent to Batavia to serve as soldiers, but finally the three survivors were permitted to go home by way of South Africa, Leguat arriving in England in 1698, Paul Be——le settling in Amsterdam, and Jacques de la Case ending up in America. It was a fascinating narrative which provided much information about the places visited.

Leguat's natural history facts were considered so important, in particular the descriptions of the "Gelinotte" and "Solitaire"

"A sailor giving a Patagonian woman a piece of bread for her baby."

[Frontispiece of the first account of Admiral Byron's circumnavigation of the globe, Paris, 1767.]

"The graves of very tall human beings, whose skeletons we found, 10 and 11 feet long. . . ."

[Explanation for "H" in center of picture as found in the *East and West Indian Mirror*, 1619, plate 22, p. 180.]

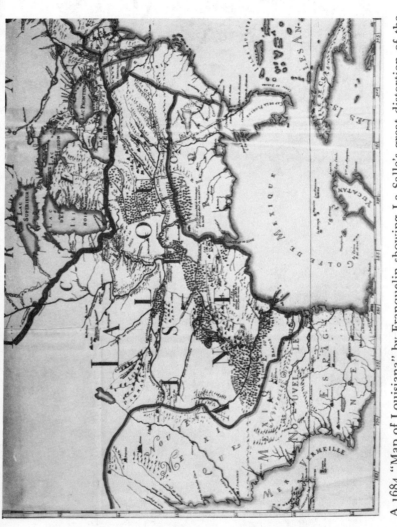

A 1684 "Map of Louisiana" by Franquelin showing La Salle's great distortion of the Mississippi River.

[As reproduced in the frontispiece to Vol. LXIII of *The Jesuit Relations*, ed. Thwaites, Cleveland, 1900.]

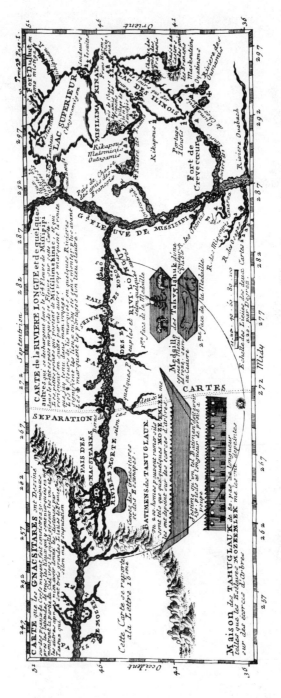

Lahontan's "rivière Longue," shown to be far north of the Missouri River and even of the Wisconsin River.

[As found in the French eds., Amsterdam 1705 or 1741.]

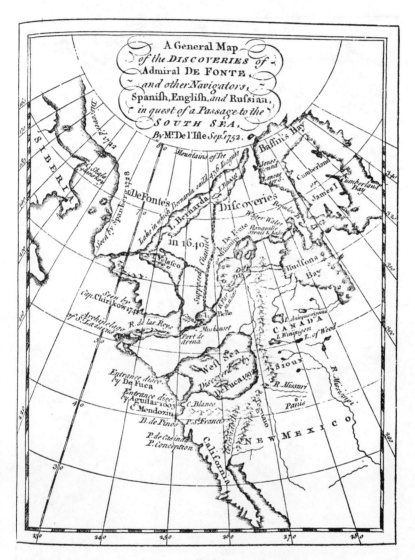

Delisle's 1752 map sent by Franklin with his letter of 1762

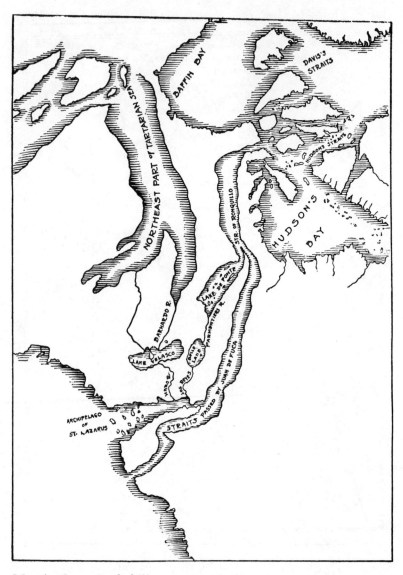

Map in *Great Probability of a North West Passage*, London, 1768.

[See note 23 to chap. iv.]

DANIEL DEFOE: "He made fiction seem like truth and truth like fiction."

[H. C. Hutchins in CBEL.]

Hottentot woman with enlarged
"lèvres des parties de la femme."

[Le Vaillant (Paris, 1790),
II, 346; or 1798, II, 351.]

The same Hottentot woman, but
with an apron that spoils Le Vaillant's reason for having a picture.

[As found in the translation by Elizabeth Helme (London, 1790), II, 50.]

birds on Rodriguez, that in 1891 the Hakluyt Society asked Captain Pasfield Oliver to edit the *Voyage*. In spite of science's approbation, however, and the dignity of being in the Hakluyt Series, from its very first appearance the journal inspired some doubts as to its authenticity. Jacques Bernard, although reviewing it favorably in his *Nouvelles de la république de lettres*,[50] asserted that the preface was not by Leguat and that two correspondents had written in to point out that the book iself was "a tissue of rubbish, which so obscures the real adventures, that it is necessary to recast it altogether in order to correct it, which someone will, perhaps, do some day." Père Casimir Freschot, another contemporary, attested that the preface was the work of François Misson, French Protestant author of the widely read *Nouveau voyage d'Italie*, and that the book itself was not by Leguat but by one of the other two surviving colonists, Paul Benelle of Metz. But Freschot, who had been attacked in the much-discussed preface,[51] has usually been dismissed as a biased commentator. Still another contemporary called Leguat's *Voyage* "fabulous travels which have no more reality than the dreams of a fevered brain." [52] In 1819 the French compiler of a collection of voyages,[53] without producing any evidence, claimed that Leguat's book was masterminded by a defrocked Benedictine monk named Gabillon, a literary adventurer who was supposed to have taken advantage of the "simple-minded" Leguat, apparently in much the same manner that George Innes had dealt with Psalmanazar three years before. And finally, in spite of the copious notes and the long introduction which he provided for the two-volume Hakluyt edition in 1891, Captain Oliver had strong reservations about the credibility of Leguat's journal, comparing it with Misson's "previous work" and showing that the two contain many of the same ideas, prejudices, facts, and expressions. However, Thomas Sauzier, by finding and publishing the official document [54] pertaining to the scheme of settling Rodriguez, by showing that a man named Leguat actually died in London in 1735, and by uncovering other external evidence, persuaded Captain Oliver to call the book authentic even while concluding, "Nevertheless, M. Sauzier's arguments, forcible as they are, will not convince other critics who hold to their opinion that Leguat's MS was largely manipulated by M. Misson." [55] Six years later, after reading and editing other travels in the Indian Ocean, the editor of the Hakluyt *Legaut* was even more suspicious of the origins of that "MS" and believed that it needed to be restudied.

In 1922 Geoffroy Atkinson did restudy it, publishing a complete exposé in which he showed, by parallel quotations, that after setting aside Misson's philosophizing, preaching, and anti-Catholic propaganda and, more particularly, after taking out everything that the journal had copied or reworked from other travelers, nothing remained for Leguat to have seen or done. For the trip to Mauritius, the ambergris episode, and the account of South Africa, Misson borrowed, often line for line, from Tavernier, while the description of Batavia is from the same traveler and two other Frenchmen. Even Leguat's real ornithological specimens, such as the famous "solitary bird," were shown to have been taken over, with the same or different names, from Du Quesne, Dubois, and Carré; and some of the curiosities, the *"gelinotte,"* for example, were invented by Misson, who borrowed its characteristics from real birds described by Du Quesne and Cauche. In a passage on the manati, or lamentin, a large sea animal to which Leguat devoted three pages, which he saw "often in numerous troops" in the bays of Rodriguez, but which no one else has ever seen there, Misson— like Psalmanazar before and Defoe after him—took previous authorities to task and, at the same time, amusingly, perhaps knowingly, revealed his own methods.

[The head of the lamentin] is extremely like that of a Hog, whatever is said in M. Corneille's *Dictionary of Arts and Sciences;* for in the Article of this Fish, . . . he is apt to erre frequently and grosly, as is the least imperfect Dictionary that ever was. He borrows the Head of an Ox, of a Mole, of a Horse and a Hog to Compose that of a Lamentin; and in this case falls into the same Confusion, which happens to all that undertake to describe things they never saw, and have no distinct Idea of. As for myself, I carefully and nearly examin'd several; wherefore I say again, that not only I, but my Companions also found the Head of a Lamentin was altogether very like that of a Hog, excepting that its Snout was not so sharp.[56]

The long description of the lamentin which followed this audacious paragraph is taken almost entirely from the maligned *Dictionary*, the added facts being found in du Tertre and Rochefort, two travelers to the Antilles, a quite different part of the world, from whom Misson borrowed elsewhere in his book and from whose accounts the dictionary article itself was constructed.[57] Like the head of Corneille's lamentin, Misson's *Voyage* is composed of pieces put together from many sources.

Although the narrative of Leguat has been proved apocryphal, the myth that came into existence with it has not yet been laid to rest. After the publishing of the Hakluyt edition, scientists became even more interested in Leguat's ornithology. Alfred Newton's *A Dictionary of Birds*, appearing in the 1890's, described the *Pezophaps solitarius* as "the *Solitaire* of Leguat, a Huguenot exile who, passing some time in 1691–1693 on Rodriguez, has left, with a very inferior figure, a charmingly naïve account of its appearance and habits . . . ," [58] and in 1899 the *Cambridge Natural History*,[59] making no mention of the travelers from whom Leguat took his *solitaire*, gave him credit for first describing it. His fictional *gelinotte*, a composite of three real birds, had to have a scientific name, even though it was dubbed "extinct." So it was classified with the rails and a French naturalist suggested it be called *Erythromachus Leguati*, a term later adopted by the *Cambridge Natural History*; two British scientists preferred *Aphanapteryx Leguati*; and Newton's *Dictionary of Birds* gave this "singular Rail" the title *Miserythrus Leguati* but agreed that it was "not generally distinct from the Mauritian *Aphanapteryx*." [60] *La Grande encyclopédie*, published before Atkinson's discoveries, still contains a biography of Leguat, taken of course from the only source that has ever been available—Misson's forged journal. And as late as 1939 the *Encyclopædia Britannica*, although it ran no article on the supposititious traveler himself, was still listing him as the most important source for the early history of Rodriguez and concluded with the statement that "his description of the solitaire is unique." [61] Most surprising of all is the fact that at least two writers—both in the 1920's and both without real evidence—can be found who refused to accept the convincing conclusions of Oliver and Atkinson.[62]

Misson's cold-blooded but delightful invention has left its marks—in geography, in natural history, and in literature. And one of the widest of those marks, made so by its blending with the traces of the d'Aulnoys, the Psalmanazars, the Courtilzes, and the contrivers of South Pacific romances, is the one left on the work of Daniel Defoe.

FIRESIDE TRAVELERS,
Defoe and After

"The travelling I mean is in books, the only way of travelling by which any knowledge is to be acquired." [1]

DEFOE DID NOT BEGIN writing his novels and fireside travels until he was almost sixty, *Robinson Crusoe* in 1719 being the first; but long before then he had been gathering the knowledge required for such literature. As a young man, if we can trust his own statements, he learned something of the world by going to Spain and, more than once, to France. And for years, as merchant, as editor of the *Review,* and as secret agent for the Tory Minister Harley and for Harley's Whig successors, he traveled by horseback over England and Scotland gathering facts that in 1724–1726 resulted in the best description of his country produced in the entire century—*A Tour thro' the Whole Island of Great Britain.* Even more astonishing than the wealth of detail he secured for his one authentic travel book is the mass of information he acquired about foreign places, especially the darker continents and distant islands. He was always interested in the colonizing of the Southern Hemisphere, submitting detailed plans for such ventures to King William and again to Harley, and late in life writing *A New Voyage round the World* partly as propaganda for such schemes. Because of this interest in foreign lands, his library, as far as we can judge,[2] was well

stocked with volumes of travel, history, exploration, and piracy.
He always considered himself an authority on these matters,
making gentle fun of his rival John Macky's knowledge of
England, jesting at all geographers,[3] even at his friend and possible collaborator, the great Herman Moll,[4] and writing the
biographies of certain well-traveled buccaneers such as Captain
Avery and John Gow. And in recent years convincing evidence
has been advanced to show that he was also the author of *A
General History of the Pyrates,* the most honored book ever
written on the subject.[5] In *The Compleat English Gentleman,*
Defoe was obviously describing himself when he said, "The
studious geographer and the well-read historian travels not with
this or that navigator or traveler, marches with not this or that
general, or making this or that campaign, but he keeps them all
company." Other people also looked upon him as an authority
on distant lands. As early as 1708, before Alexander Selkirk
returned from his stay on Juan Fernandez Island, Captain
Thomas Bowrey, needing expert advice for a project having to
do with that island, sought it from Defoe.[6]

In addition to the knowledge which he derived from traveling
and studying, Defoe early developed certain talents and displayed certain characteristics that were later to be useful in a
period of successful fireside wandering. In 1705 he began composing imaginary voyages like those by Godwin and Cyrano de
Bergerac, one of which was a satire called *The Consolidator; or
Memoirs of sundry transactions from the World in the Moon.
Transpos'd from the Lunar Language.* These were not very
good but they looked ahead to better, more earth-bound, but
still fictitious voyages. Another talent was his ability to play a
part, to identify himself—as Courtilz did—with some character
whose name or personality he assumed; in fact, after 1710 only
two of his many works were issued as his own. It has been
shown [7] that Defoe used four favorite methods to remain
anonymous: he would suggest a vague, unspecified author—"a
Gentleman"; he would use a fictitious name—"Andrew More-
ton, Esq."; he would offer a misleading identification—"Written
by a converted criminal"; he would give no information what-

soever about the author. Like his contemporary Swift, he had a
mask for every occasion.

This duplicity is one of the most unusual and controlling of
Defoe's many characteristics; it is one about which all his biographers must make a decision; and it is important for an understanding of his fireside travels. Believing himself to be religious
and highly moral, he was a good friend, a patriotic Englishman,
and a man who loved his family; but on the other hand, as a
journalist and a government spy fighting to keep his liberty and
even his life, he was for two decades forced to be a deceiver. He
was most underhanded in his political dealings during the five
years just prior to his great period of voyage literature, serving
as a Whig spy among the Tories and Jacobites whom he had
formerly served, even working for a Tory newspaper in order to
remove its sting. Only "blinded partisans," W. P. Trent has said,
can excuse Defoe's duplicity here.[8] Consequently, when he came
to write the books that have made him a figure in world literature, he found it easy to continue to change his mask at will—
to be a Robinson Crusoe, or a Captain Singleton, or a merchant
on a voyage of discovery, or perhaps a Charles Johnson, who
would be an authority on pirates. And it was especially easy because of the literary tradition into which he entered, one of
invention for the purpose of deception, with its Vairasses, its
d'Aulnoys, its Psalmanazars, and its Missons.

Considering all these facts, *liar* may be too harsh a word for
Defoe as the supreme creator of literary hoaxes. But it was not
always so. In his own day, rival writers "exposed" him as Courtilz
had been "exposed." An enemy like Charles Gildon might
publish a satire that permitted Robinson Crusoe and Friday to
toss their mendacious creator in a blanket,[9] while another Defoe-
hater, *Read's Journal,* could speak sneeringly of "the little art
he is truly master of, of forging a story and imposing it on the
world for truth." [10] A more humorous example, but less well
known at the time, would be that of the Earl of Oxford, son of
the Tory statesman whom Defoe served as spy. In 1732 the young
Earl kept a journal of his tour of England, and in it, thinking
that John Macky had written Defoe's *Tour,* he accused Macky

of being a liar.[11] Such attacks, although frequent in his own day, largely subsided during the century after Defoe's death, when as a novelist he was not a popular subject for criticism.[12] But when he was rediscovered his methods proved shocking. By the end of the Victorian era, Sir Leslie Stephen credited him with "the most amazing talent on record for telling lies," and George Aitken could say, "We are now told that he was a consummate liar." Later critics have been more concerned with the ways in which Defoe achieved such perfect verisimilitude and less concerned with the morality of his approach. Professor Arthur Secord's classic study favors a lenient judgment because Defoe used real historical and geographical facts even while inventing a framework for them.[13] And one recent student of eighteenth-century travel literature concludes with the defense that Defoe had "a genius for parquetry, piecing together bits from everywhere in new designs" and that, consequently, "No longer magician or liar, he now stands before us as the journalist par excellence." [14] In other words, Defoe is to be classed not with Psalmanazar, who made up his description of Formosa almost completely, but with Misson, who invented almost nothing about the lands he described. The author of *Robinson Crusoe* defended his "parquetry" on still other grounds. From the point of view of the reader, such writing, he said, was "allegoric history . . . designed and effectively turned for instructive and upright ends." [15]

Nevertheless, Defoe intended to deceive the public when he put his books together. Some of them were better as realistic fiction than as apocryphal voyages—the first part of *Robinson Crusoe, Moll Flanders, Colonel Jacque,* and *Roxanna,* for example—since they fooled only a relatively few people and had little to do with geography and history. Others were more successful as hoaxes and have caused not only much pleasure to the general reader but often much anguish to the scholar. These include at least six books, not counting *A History of the Pyrates,* "by Captain Charles Johnson," but the latter seems to belong to real voyage literature—romanticized as it very well may be— rather than to the extreme kind of fireside travels.

The *Memoirs of a Cavalier* (1720) and *Captain Carleton* (1728), both of which are of the school of Courtilz and Mme d'Aulnoy, are pretended autobiographies of soldiers who toured Europe fighting in various famous real battles under well-known leaders. The first of these has had little trouble being assigned to Defoe, although the second edition, published some ten years after the author's death, claimed that the "Cavalier" was in reality Sir Andrew Newport, and in spite of such endorsements as the famous one of Lord Chatham, who, until he was disillusioned, considered these *Memoirs* the best firsthand account of the Civil Wars.[16] However, on investigation Andrew Newport was revealed to be only eight years old at the time of some of the battles he described; no such cavalier could be found to have held the positions assigned to this one under Gustavus Adolphus and Charles I; and the entire book turned out to be cleverly put together from the best-known histories of the day. Yet the preface which Defoe wrote anonymously for his book insisted that it was better than the histories. "Do those relations," he asked, "give any of the beautiful ideas of things found in this account? Have they one half of the circumstances and incidents of the actions themselves that this man's eyes were witness to, and which his memory has thus preserved?" And then with the greatest audacity, Defoe continued, "In a word this work is the confutation of many errors in all the writers upon the subject of our wars in England." One of the "confuted" writers mentioned by the "editor" was the Earl of Clarendon, whose classic *History of the Rebellion* was itself a major source for the *Memoirs of a Cavalier*.

Captain Carleton—the setting for which is in England and Spain—with the same sort of profession of truth as that in the *Memoirs of a Cavalier* and with the same perfect air of reality about it, has had a very hard time getting into Defoe's bibliography.[17] Many readers are unable to accept the fact that during his last twelve years Defoe wrote more than any other person in all literature has been able to do in a similar period—even Honoré de Balzac—and as a result they become suspicious of efforts to assign so many books to him without much external evidence. Furthermore, there was a Captain Carleton, just as there was a François Legaut, and the real captain's descendants have often joined with scholars to attempt establishing his connection with the *Memoirs*. However, in recent years Professor Secord has shown that while the story does in some ways follow the career of the real person, it often departs from that career to describe battles the actual Carleton never participated in and to change history in order to make the fictitious facts hang together. Books by Abel Boyer and John Freind were the sources for that part of the captain's *Memoirs* dealing with England; and for his supposed trip to Spain, the Countess d'Aulnoy's fireside *Travels in Spain* provided both real scenes and personal adventures. Dr. Johnson believed Carleton's story to be authentic. Sir Walter Scott published it as history, and in 1929 an editor,[18] apparently without knowing of Secord's convincing demonstration of five years before, brought out the *Memoirs* as authentic, thus renewing a controversy that had seemed to be settled.

The hero of *The Life, Adventures, and Piracies of the famous Captain Singleton* (1720) apparently existed only in Defoe's imagination, but Captain Roberts, like so many men about whom the eighteenth century built false travels, was a real person who actually went to at least some of the places described in his *Four Voyages* (1726).[19] In spite of its dependence on authentic travel books, Defoe's account of Roberts was in 1745 accepted by Thomas Astley's *A New Collection of Voyages and Travels* as the chief authority on the Cape Verde Islands, even though Astley was forced to correct so many errors that he became somewhat suspicious. Captain Singleton's is a better story and has even been called "the best geographical romance which has ever been written."[20] The first half recounts Singleton's early life at sea, his being set ashore on Madagascar with other mutineers, their escape by small boat to Africa, and their unprecedented march across that continent to safety on the other side; the second half concerns the later life of Singleton as a pirate accompanied by his faithful Quaker friend William Walters, and deals with their subsequent "repentance" which led them to retire with all their ill-gotten gains to London, where Captain

Singleton married the Quaker's sister. It has sometimes been said that the account of the trip across Africa was astoundingly ahead of its time in geographical knowledge, but again Professor Secord has demonstrated that, as usual, Defoe followed sources available to everyone—the *Atlas Geographus* (1717), his own earlier stories of pirates, William Dampier's voyages, and for building the boat and leaving Madagascar the *Voyage of Leguat,* another fireside travel book. And, as usual, the resulting composition was so successful that at least one nineteenth-century writer accepted Singleton as a historical person and suggested that he be considered a "claimant for the honour of the discovery of the sources of the White Nile." [21]

Of all Defoe's fireside travels the most discussed, the most influential, and the most nearly approximating the type of Misson's *Leguat* is *Madagascar; or Robert Drury's Journal, during fifteen years captivity on that Island* (1729). The 1719 story of Robinson Crusoe owed its inception to the account by Woodes Rogers of the life of Alexander Selkirk on Juan Fernandez Island; and in much the same fashion, it has been shown, the main ingredients for the 1729 *Journal* seem to have been found in a newspaper notice:

> A boy lately arrived in a galley from the Indies gives account that the Degrave, an East India Ship of 800 tun, valued at [£]100,000, sprung a leak some time since on the coast of Madagascar, where the men landed, with their effects, and also carryed their guns on shore, but could get no provisions of the inhabitants, who said 'twas not customary to supply strangers till they delivered up their arms; which they had no sooner done but those barbarous people killed them all but the boy now come over.[22]

Defoe, apparently starting with this suggestion, perhaps after talking with the boy and other sailors, developed a story in the usual fireside manner by making a personality of his character Drury, changing the boy's time of return from Madagascar to 1717, permitting him some of his own experiences and adventures, giving him others that could be found wholly or in part in the voyages the author knew so well, from the same books providing realism in plants, animals, native customs, and native languages, and writing a preface that both defended Drury's truthfulness and supplied authenticating evidence that the journal could be trusted. One of these "authentications" was said to be from an actual Captain William Mackett, whom Defoe quoted as believing the narrative because he had brought Robert Drury home after the fifteen years' captivity. Then Defoe hastened to give his own editorial opinion that Captain Mackett was "a person of the highest Reputation for Integrity and Honour" and would not "countenance any trifling Fables or Impositions." [23] This honest captain, whose style was so much like that of Defoe, pops up again as a slave-trading friend of filibusters in the *History of the Pyrates*.

Robert Drury's Journal was seemingly not questioned seriously in the eighteenth century, although some doubt about it must have existed since the bibliography to Pinkerton's *Voyages and Travels* of 1814 asserted that "the authenticity of this amusing work seems now fully established." [24] But Emile Blanchard in 1872 and Captain Pasfield Oliver in his edition of the *Journal* (1890) were convinced that much of it was taken from such works as de Flacourt's *Histoire de Madagascar* (1661) and that the "editor" borrowed other information from, and repeated phrases and ideas found in, some of Defoe's writing, for example, *Captain Singleton* and *The True-Born Englishman*. As a result, ever since the issuance of Captain Oliver's edition of *Drury,* Defoe has been accepted as at least a collaborator. In 1939 and 1943 Professor J. R. Moore [25] added other important sources for Drury, pointed out its endless Defoe mannerisms, showed how inconsistent the character of the narrator was, proved that the map Defoe provided was not only borrowed but did not always accord with the *Journal,* and concluded that:

1. The *Journal* is clearly a work of fiction, expressing many of Defoe's own interests and observations and written throughout in his own style—and yet it gives one of the most realistic accounts of Madagascar in existence.

2. The *Journal* is largely based on printed sources, some of which can be identified beyond question—and yet it is colored and

sometimes even shaped by an undercurrent of details which must have come to Defoe from oral transmission or from unpublished manuscript material.[26]

One of the chief inconsistencies in the character of Drury resides in the fact that Defoe made him an ex-slaver and an ex-pirate, who not only never went to school but for some fifteen years spoke no English, and then endowed him with the ability to draw up a long vocabulary of English and Malagasy words in parallel columns.[27] This vocabulary also provides more evidence for Defoe's ability at "parquetry." While much of it was taken from previous books about Madagascar, it has words that are original and that must have been obtained from the many pirates and sailors Defoe knew, for example, from the same Captain Bowrey who in 1705 had asked Defoe's help in a project about Juan Fernandez and who in 1702 had been in the process of using his sailors to assist in making a record of the languages of Madagascar.

The chief sources for *Robert Drury's Journal* are finally shown to be several. Some of its facts could have been taken from any one of several compendia of the day, for example, John Ogilby's big volume on Africa (1670), or the *Atlas Geographus* (1717),[28] which had been studied for the writing of Captain Singleton and which the "editor" of that book admitted to having read only to disagree with or add to. But for other bits of curious knowledge and dozens of incidents, the author could have gone only to the twenty-four pages of *A Relation of Three Years Suffering of Robert Everard, upon the Coast of Assada near Madagascar*,[29] which was not published until three years after *Drury's Journal* made Madagascar popular but which had been in manuscript for three decades and may have been known by numerous people, including Defoe. For example, in each story, when the king approached, women danced out to meet him with cow's tails attached to sticks in their hands; Drury and Everard were cured of the yaws in the same fashion; and fighting, circumcision, fire-making, wild-hog hunting, and many other customs and events were the same. But in putting the *Journal* together,

Defoe made most use of Robert Knox's *An Historical Relation of the Island of Ceylon* (1681),[30] a book that had also been an important source for *Robinson Crusoe* and *Captain Singleton*. Both Drury and Knox went to sea before age twenty and were captives on an island to which they had gone to trade for slaves; both returned to London, where in old age they related their adventures; each was lured inland and captured by a native king; each made a very dramatic flight overland to the coast, later on indicating on a map the line of escape; each told of writing on tree leaves; each drew up a vocabulary, Drury's much the better; and both books contain certificates of authenticity, Knox's from the Royal Society and Christopher Wren, Defoe's from the relatively unknown Captain Mackett. In composing *Robert Drury's Journal,* Defoe was such a "studious geographer and well-read historian" that he produced an imitation that has been read and quoted more than any of the real travels it imitated and adapted.

Since its first publication it has been reissued six times, and until recently it has been a prime source of information for almost every work on Madagascar. Although Dr. John Campbell, one of the great eighteenth-century compilers of voyages, refused to use any of Defoe's writings about piracy, he quoted *Drury's Journal* extensively, believing it authentic.[31] A traveler to Madagascar in 1792, putting his account together years later, continuously vouched for its accuracy.[32] A hydrographer of the twentieth century quoted it.[33] In 1891–1892 *La Grande encyclopédie* ran a short biography of Robert Drury, employing the *Journal* as its source, but three years later, after the research done by Oliver had taken effect, omitted the *Journal* from a list of authorities cited for the article "Madagascar." And now all encyclopedias, aware of the latest scholarship, avoid mentioning Drury's name or the book about him. He has become a myth, but a myth that will almost certainly be kept alive by its originator's reputation.

A New Voyage round the World by a Course never sailed before (1724) is different from Defoe's other apocryphal travel books. For it the author invented a merchant captain and sent

him on a trip that was designed to discover new lands in the
South Pacific and bring in rewards both from trade and from
captured Spanish ships. The captain, who was also narrator of
the story, went first to South America, then, after gently quelling
a mutiny near the spot where Magellan and Drake had hanged
their mutineers, reversed the normal route for circumnavigations and sailed east. He touched at Madagascar, about which
Defoe probably knew and wrote more than any other person,
had adventures and narrow escapes among uncharted islands in
the region of Australia, spent much time on the coast of Chile
and Peru, encountered storms on the southern tip of South
America, and then before sailing home with booty for himself
and his lucky crew, had a rendezvous in Argentina with a large
detachment of his men that had hiked through a pass in the
Andes and all the way to the east coast, stopping here and there
to gather gold from river beds. *A New Voyage* is obviously an
outgrowth of its author's active interest in getting England to
compete with Spain in developing South America. He had drawn
colonizing plans for King William, burned them, and then
redrew them for Harley in 1710, being more responsible than
any other person for that statesman's reluctant acquiescence in
the policy that led to the South Sea debacle and the adverse
criticism the policy drew after 1720, as related, for example, in
the third part of *Gulliver*.[34] But while the voyage and events
make the book different, it was manufactured in much the same
old fashion, by the author's employing his talents and his
library of travels, such as those made by Sir John Narbrough,
Frézier, the early Dutch and English circumnavigators, and
William Dampier, the title of whose *A New Voyage round the
World* Defoe parodied and from which he took many suggestions. This hoax by Defoe was exposed very early and has never
had the influence nor the popularity of some of the others—
Carleton, Drury, and *Singleton,* for example.

Each of the fireside travels that Defoe authored has its distinctive traits, but each also clearly shows his hand. Taken together
they display a set of peculiarities in style and philosophy that are
invaluable, not only to the scholar trying to establish Defoe's

bibliography, but also to the critic who wants to study his technique, the biographer who wishes to understand the man, and the librarian who must catalogue him. Many students of Defoe have worked at the really fascinating job of finding him in his novels—Aitken, Trent, Secord, Dottin, and Moore, to name only the most important. They have shown that from *Crusoe* to *Drury* he imitated and borrowed from dozens of geographies, histories, and travel writers, but most of all from Dampier, Frézier, Knox, the *Atlas Geographus,* and the accounts of the buccaneers, including the *History of the Pyrates,* which he probably wrote himself. They have found the recurring prejudices and the repeated ideas [35]—defense of Protestantism and the married state, opposition to the divine right of kings, a puritan-like morality, an interest in and display of languages, and a dislike of horse racing, cockfighting, and the Portuguese. They have segregated his distinctive traits of style—digressions with apologies, dialogues for realism and life, the historical present, and a frequent use of irony. And they have put together a list of Defoe's dozens of definitely peculiar expressions—"surprised with joy," "growing old and crazy," "put the enemy into confusion," and "for now I must call it so." All of these kinds of internal evidence provide excellent support for whatever external evidence is available and determine with a high degree of certainty which of the apocryphal voyages belong to the Defoe canon and which of those that have been attributed to him must be kept out, as, for example, *Signior Rozelli, Robert Boyle,* and *Mother Ross.*

In the third part of *Robinson Crusoe,* Defoe argued that "this supplying a story by invention is certainly a most scandalous crime." The most widely read inventor of fireside travels was not tongue-in-cheek condemning himself. His criticism was directed at the popular seventeenth-century French romances and not at his own "histories," as he called them, which were set in actual places, which contained characters with the qualities of real people, and which, to him at least, were didactic. Even while titillating the reader with salacious details in *Moll Flanders,* or leaving Captain Singleton with the profits from his piracy, or condoning the semifilibustering activities of Colonel Jacque, he always emphasized this element of didacticism; and in 1722, his *annus mirabilis* in productivity, he defended with some pride the current "fashion" of writing fictional, but realistic, travel biography by saying that "the history of men's lives may be many ways made useful and instructive to those who read them, if moral and religious improvement and reflections are made by those who write them." [36]

<h3 style="text-align:center">A FRENCH DEFOE: FRANÇOIS COREAL</h3>

In the very fruitful year in which Defoe was offering this defense —unnecessary for most readers but directed at enemies like Charles Gildon—a French travel book was published that contained nearly all the elements and displayed most of the personal characteristics found in the fake voyages of the English master, including in particular the vaunted didacticism. Called *Relation des voyages de François Coreal aux Indes Occidentales* (1722), this book came out in Paris in two volumes, appeared simultaneously in Amsterdam in three, was popular enough to undergo a reprinting in Brussels in 1736,[37] and was one of the chief influences on Rousseau's theories of primitivism, especially in the *Discours sur l'inégalité*.[38] The first half purported to be a translation of an English manuscript of the Spaniard Coreal's travels in the Antilles, Florida, Mexico, and Central and South America between the years 1666 and 1697; the rest of the set was filled in with reprintings of voyages by Raleigh, Narbrough, and other very real people. It is the first half only that was manufactured in the fashion of Defoe. Whoever the author was, he covered his tracks so successfully that he has until now remained unexposed. And he demonstrates the popularity of a type of literature that becomes more important historically with each new revelation of its kind.

Most readers of Coreal have accepted him as authentic; others have been puzzled. The only contemporaneous review of the book, that given in *Mémoires historiques et critiques*,[39] a respectable Amsterdam periodical, ran through two issues and was quite favorable, summarizing Coreal's life as given in the

Relation and quoting long excerpts from his voyage. But all successful hoaxes—*Leguat,* the *Travels in Spain,* the *History of Formosa,* and *Robert Drury,* for example—raised doubts before their contrivers were unmasked. Coreal's volume of voyages went through such a period of doubting too, for in the middle of the eighteenth century Prosper Marchand announced categorically that it was only a collection of "fragments taken from several effective accounts by some starving compiler." [40] However, by the end of the century bibliographies of travels and dictionaries of biography, although aware of Marchand's opinion, were praising Coreal and including long accounts of his life, taken, of course, from the only source available, the fictitious book itself.[41] In the middle of the nineteenth century Rich's *Bibliotheca Americana nova* made the statement [42]—to be repeated many times by other commentators and to be typed in on many library cards—that "there appears no reason to doubt of the identity of Francis Coreal, or of the fact of his having visited the countries he describes. The only motive for such a doubt arises from the work never having been printed in Spanish, and from the French editor making no mention of the source from whence he obtained the original." *La Grande encyclopédie* stressed the doubt even while giving a biography, but the great Spanish Espasa pointed out that the theory that Coreal was a pseudonym "is not founded on any real evidence." The twentieth century has continued both traditions, Joseph Thomas' biographical dictionary accepting the man and the book and the *New Century Cyclopedia of Names* concluding that "the work is generally believed to be fictitious." [43] However, the majority of the commentators have not believed it fictitious, and those who have thought it was—from Marchand to the *New Century*—have offered no real evidence. That evidence can now be provided.

There are a number of reasons why readers of travel literature might suspect Coreal's origins. First, as the *Bibliotheca Americana nova* pointed out, the book was published only in France, even though the author was said to be a Spaniard and his manuscript to be in English. This set of conditions reminds one immediately of such English inventions as the unbelievable *Voyage of Domingo Gonzales to the Moon,* of the believable *Voyage of Don Manoel Gonzales . . . to Great Britain,* with which Defoe had something to do, and of the long tradition of letters by fictitious foreign observers, such as Marana's Turk and Montesquieu's Persians. Second, after some two pages of very general biographical details and sailing directions, the first-person narrator made only a few weak attempts to record personal experiences. These consist of statements that he was with the buccaneers in the West Indies and Central America in the 1680's, of reports given him by someone named Dom Pedro de las Fuentes of Quito or a learned Fleming in Peru, and of claims that "I ate this," "I heard this but don't believe it," or "I can say this from having been there." Third, and closely related to the lack of personal experience, the book is almost entirely a compilation of social history, natural history, and geography, exactly the kind of information that could have been taken from other books. Fourth, this supposed travel account contains much unnatural propaganda. Its author, while claiming to be a good Catholic and a loyal Spaniard, constantly criticized the Church and repeatedly pointed out how Spanish America could easily be conquered and settled by other nations. Fifth, most of Coreal's maps, drawings, and pictures are to be seen in earlier travel books by Froger, Careri, Frézier, and Feüillée. And sixth, many passages in the *Relation* seem so familiar that one becomes convinced he can find them in these same sources or others like them. Such a search will show that throughout his book Coreal seemed to be borrowing from over a dozen of the best known of previous travelers and historians, among them Careri, Gage, Nieuhoff, Frézier, and Dampier. A list of sources so formidable would not only require a compiler to have a rather extraordinary library of travel books but it would demand that he go easily and yet thoroughly through this library, extracting and arranging systematically for each country described. Knowing that this system was followed by the many eighteenth-century geographies, one might suspect that to save time Coreal's inventor used such a book. And that is what he did, for almost everything in the *Relation* was taken, never with an acknowledgment, from the fifth volume of the *Atlas Geographus,* published in London five years earlier and a favorite source for other apocryphal voyages, such as Defoe's *Captain Singleton* and *Robert Drury.*

Although the author of the *Relation* attempted to avoid detection by manipulating his source in a variety of ways, there are countless examples of outright copying of passages almost word for word. The first place Coreal described at any length was Cuba. After locating it by references to five geographical points around it, exactly the same five and in the same order used by the *Atlas Geographus,* and after giving other information from that book, he pointed out two "remarkable things," a valley full of rocks so round that they were used as cannon balls, and a natural fountain that produced pitch fit for calking ships. The same two "things" are told of, often in the same words, by the *Atlas.*⁴⁴ For examples of other close borrowings in other parts of the *Relation* one could turn to Coreal's statistics on the great cathedral of Mexico City, found not only word for word in the *Atlas* but also word for word in Woodes Rogers, the *Compleat Geographer,* and Gemelli Careri.⁴⁵ The difference is that Rogers and the two geographies recognized their debt to Careri while the fictitious Coreal thanked no one. Or his thirteen Brazilian animals could be inspected and twelve of them found, sometimes changed a bit and in an entirely different order, on three pages of the *Atlas Geographus,* which had painfully collected them from real travelers such as Nieuhof and Acosta.⁴⁶

But most of the borrowing done by the compiler of the *Relation* was of a sort that is more difficult to recognize. In general, his method was to read an entire section and then rewrite it, rearranging, selecting, sometimes padding, sometimes copying the original. Thirty lines on Jamaica, its soil, plants, grasslands, and wild herds of formerly tame animals, were extracted from four big double-column pages in the *Atlas'* treatment of the same island.⁴⁷ At the beginning of his account of Florida, Coreal says, "In 1669 I went to Florida, and I lived there for some months. During this time I attempted to find out as exactly as

possible the condition of this great country which is not so well
known as Mexico and Peru and the interior of which is not in
our [meaning Spanish] possession." Then he told of the coasts,
rivers, trees, animals, birds, capes, islands, and especially of the
Indians—their marriage customs, wars, medicine, religion,
priests, crops, and even their sodomy—all of which he found
in the single big source.[48]

One original feature of the *Relation*—a disconcerting one to
the detective—was its author's occasional supplying of names
not found in the *Atlas,* even though all the facts that go with
the names are there. For example, in its section on Florida, the
Atlas tells of the Indian priests and Indian chiefs without giving
them a title. Coreal called them *jaounas* and *parouistis,* names
that, because of the spelling, were apparently taken from the
Sansons' French geography,[49] which was often quoted by the
Atlas Geographus but which was far too sketchy to be of much
assistance in putting the *Relation* together. Infrequently Coreal
took a name from some other, unknown source, as when he
provided the Spanish word *tabardillo* for the deadly typhus
fever of Central America,[50] although the *Atlas* had all the other
information about it he needed. But such additions are quite
rare and insignificant and necessitated only the opening of a
dictionary or another geography book.

Just as disconcerting was Coreal's trick of taking from the
Atlas something having to do with one country and transferring
it to his account of some other country. For example, in describing the amphibious manati—Leguat's lamentin—of Nicaragua,
he told an interesting story of how a certain tame one of which
he knew was so gentle it would let children ride on its back in
the water. His source told the story in its article on Hispaniola,
not Nicaragua.[51] Elsewhere the *Atlas* quoted Peter Martyr to the
effect that Amazons once inhabited Martinique. Coreal repeated
the tale and then added that periodically these Amazons mated
with cannibals from neighboring islands. His addition came
from an account of Columbus' visit to the island of Guadaloupe,
which appeared over four hundred pages away in the *Atlas.*[52]
Such changes as these show that the author of the *Relation* was

guided by at least two motives—to make his travel book interesting and to cover up his tracks.

Another device for throwing the reader off the scent, used only once, was to quote a fake source. His "two remarkable things" on Cuba, the rocks and the pitch, Coreal claimed falsely, were taken from "our Gonsalo Ovetano," meaning, no doubt, Gonzalo Ferandez de Oviedo y Valdes, the author of the great *Historia general y natural de las Indias,* a storehouse of information for many books about America, and sometimes referred to by the *Atlas.* Giving such false leads had already been proved successful by other eighteenth-century contrivers of fictitious travels, for example, Defoe, who in *Captain Singleton* had gently argued with his source, the same *Atlas Geographus,* about details of topography, and Misson, who borrowed a passage on the manati and then condescendingly corrected it.[53]

The author of the *Relation* had an even more brazen way of handling sources. Although he took both a description and a drawing of a South American Indian boat called the *balza* from Father Feüillée and admitted doing so,[54] he was not anywhere else so scrupulous. In his treatment of Peru and Chile, Coreal twice referred in footnotes to M. Frézier, the latest important traveler to have gone to South America. In one instance the note simply mentioned the man and his *Voyage de la Mer du Sud,* but in the other the reader was asked to look into "Fraizier" for a "confirmation of all this." [55] Actually the passages in question, having to do with religious hypocrisy, especially of the priests in Peru, are so much like some in the earlier travel book that "confirmation" is not at all the right word. Furthermore, Coreal, without any acknowledgment, found Frézier to be a good supplement in many ways to the *Atlas Geographus,* which was published too early to include that writer's information. Since Frézier, like nearly all travelers, made some use of previous authorities, including the Inca historian Garcilaso de la Vega and others ransacked by the *Atlas,* one can not always be sure which of the two books Coreal was indebted to for a particular passage in his section on Peru and Chile—a description of the houses, streets, and canals of Lima, for example. But one can be quite sure that Frézier was the original for facts about Peruvian sex life; and certainly he provided Coreal with a chart of Callao, while either he or Feüillée supplied one of Lima.[56] In considering Coreal's use of these two French travelers, one should not forget two facts, however. What he took from them for his account of the eastern coast of South America is very little in comparison with what he found in the *Atlas Geographus*—distances, cities, Indian customs, natural history, silver mines, and the history of the Incas. And other writers of fake voyages—the creator of Admiral de Fonte, for example, but Defoe in particular—knew the value of mixing truth with their fiction, of sometimes mentioning some trustworthy real traveler. It helped to allay suspicion and, by association, it lent dignity to the venture. Furthermore, French readers could be expected to recognize something stolen from Feüillée and Frézier more easily than they would be expected to know something derived from the English *Atlas Geographus*.

Occasionally the compiler of the *Relation* altered the facts taken from his big geography, sometimes out of ignorance, sometimes to make a correction, sometimes to add spice. For example, in describing the much-talked-about *colibri*, he tried to be original by adding that its "melodious song" is "similar to that of a nightingale," when actually this little hummingbird's sound is produced by the whirring of its wings. Once he carefully corrected the spelling of the *Atlas'* "Guiabea Tree" to "Guiac" and then gave, from some undiscovered origin, full details about how this then very famous plant was used as an antidote to "*la verole*," or syphilis.[57] All around this unusual insertion, however, are close borrowings from the *Atlas*. To provide a bit of local color, originality, and drama to the *Atlas'* account of the great Guatemala earthquake of 1541, he ignored a story of how the earthquake was caused when an unhappy woman blasphemed too strenuously, and in place of it he put one that told how several hours before the catastrophe happened some natives came to warn the governor and were laughed at for their pains. But even this substitution is hardly original, for in its article on Nevis Island in the Antilles, the *Atlas* had told of the inhabitants escaping such an earthquake because they paid attention to the warning of the Indians.[58]

Less excusable were some of Coreal's tamperings with the statistics he found. Succumbing to the chief sin of the real traveler—exaggeration—he insisted that the manati was often forty feet in length, although neither his source nor any of the many voyagers who described this sea animal would give it more than twenty or twenty-five feet,[59] and scientists will not allow it more than thirteen. In treating the city of Lima, Coreal retained the *Atlas'* 40,000 Negro population but altered the number of Spanish inhabitants from 50,000 to "more than 12,000 to 15,000." [60] One's first impulse here is to think that the *Relation* was depending on some other authority; but no other possible source gives the number 40,000 for the Negroes, and none has such a disparity between the whites and the blacks as Coreal claimed.[61] The reason why he decreased the Spanish population so drastically may be that he was a victim of his own anti-Spanish propaganda. Throughout his sections on Mexico, Central America, and South America, he kept before his readers a claim emphasized not only by French explorers like La Salle but by English writers like Thomas Gage and Daniel Defoe—the claim that Spanish America could easily be overcome by invading forces because the natives hated and outnumbered their masters and would be willing to follow leadership in a rebellion. For example, earlier in his book, among the details on Guatemala and its preponderance of persecuted natives, Coreal prophesied that one day the Indians would rise up and take that country. And immediately after the false figures on Lima's population, he added that these 40,000 Negroes belonged to a race "that multiplies extraordinarily . . . and I am astonished that it has not yet been aroused to an angry revolution; for these Negroes are warlike and very clever." Then, five lines further, after following the *Atlas Geographus'* description of the walls of the city, he added what neither his source nor any real traveler had said, "Thus one can say that Lima is without any defense." Rather obviously his thesis was better if the Negroes of Lima outnumbered the Spanish: they would be potent allies in an attack on this supposedly undefended city.

But the tenor of the *Relation* as a whole is far from being one of deceit, even though as a book it is all a big hoax. In fact, its author insisted on morality quite as strongly as Defoe did. After all, Exquemelin, Dampier, and Lionel Wafer had been pirates, written books about their travels, and lived to be so respected that they became prime sources for all later travelers, geographers, and collectors of voyages, including the editors of the *Atlas Geographus*. So it is not entirely strange to hear an ex-buccaneer preach long sermons on the white man's cruelty to Indians, on hypocrisy in religion, or on laxness in the sex life of Europeans in America.

Yet these sermons are not dull, for their composer knew how to select his facts and then dramatize and color them with wit. One of his favorite themes was the false position assumed by the Europeans who while attempting to teach the American Indian how to control his sex life were at the same time not willing to control their own. Coreal cleverly presented his case from the Indian point of view. Early in his book, after recording the marvelous powers of the guaiac tree in healing syphilis, he let a Porto Rican native say sarcastically, "God has been very good to the Spanish to give them our gold and our women, and at the same time, our Guaiac." [62] According to Coreal, in this dissolute Spanish America syphilis was a universal curse, but so great was the depravity that men were unable to resist visiting their contaminated mistresses and so made it a point to go first to church and pray to the Virgin Mary for protection against the disease.[63] And in a hard-hitting chapter called "Of the Customs and Religion of the Creoles and Spanish," which does much with only a few facts from the source, Coreal allowed an embittered Indian to defend his people's ancient marriage customs by pointing scornfully at the European's boasted monogamous system that condoned mistresses.

All of this contrast between the primitive innocence of the American Indian and the decadent corruption of the European interloper was grist for the mill of a Jean Jacques Rousseau. The book Rousseau was depending on, however, was not authentic. Its author gave no eyewitness account but was as much a fireside philosopher as Rousseau himself. And, ironically, his thesis was not the attractive life of the Noble Savage but the misrule of the ignoble Spaniard, who should be driven out of America to make way for nations with better morals and better merchants. In other words, the inventor of Coreal was not advancing primitivism but promoting progress.

Coreal's humor was not all directed at hypocrisy in matters of sex. He even subjected to ridicule some of the traditions and beliefs of the Church. In fact, this professing Roman Catholic, who hoped to die "in the Communion of the Church our Holy Mother," [64] had absorbed a great deal of Protestantism while beating around the New World with his English buccaneers. In an especially bitter attack on the Spanish and Roman Catholic oppression in Nicaragua, he told a dramatic story of how a greedy priest persuaded two ignorant Indians to compete with each other in praying and giving to their patron saints, one to Saint Dominique, the other to Saint Ignatius. So hot did the competition become that the Indians arrived at blows and ended up with mortal wounds. "The saints," Coreal abruptly concluded his parable, "did not appear, and kept to their rest during the battle." [65] Even more obviously invented was his account of how ignorant the inhabitants of Spanish America were because of the Church and state ban on books:

At Porto Bello a Creole by chance found a copy of Ovid's *Metamorphoses,* which he could not understand. He took it to a Franciscan monk who probably did not understand it any better. Perhaps out of malice, perhaps out of ignorance, the monk led the people of Porto Bello to believe that the book was an English Bible, and in order to prove it he showed them the pictures of the metamorphoses and said, "Look how those dogs worship the devil, who turns them into beasts." After that the so-called Bible was thrown into a fire lighted expressly for it, and the monk preached these good people a fine sermon which consisted of thanking Saint Francis for their happy discovery.[66]

Dramatic touches of this sort, including the irony and sarcasm, are to be found in other apocryphal travels of the time, especially in Tyssot's *Jacques Massé* of 1710 and in Defoe's many successes.

And it is with such books that the *Relation des Voyages de François Coreal* must now be placed. In fact, the talents, tricks, and prejudices of its unknown author were so much like those of Daniel Defoe that one is tempted to add it to the already amazing number of volumes produced by that English writer in his busiest year. Like Defoe, the French hoaxer knew and used the *Atlas Geographus*. Both could extract information about places, things, and people and bind that information together with the life of a fake traveler. Both knew the Antilles and South America especially well. Defoe was the world authority on pirates of the West Indies and Central America; Coreal claimed to be one of those pirates. Both were witty and clever ironists. Both were highly moral, even on topics that often titillated the passions. The second volume of Coreal's *Relation* reprinted the voyage of Narbrough, whom Defoe often used, and the voyage of Raleigh, whom Defoe honored especially and with whom he claimed kin. The two writers sometimes expressed the same prejudices, for example, against the Portuguese. The supposed Spaniard Coreal, showing no specific knowledge of Spain, praised Defoe's England and the English,[67] used the English Channel as a comparison, and referred, as Defoe often did, to the story of English King James II's loss of his crown. And finally, the author of the *Relation* was a militant follower of the tradition that combined religion and economics to write propaganda concerning Spanish cruelty in America and the moral and financial necessity of wresting trade and colonies from Spain, cleverly putting his attacks in the mouth of a disillusioned Spaniard. This tradition was strongest in England, and although John Phillips was perhaps its best representative, with his oft-reprinted *Tears of the Indians,* a sort of translation of Las Casas, Defoe was one of its staunchest supporters, with his *Essay on the South Sea Trade* (1711) and his *New Voyage round the World* (1724), the latter a fictitious travel book much like the *Relation*

of Coreal published two years earlier. Such a parade of similari-
ties in technique and subject matter almost persuades one that
at his busiest time of life Daniel Defoe was even sending manuscripts abroad for publication, as he did in 1725 when he issued
The Complete English Tradesman in Dublin.

But the evidence is not convincing enough. One must remember that many of the *Relation*'s techniques, ideas, and aims
can be found not only in Defoe but also in one or another of his
French predecessors such as Tyssot and Misson. Also the most
liberal translation of Coreal's French would fail to reveal any
of Defoe's distinctive speech characteristics, even in the passages
that are least dependent on the *Atlas Geographus*. Furthermore, Defoe apparently never had dealings with agents or publishers in either of the two cities in which the French fabrication
appeared. And finally, since England would have received the
anti-Spanish propaganda even more cordially than did France,
an English author would have seen little reason to seek a market
outside his own country. But whatever the nationality of the
compiler, he was remarkably like the most facile of the fireside
travelers.

AFTER DEFOE

Defoe and the anonymous author of Coreal's *Relation* flourished near the beginning of the eighteenth century, but the type
of travel book that they and their predecessors were so successful in putting together continued to be written. Some of these
imitation travels are listed in Philip Gove's excellent bibliography of the *Imaginary Voyage*. Often they suggested their
spurious origin by using titles containing such words as "remarkable adventures" or "strange life." There are others, however, that have not been called imaginary voyages because they
followed the rules of the game completely, refusing to leave any
very strong hint as to their nature and hoping to pass as authentic.
Again there are representatives from every nation—England's
Richard Castleman (1725) and *Thomas Anbury's Travels
through North America* (1789), for example; or the *Neue Reisen
. . . in England* (1784) by Germany's Johann Büschel; [68] or

P. N. Chantreau's *Voyage philosophique, politique, et littéraire fait en Russie* . . . (1794), which claimed to be "translated from the Dutch" but was actually stolen from a British book and then, ironically, translated laboriously back into the language from which it was taken.[69]

One of the most confusing of all these later pseudo travel books was that by St. Jean de Crèvecoeur, written at the end of the century and published in 1801 as *Le Voyage dans la haute Pensylvanie et dans l'état de New York*. Crèvecoeur pretended to have found three volumes of manuscripts that were water-soaked from a shipwreck and written by an anonymous, middle-aged, experienced narrator who, accompanied by a young, naïve German, traveled in the less populated, frontier regions of New York and Pennsylvania, talking with settlers, visiting Indian councils, listening to native legends, describing natural phenomena, and experiencing a variety of adventures. The guise of traveler-author is retained to the end, when young Herman sails for Europe.

What is confusing about the book is that the real author made wide use of previous writers, never crediting them with any of the information taken but never claiming it for his own. For one chapter he condensed William Smith's history of Bouquet's expedition into the Ohio country and said it was an account given him by a certain Frederick Hazen, aide to Colonel Bouquet at the time. He summarized William Bartram's travels in the southern United States and attributed the material to the same nonexistent Hazen. He took Jonathan Carver's Indian lore, much of it already secondhand, and insisted that it came from George Croghan, a well-known Indian scout and trader who was dead and unable to defend himself. And, as we shall see, he composed a speech for Benjamin Franklin, also dead, by using Gilbert Imlay's compendium of knowledge about America.

The transformation that Smith underwent is typical of Crèvecoeur's methods, as well as those employed by his fellow fireside travelers.[70] For the first few pages the invented Hazen followed Smith's history of the Bouquet expedition carefully. Then

Crèvecoeur began to leave out long sections of his source, omitting, for example, the entire second day's fighting at the Battle of Bushy Run. Because of its sentimental nature he was more interested in the last part of Smith's story and required as many pages to describe the touching scenes of prisoners returned at Muskingum, of the white friends and relatives who met them, and of the Indians who had to give them up, as he needed to tell of the entire campaign and the conferences that followed it.

But he was guilty of more than plagiarism; occasionally he altered, added to, or embellished the original. For example, he made the Indians more humane by increasing the number of prisoners they were kind enough to return and inserted an incident about an Irishwoman who refused to leave her former captors. In fact, she made such a stirring appeal for the life of the Noble Savage that Colonel Bouquet permitted her to return to the forest. There is nothing like it in Smith. One intriguing embellishment is the story of the mother who, while holding one of her children, discovered another who had been captured by the Indians. Smith, depicting the mother's joy on seeing the long lost child, told of how she let the one in her arms drop to the ground. The tenderhearted Crèvecoeur could not stand such a thought and permitted the falling infant to be saved by "the incredible quickness of Captain Percival, who, finding himself beside the mother, prevented the fall." While the father of the two children, in Smith, is rescuing the fallen one, the mother, in Crèvecoeur, is saying to the gallant Captain Percival, "Heaven bless you a thousand times! . . . When I am in such a state of mind, how can I know what I am doing?"

The confusion brought on by all this peculiar use of sources was compounded because Crèvecoeur dramatized incidents and introduced characters taken from his own thirty years of living in America as soldier, surveyor, farmer, and consul, an experience that had already produced *Letters from an American Farmer,* which a few years before had been the most widely read book on America. These original sections make the *Voyage* valuable both as history and literature. Because of its method, however, unique but in the tradition of *Drury* and *Coreal,* it has too long been avoided. Now that its borrowings have recently been exposed and its originality pointed out,[71] it should assume its rightful place as an important study of early America.

Although Crèvecoeur was not the last writer to invent a traveler who would be the vehicle for a body of knowledge about foreign countries,[72] the great age for such literature was over with the advent of the steamboat and the steam locomotive, when real travelers became so numerous that false ones were both less necessary and more easily exposed. But the fireside travelers of the eighteenth century continued to exert their influence. Historians and geographers labored on the one hand at picking the original from the unoriginal in the works of those writers who actually went somewhere but still padded their notes after getting home and on the other hand at determining whether certain books were products of actual experience or simply the results of good compiling. Another kind of influence, more pleasing but less easily ascertained, can be seen in the methods of fiction. The historical and adventure novels, from Smollett's *Roderick Random* to Cooper's *Afloat and Ashore* to Waltari's *The Egyptian,* have learned from the school of Defoe that by applying the tools of the scholar they can add color, concreteness, and verisimilitude to the lands where their heroes go. In fact, more and more recent unmaskings of fake travel books—Defoe's *Drury,* d'Aulnoy's *Travels,* Misson's *Leguat,* and Coreal's *Relation*—all demonstrate how closely fiction and travel literature were related in the eighteenth century. And finally, these exposures make it impossible to say now, as a writer in *Harper's Monthly Magazine* said in 1907, "Of stories of travel which are actually meant to deceive, which are pure fiction from beginning to end, passed off as fact, happily there are not many examples." [73]

VII

FANTASTIC MEMORIES

By telling of it,
Made such a sinner of his memory
To credit his own lie.[1]

NEARLY ALL EIGHTEENTH-CENTURY travelers who told
their stories did so after returning home to sit down with their
notes, their formal journals, or their sometimes accurate, sometimes perverse memories. Few of them let the public see their
unedited, on-the-spot reports of what they experienced; and
those few wrote letters posted from some place in Europe, as
did Lady Mary Wortley Montagu when she sent back to London
wonderfully detailed accounts of life in Turkey that were passed
around among her friends. Occasionally the returned traveler
did not publish his own story but told it to some recorder who
had sought him out for interested reasons. In that case his vanity
was easily piqued. At other times he made it a point to find
the proper people and arouse their interest. In that case he was
probably motivated by a desire for money. But in either case the
impulse was great to change, or at least exaggerate, the facts as
the traveler attempted to recall them. And if he was an old man,
it was even easier for him to manipulate his memory.

Not that the liars of the eighteenth century were unique in
the artful management of this function of the mind. It has
long been a truism, at least since the time of Quintilian in the
first century A.D., that "a liar should have a good memory."

Here *good* may have been used seriously to mean *retentive,* since a liar who does not want to get caught must remember what he has said; or it may have been used sarcastically to mean *inventive, adept, pliable.* Nor was the eighteenth the only century in which old, retired travelers, by twisting and padding their memories, aroused and influenced important decisions. Among the most influential of aged travel liars of anterior times were the Englishman David Ingram and the Greek Juan de Fuca, both of whom lived in the days of Queen Elizabeth and her venturesome Sea Dogs. Their stories will help to demonstrate the universality of the old traveler with the fantastic memory.

In 1582, at the height of Elizabethan interest in finding a Northwest Passage for trade with the Orient, a group of outstanding Englishmen met in London to talk with an elderly sailor about his knowledge of the New World.[2] One of the men was Sir Francis Walsingham, Secretary to the Queen, important politically, and a prime mover in many colonial ventures. Another of the men was Richard Hakluyt, whose name has been immortalized because of his activities in urging and backing voyages of discovery and, more particularly, because of his world-famous collections of travel accounts. A third person present was Sir Humphrey Gilbert, mariner, graduate of Oxford, and author in 1576 of the widely read *Discourse on the Northwest Passage.* The object of their attention was David Ingram, who had sailed with Sir John Hawkins on the disastrous expedition of 1567–1568 when the English fleet had been largely destroyed by the Spanish near Vera Cruz, forcing the commander to leave about a hundred of his crew on the coast of Mexico. According to Ingram, he and two others of the abandoned men made their way north along the coast, then westward, and finally overland through what is now the United States and southern Canada to a point near Cape Breton Island, where a French fur ship rescued them. The two companions had died and were not present to verify the report.

The most surprising fact about David Ingram is not that he walked from the Rio Panuco to Acadia in less than a year's time, through pathless forests, past savage Indians, and along rivers that for the most part flowed the wrong way, nor that he reported seeing so many marvelous sights, but rather that such intelligent men would have believed him. However, they were all partially convinced already, not only that there was a waterway across northern America but that America itself was valuable. And so the old sailor, flattered by all the attention bestowed upon him, gave his listeners what they wanted. He assured the seekers of Northwest Passages that there were "manie great rivers in those Cuntries . . . some 4 some 8 some 10 myles over, whereof one was so large that they cold scarse cross the same in 24 howers." And, much less plausible, but mixed with much that can be accepted, he told of having seen large "cities" at short distances from each other all across the continent, of gold and silver and pearl, of Indian kings who "weare great precious stones which commonly are rubies about VI ynches long & 2 ynches broad," of "Elephants," and of many other curious and wonderful sights. It is easy to see that, although Ingram may have made his tremendous trek, the story which he composed years later contained more than actual experience. There were at least two other ingredients: hearsay about the reputed riches of the Spanish in New Spain, and the fantasies of an imagination working on a malleable memory.

The total effect of this narrative cannot be measured, since it was by no means the only evidence that explorers in North America relied upon. But one man who listened to it, Walsingham, became in the next five years the chief backer of John Davis in his three unsuccessful voyages to the waters of Canada and Greenland. A second listener, Hakluyt, within seven years published the first edition of his *Principal Navigations,* chapter v of which was called "The Narrative of David Ingram." However, the second edition, that of 1598, omitted the story because more advanced knowledge caused the editor to recognize its "incredibilities." The third important member of Ingram's audiences, Sir Humphrey Gilbert, within a matter of months sailed twice to North America, losing his life on the second voyage. No doubt other explorers and colonizers, such as Raleigh and White, were attracted by the old sailor's yarn.

At least one historian credits him with a share "in drawing to Virginia the luckless settlers who made England's first colonial adventure there." [3] In the nineteenth century the "Narrative" was rediscovered and twice published,[4] one editor attempting to explain and defend some of its improbabilities while at the same time recognizing that some others could not be defended.

The story of Juan de Fuca is today much better known than that of Ingram, and its greater influence, especially on the eighteenth century, is more easily estimated.[5] It begins with Michael Lok, an English merchant-mariner who traveled to many countries and knew many languages well. While in Spain and Portugal he was filled with enthusiasm for western exploration and trade and returned home to become the outstanding merchant backer of voyages of discovery, for example, with his own funds sending Martin Frobisher to the North Atlantic three times, even going to prison for a debt incurred while making ready for the third of these expeditions. His fortune gone, he went to Italy in 1596 hoping to obtain payment of money owing him, and in Venice he met a Greek named Apostolos Valerianos, commonly called Juan de Fuca, a man of threescore years who claimed to have spent forty of them sailing in the West Indies.

De Fuca related a long story to the eager English merchant. He told first of a voyage from China to New Spain on which he had been robbed by Captain Cavendish of 60,000 gold ducats worth of goods. Then he told of being commissioned by the Spanish to go as pilot on a sailing expedition along the California coast "to discover the Straits of Anian," the mythical, long-sought-for waterway across the top of North America. Unsuccessful on this trip, he was sent out again in 1592; and this time, he said, he found an inlet at 47° North Latitude that, after turning in every direction but west, led him twenty days later into the North Sea. "Also," the old man insisted that "he went on Land in divers places, and that he saw some people on Land, clad in beasts skins; and that the Land is very fruitful, and rich of gold, Silver, Pearle, and other things." Returning to Mexico, then to Spain, the intrepid navigator failed to receive the expected reward for his discovery. Now he was ready, according to his discoverer Michael Lok, to give his services to England, that is if Queen Elizabeth would make him pilot on a ship that would go to America and if she would restore the 60,000 ducats which had been stolen from him some twenty years before by the English Captain Cavendish. Lok's letters to London aroused the interest of such men as Sir Walter Raleigh, Lord Cecil, and Hakluyt; but when no money was sent to bring the old sailor to England, he lost interest in the affair and went home, from where, until his death in 1602, he corresponded with Lok.

It is an almost certain fact that Juan de Fuca existed and was in New Spain during the last quarter of the sixteenth century, because Michael Lok was not the only person to know of him and because certain incidents in his story are like some that really happened—but to other people. For example, Drake, not Cavendish, captured a Spanish boat piloted by a Greek named Juan and from it removed 24,000 pesos, not 60,000 gold ducats, worth of goods. Furthermore, de Fuca told how on his first trip to discover the Strait of Anian, "shortly" before 1592, one of the captains was brought back to be tried for "sodomie." Actually the captain of a Spanish ship sent to the peninsula of California had been tried for "an unnatural crime." But even if there was such a person as de Fuca, he could never have found the body of water that he described. Not only did he lie about the riches he saw on the shore of the strait, but his geography and his sailing directions were impossibly wrong, even for the strait between Vancouver Island and the mainland, which bears his name and is the likeliest to fit his description but which leads not into the North Sea but back into the Pacific. And Spanish records have failed to reveal anything about a voyage like the one he was supposed to have made.

However, in spite of its falseness, the fable of Juan de Fuca went far and lived long. One cannot say what its influence was on the English flotillas sent out between 1602–1607, but shortly before that time Lok himself had planned to sponsor a ship that would be piloted by the old Greek. In 1625 Samuel

Purchas' *Pilgrimes,* the most important collection of travels after that of Hakluyt, included the narrative of de Fuca's voyage. Thereafter, it remained uncited as evidence, but not unread, until in the 1740's and 1750's Englishmen like Arthur Dobbs and Frenchmen like the geographers Delisle and Buache resurrected it as important evidence for their theories concerning a Northwest Passage, and as support for the much discussed de Fonte hoax, which is actually in no way like it, describing a passage supposedly found from the Atlantic rather than from the Pacific side and much farther north. But while in general the eighteenth century finally and unanimously discredited de Fuca's story, its influence was occasionally felt long afterwards; for as late as 1901 an editor could be found referring to it with such mild terms as "doubtful." [6] Perhaps the unfairest effect of all is that it caused some people to doubt the word and defame the memory of Michael Lok, whose devotion to discovery has caused one historian to believe, "There is no doubt that Lok was actuated primarily by scientific interest," [7] but whose publicizing of an old sailor's narrative caused another historian to say, "All that Fuca knew was something about a voyage up the Gulf of California, I think that Michael Lok did the rest" because "he was looking for information to verify his theory of a Northwest Passage and possibly the Greek was quite willing to supply it and thus gain employment." [8]

In the period from 1660 to 1800 there are to be found numerous examples of travelers who followed the pattern established by such men of former ages as Ingram and de Fuca. In each case an old man who had been back in Europe for some years without publishing an account came forward at the appropriate moment to offer his evidence.

The first of these stories in point of time as well as influence was that of a Spaniard named Diego de Peñalosa, a real adventurer and fabricator of falsehood, one of the school of Lahontan and Father Hennepin, but one who did not influence geography so much as they did.[9] Born in Peru, Peñalosa in 1660 was sent to Santa Fe to be Governor of New Mexico for four years. Back in Mexico City he was tried and condemned by an auto-da-fé but escaped with his life and went to London, where in 1671–1673 he was scheming to persuade England that she should seize the Spanish ports in the West Indies. Failing in this attempt, he went to Paris and there had such success that one historian goes so far as to say that there is "little doubt" that the proposals of Peñalosa "led to the La Salle enterprises." [10]

He claimed to have explored Quivira, the mythical city of fabulous wealth sought by Coronado over a hundred years before, and as evidence he offered a faked relation supposedly written by a Spanish friar. With these credentials he gained access to the councils of Louis XIV's minister Seignelay, in whose library was later found a copy of the *Relation* of Peñalosa. The Spanish adventurer was introduced by Seignelay to La Salle and no doubt provided the great explorer with at least part of his information about New Spain and with some of his hopes of wealth. But while the king's minister continued to be impressed by Peñalosa, others saw through his designs and refused to have more to do with him. However, one La Salle biographer [11] believes that the Spaniard's attempts to relate his fortunes to those of La Salle not only caused the Frenchman's reputation to suffer but made his success more difficult to achieve.

Just at the beginning of the eighteenth century, a few years after Peñalosa had met with far too much credence in France, Iberville, Bienville, Le Sueur, and others were exploring the Gulf Coast region of what is now the southern United States, discovering the mouth of the Mississippi from the sea and leading expeditions into the interior. Forty years later a man from La Rochelle named Pénicaut, who had accompanied Iberville as a carpenter, put together what he called a journal of these important events.[12] The moment was propitious because in France and England there was a great interest in writing the geography and history of the New World. Furthermore, the old man was going blind and needed money. At any rate, writing long after the incidents occurred, he was the victim of a very bad memory.

In fact, Pénicaut's journal is filled with "muddled Chronology, misstatements, and confused sequences," [13] as one scholar has shown by comparing the old man's version with others that were written while the history was being made. Pénicaut exaggerated the number of children whom the Taensa Indians sacrificed to appease an angry god, he mistakenly credited Iberville with discovering the mouth of the Mississippi, and he insisted that Bienville made four voyages instead of three. All of these and many other errors could have been the result of "a failing memory and not a deliberate attempt to falsify"; [14] but one can hardly be so generous with, for example, Pénicaut's telling, as if he had participated in them, of events that took place on two different trips made at the same time, one led by Le Sueur up the Mississippi into Minnesota country looking for minerals, the other guided by Iberville and designed to explore the country farther east.

A copy of this mixed-up but unpublished journal was given to Charlevoix, one of the great French historians of the eighteenth century. He was the first, therefore, to use it,[15] accepting uncritically all of its misstatements, such as that about Iberville's fourth voyage and another concerning a false date for Le Sueur's expedition to the Sioux country. The complete relation was published in the nineteenth century [16] and, until its exposure in 1941, was used by a number of writers, particularly historians of the southern United States.[17]

Of all these men with fertile but untrustworthy memories, perhaps the oldest was an ancient ship captain named Reainaud. And his story was one of the most appropriately timed. At age eighty-four he was discovered by the Abbé Coyer, member of the Royal Society and the Academy of Nantes and the first important writer to take up the subject of the Patagonian giants during its revival in the eighteenth century. Writing in 1767, a few months after the return of Admiral Byron's ship, the *Dolphin,* Coyer told how he had by chance run across the old captain in Marseilles and had by him been convinced of the existence of the giants two years before Byron's men were arousing the interest of the world. According to Reainaud, he had sailed a tiny boat across the Atlantic to the Strait of Magellan, where he had found the fabled Patagonians and measured them.

The men, he said, were "twelve spans, that is to say, nine feet, a little more or a little less; the women and the children in proportion." [18] The voyage had been made in 1712, fifty-two years before the time of narration. But, the Abbé hastened to say, the aged man was not talking out of a weak or diseased mind, for in spite of his eighty-four years he was vigorous and had all of his powers of intellect. Captain Reainaud's testimony was placed alongside that of a dozen other travelers to South America, from the sixteenth-century Italian Pigafetta to the eighteenth-century English officers of the *Dolphin,* and soon it was standard fare for those who, like Dom Pernetty and the editor of the *London Chronicle,* accepted the existence of the giants.[19]

One very popular twentieth-century history of explorations, while dismissing these same Patagonians in a single sentence, concludes that although they were only "tall and stalwart" they were "afterwards magnified by fantastic memory into giants." [20] As we have shown in another chapter of the present study, fantastic memory alone was not responsible for that legend, nor was it wholly responsible for any great mistake resulting from travel accounts, but it often played a prominent supporting role in history. Perhaps its role, as in the stories of our aged voyagers, was to hoodwink statesmen, or cause scholars to commit errors, or tempt businessmen into spending their fortunes, or assist the world in crystallizing a legend. Or perhaps it even led, in part, to desirable ends, such as the exploration of unknown Canadian seas, or the discovery of the lower Mississippi, or the settlement of Virginia.

A fantastic memory has been part of the equipment of many travel liars, but it has existed in a peculiar way in the minds of those who were old and retired, some of whom would have remained simply travelers—but unheard-of travelers—if they had not been called from their retirement to corroborate a theory or give moral support to a venture. It is true that nostalgia, reminiscing, the "memories of eld" are all congenial to fantasies, to wish fulfillments, and to exaggerations which are not always considered lies. But somewhere along the road of resurrecting the past, exaggeration becomes untruth, the pleasing picture becomes so distorted that it is false, and the travelogue becomes the travel lie. However, while the tendency to make the old times good is a universal characteristic, and while some of these aged travelers must have shared it—David Ingram and Captain Reainaud, for example—all of them were apparently actuated even more by characteristics less forgivable but nevertheless just as universal—the wish to have money and the wish to be important, influential, the center of attention. These men who had been so active in their youth, in order to avoid sterility in what may have seemed the cruelest time of life, in order to live again in the wasteland of old age, were "breeding lilacs out of dead land, mixing memory and desire."

PECULIAR PLAGIARISMS

But they are the wiser who put out other men's works for their own, while relying on the hope that even if they are finally and fully found out they will have temporarily enjoyed the pleasure of their plagiarism.[1]

WRITERS OF FORMER TIMES were notorious plagiarizers, and once upon a time scholars delighted in publishing not only newly discovered sources but even parallels and other possible evidence of indebtedness. Such scholarship is perhaps negligible if it does not help to indicate something about a writer's methods or throw light on social attitudes or set history straight. But to be eclectic is not to plagiarize. Often great literary figures, dealing in emotions, actions, ideas, have borrowed from earlier literature, not to obtain money or fame by placing their own names on somebody else's work, but by reshaping and recombining to create something which in its total effect is aesthetically and intellectually original. Virgil, Chaucer, Shakespeare, Racine —writers such as these have always made use of other writers, and frequently they have been incorrectly called plagiarizers. Some of the great figures of the eighteenth century belong to that group, among them Swift and Voltaire, both of whom, for example, wrote imaginative stories that parodied the popular travel literature of the day and both of whom took suggestions from specific travel accounts. But, at the same time, there was that other kind of borrower, one who removed whole sections of books, sometimes whole books, without acknowledgment and with little or no thought of adding anything factual or creative of his own.

Most of the time this writer was a practical person who preferred to deal in facts, not in art, and his motive was usually money. The period that we are studying had many such plagiarizers, especially among the voyagers to more distant countries. While in a sense all such travelers can be classed as liars, since they claimed to have done something which they did not do, their story is an old and sometimes boring one and need not be repeated. But there was a peculiar kind of traveler-plagiarizer who compounded both his guilt and the resulting confusion by stealing from one source and then acknowledging another. Such people were doubly liars and need to be included here, not only because of their intrinsic interest but because of their influence on history. The representatives of this type, luckily few in number who worked on a grand scale, seem to have been attracted almost exclusively to America and included a Swiss, an Englishman, and a Frenchman. Perhaps this kind of traveler was a propagandist who desired to impress his readers by claiming that certain facts were furnished him by a well-known authority when in actuality they had been obtained elsewhere. Such was the case when one Samuel Jenner borrowed the name of William Byrd, the prominent Virginia landholder and statesman. Perhaps the traveler pretended to be publishing a compilation when in reality he had only rewritten some well-known book, making just enough changes and additions to escape immediate detection. Such was the case with Dr. John Brickell and his *Natural History of North Carolina.* Or perhaps the compiler was on the whole original but wished, like the propagandist, to make whatever information he did borrow appear more authentic and so attributed it to men of greater world-renown than that possessed by the authors of the rifled books. Such was the case when St. Jean de Crèvecoeur made use of the name of Benjamin Franklin. By pretending to sources other than the real ones, these three travelers gave such an appearance of honesty that they not only were misleading at the time but they have been successful in confusing historians ever since. Their stories reveal much about the methods of the travel writers and pseudo travel writers of the eighteenth century.

SAMUEL JENNER OR WILLIAM BYRD?

In 1736, when he was in his sixty-second year, land-rich and heavily in debt because of assuming his father-in-law's obligations, William Byrd busied himself in an attempt to make money by persuading a colony of Swiss to settle on his vast lands along the Roanoke.[2] After one unsuccessful and disappointing experience that ended with the expected colonists going to the Carolinas, Byrd succeeded in selling over 33,000 acres to a Swiss named Samuel Jenner, who was apparently acting as an agent, the price to be £6,000. As a result of this sale, 250 prospective colonists left Switzerland in 1738 and embarked for America with the intention of settling on the Roanoke land. But this venture, while financially not disappointing to Byrd, turned out tragically; for the ship bearing the Swiss immigrants went down in a storm off the coast of Virginia, taking with it the majority of the colonists.

In order to interest his countrymen in the newly acquired territory in Virginia, Samuel Jenner had in 1737 published a book of 228 pages, written in German and called *Neu-gefundenes Eden,* the "Newly-Discovered Eden." Its title page claimed that it was "a Detailed Report on South and North Carolina, Pennsylvania, Maryland, and Virginia. Sketched through two journeys made to these Provinces and based upon a journal of travel and many letters." After the "Report" and Jenner's account of his visits in Virginia and elsewhere in America, the author announced on page 96, "There follows now a short description of Virginia, . . . a true report, which I have received from the President himself and have translated as well as I was able from English into German." The "President" was, of course, William Byrd, although Jenner was not quite accurate in using the title since Byrd was not then "President of the High Royal Council of Virginia," as he claimed in the purchase contract signed over to Jenner on August 18, 1736.[3]

Because of the statement that Byrd had supplied the information on Virginia and that this information was simply "translated," the "short description" of that colony, running to almost a hundred pages, has been taken from the *Neu-gefundenes Eden,* put into English, and published as *William Byrd's Natural History of Virginia or The Newly Discovered Eden.*[4] Since its publication this volume has been added to the Byrd canon and may well become important evidence for the already obvious versatility of its reputed author.[5] However, at least one scholar was indicating a slight uneasiness in accepting the book's authenticity when he pointed out that it lacks the literary qualities of Byrd's prose and reveals him "as a much more respectable student of natural history than do most of his letters to the Royal Society."[6] One might defend Byrd's knowledge of American flora and fauna by referring not to the Royal Society correspondence but to his best-known work, *The History of the Dividing Line,* with its eyewitness accounts of the buffalo, the bear, the opossum, the beaver, snakeroot, hickory nuts, and cane brakes. But no matter where we go in Byrd's writings we shall not find the detailed knowledge of animals, plants, and fish that is displayed in *Neu-gefundenes Eden,* for a better naturalist than Byrd supplied the facts translated by Jenner. They came, with few exceptions, from John Lawson's *History of Carolina.*[7]

Lawson's was the logical book for a Swiss promoter to use in pilfering information about America. It had been popular in England, where there were four different issues to its credit before Jenner wrote; and it had been translated into German, one of the two German editions having been available in Switzerland. Furthermore, Lawson's name was not unknown in Switzerland because of the part he had played twenty-six years before as surveyor and planner for the settlement of New Bern, North Carolina. And finally, Jenner, looking for a full account of the climate and natural resources of his newly purchased land in Virginia, an account that would be of interest to prospective settlers, easily found Lawson's book on North Carolina, next door to the Roanoke property, to be the most complete and satisfactory survey of the subject.

Ignoring almost completely the "journal of a thousand miles traveled" into the interior, which begins Lawson's *History of Carolina*, as well as the very full account of the Indians that closes the book, Jenner concentrated on the middle section, because it provided such complete descriptions of vegetables, trees, animals, birds, and fish. He omitted one part which a propagandist would wish to deëmphasize, however, that called "insects," a category which included, strangely enough, nineteen varieties of snakes. Nor did Jenner always use all of Lawson's information about a particular plant or animal, but—with the exceptions to be noted—he never added facts to those he found in *The History of Carolina*, although he occasionally made errors, exaggerated on the attractive side, or supplied propaganda sentences that contained no real substance.

Two examples will illustrate his methods. In reading the parallel passages given here one must continually bear in mind that the Jenner passage is always the product of two translations, since we shall make use of the 1940 English version of the *Neugefundenes Eden*. But even though the words are not always the same, the similarity in arrangement and facts is only too obvious.

Opossum. This animal is found nowhere else in the whole world except in America: it is a phenomenon among all animals living on land. Its shape and color are similar to a badger. The male's genital member sticks out in the back, because of which they turn back to each other at the time of copulation. The female bears her young in the teats. . . . If a cat has nine lives, as one commonly says, then this animal has certainly nineteen, for if all bones in its body are broken, so that it lies there as if dead, still it recovers again in a short time, and very soon gets well again. (Jenner, pp. 55–56)

The Possum is found no where but in America. He is the Wonder of all the Land-Animals, being the size of a Badger, and near that Colour. The Male's Pizzle is placed retrograde; and in time of coition, they differ from all other Animals, turning tail to tail as dog and bitch when tied. The Female doubtless breeds her young at her teats; . . . If a Cat has nine Lives, this Creature surely has nineteen; for if you break every Bone in their Skin, and mash their Skull leaving them for Dead, you may come an hour after, and they will be gone quite away. . . . (Lawson, p. 124)

Bonitos are very tasty fish, about an ell long. They stay at the mouths of rivers and banks of the seas and are caught with harpoons and eel-pots. (Jenner, p. 74)

Bonetos are a very palatable Fish, and near a Yard long. They haunt the Inlets and Water near the Ocean, and are killed with the Harpoon and Fish-gig. (Lawson, p. 164)

The latter of these selections will help to illustrate certain peculiar problems Jenner encountered. There the Swiss translator had difficulty with the word *Fish-gig.* Not knowing that it was a three-pronged harpoon, he coined, in the plural, *Reussen* [oyster-pots], which was retranslated into English as *eel-pots.*

Perhaps as convincing as any evidence that Jenner used Lawson is the fact that both describe the same types of flora and fauna not only in the same way but in almost exactly the same sequence and with no important omissions. For example, the only real difference in the two lists of nineteen trees is the naming of "Birches" instead of "Beech." It is Jenner's error, since he rendered Lawson's *Beech* into the German *Birchen,* retranslated correctly in 1940 as *Birches.* Needless to say, the two trees have the same description even though the names are different.

Another excellent bit of evidence for Jenner's plagiarism is the very ironic fact that nearly all of the many question marks inserted in the English version to indicate inability to translate the German can be cleared up by reference to Lawson. A good example is the section that lists the apple trees. Of some sixteen varieties of apples that Jenner listed, the translators were unable to find English equivalents for six and, as a result, were forced to retain the German words. A glance at Lawson will clear up five of the six; for example, Jenner's *Läder-Göller* and *Kassapffel* were Lawson's *Leather Coat* and *Cheese Apple* trees. The single unindentified variety seems to have been one of the propogandist's rare inventions.

Not only could most of the uncertain words have been translated by keeping one eye on Lawson, but a great number of errors would have been avoided in the English edition. Sometimes the error was Jenner's, as when he mistranslated Lawson's information on the fish hawk. Whereas *The History of Carolina* correctly describes it as "a large Bird, being above two-thirds as big as the Eagle," the *Neu-gefundenes Eden* says, *"Dises ist ein entsetzlich grösser Vogel und noch mehr als einmahlen grösser als der Adler."* This statement, returned to English as, "This is a terribly large bird, more than once again as large as the Eagle," is quite surprising because the fish hawk and the larger, not smaller, bald eagle were favorite subjects for eighteenth-century commentators on America.[8]

Sometimes an error in the German translation brought on another in the final, English version. One rather startling instance is the statement that "Jellyfish are . . . very good to eat,"[9] *Jellyfish* being an attempt to translate Lawson's *Cockle,* a shell fish that is edible and quite unlike the water-filled, umbrella-like jellyfish.

Although Lawson was the source for nearly all the natural history which the *Neu-gefundenes Eden* attributed to William Byrd, Jenner occasionally supplied facts not found in *The History of Carolina.* For example, after taking from Lawson information on the sturgeon and its spawning habits, the Swiss promoter added an account of the Indian method of capturing this fish by lassoing its tail. And here one who knew Byrd's *History of the Dividing Line,* unpublished in 1737, might believe that the famous Virginian did give some assistance, by letter or by word of mouth, since that book tells of an actual instance of such fishing.[10] But again we can find Jenner's source in a well-known book that was available in 1737, not written by Byrd but, ironically, by his cousin Robert Beverley, and called *The History and Present State of Virginia.*[11] Compare these two entertaining passages.

The Indians catch them . . . at times with their hands with a line, in which there is a running knot, which they are able to cleverly fasten onto the sturgeon's tale. As soon as the fish notices that he is being held, he pulls and jerks terribly, and draws the one who is holding	The Indian way of catching Sturgeon, when they came into the narrow part of the Rivers, was by a Man's clapping a Noose over their Tail, and by keeping fast his hold. Thus a Fish finding it self intangled, wou'd flounce, and often pull him under Water, and then that Man was counted

| him swiftly into the water. But the latter does not let him go free. Rather [he] takes a dip so often and swims after him so long that the sturgeon becomes so tired that the man can draw it out of the water onto land. [This] the Indians consider a masterpiece of fishing. (Jenner, p. 79) | a *Cockarouse,* or brave Fellow, that wou'd not let go; till with Swimming, Wading, and Diving, he had tired the Sturgeon, and brought it ashore. (Beverley, pp. 148–149) |

If all the natural history in *William Byrd's Natural History of Virginia* was taken from John Lawson, with a few assists from Robert Beverley,[12] what is left that could be used as evidence that Byrd "wrote, or aided in writing" the book? [13] Perhaps the some twenty pages that have nothing to do with natural history. But even here one sometimes finds strong echoes of Lawson and of Beverley.[14] The section of *Neu-gefundenes Eden* which most clearly points to William Byrd is one that tells of Byrd's earlier, unsuccessful attempts to secure Swiss settlers for Virginia.[15] But that similarity does not warrant the translating and publishing a big part of *Neu-gefundenes Eden.* Nor would the German book have been translated with such care and added to the canons of literature, science, and social history if the traveler-promoter Samuel Jenner, for the sake of borrowing prestige and an air of authenticity, had not falsely attributed it to the well-known Virginian, "President" William Byrd of Westover.

DR. JOHN BRICKELL OR JOHN LAWSON?

By a peculiar coincidence, in the same year that the Swiss propagandist took John Lawson's *History of North Carolina,* changed its setting to Virginia, and credited it to William Byrd, an Englishman named Dr. John Brickell was stealing the same book for himself, thereby perpetrating one of the strangest and most enduringly successful of literary thefts.[16] The case has been a strange one because it was so flagrant and the victim so well known. It has been successful because for over two hundred years Dr. Brickell's book, which he called *The Natural History of North Carolina,* has been an important source for students of colonial America, and that in spite of a warning given early in the nineteenth century.

Little is known of Dr. Brickell except that in the 1730's he resided for several years on the coast of North Carolina before returning to live in England and publish his *Natural History*.[17] Of the book, more is known. Although at first ignored, by the end of the century it had gradually attained popularity. For example, ten years after its publication it was not used by Emanuel Bowen in his *A Complete System of Geography*, which depended on Harriss, Purry, and Archdale for information on Carolina; but in 1771 it was an important source for *A New System of Geography*, compiled by D. Fenning and J. Collyer.[18]

The early nineteenth century provides three interesting references to Dr. Brickell's *Natural History*. André Michaux, the younger, in his description of the trees of the United States, used it twice, but both times with some reluctance.[19] Jacob Bigelow in the *North American Review*, in an article entitled "Botany of the United States," praised it as "the most complete work of this kind." [20] But shortly after these two writers had enhanced the reputation of the book, Jared Sparks attempted to annihilate it. In 1826, in an article on "Materials for American History," Sparks, after a two-page discussion of John Lawson's *History of Carolina*, had this to say:

> A book was published in Dublin in the year 1737, entitled *Natural History of North Carolina*, by John Brickell, M.D., which is remarkable for being an almost exact verbal transcript of Lawson's History, without any acknowledgment on the part of the author or even a hint that it is not original. . . . as a whole a more daring piece of plagiarism was never executed.[21]

Such an accusation, made by a noted scholar who was later to be president of Harvard University, would ordinarily have been enough to cause students and historians to be very careful in using *The Natural History*; and, in fact, for nearly a century it was avoided altogether. But Jared Sparks was not permanently successful in his attack, for two reasons: First, he put his accusation in a footnote, apparently believing it unimportant because he knew of so many such examples of plagiarism; and second, he provided no evidence.

But whatever the reason, he was unsuccessful, for in 1911 Dr. John Brickell's *Natural History* was republished in Raleigh with a preface that called it the "best description we have of the natural, social, and economic conditions in the Colony of North Carolina," complained that Sparks's charges "are only partially correct and do grave injustice to Brickell," and offered a strong defense of the book's originality.

This defense succeeded in restoring Brickell's reputation. Furthermore, the book was now more easily available and became a popular source work. One noted writer, for example, while describing Lawson as "the first historian of North Carolina," echoed the statement that *"The Natural History* was by no means a slavish reproduction"; and in 1937 a history of North Carolina, while making only limited use of Lawson, referred frequently to Brickell.[22] A year later, however, in his *Reference Guide to the Literature of Travel*, E. G. Cox repeated Sparks's charge, saying, again without the evidence, that Brickell's material "was stolen from Lawson." [23] Nevertheless, in 1946 an article called "Traveller's Tales of Colonial Natural History" [24] depended heavily upon Brickell but made no mention whatever of Lawson. Then in 1948 an important collection of early documents, entitled *North Carolina History Told by Contemporaries*, introduced its selection from Brickell by saying, "Although he copied much from Lawson's *A New Voyage to Carolina*, he went far beyond that writer and gave detailed descriptions of many things not even mentioned by Lawson." [25] And in 1954 the latest history of North Carolina made extensive use of the doctor but included no comment on his connection with Lawson.[26] Perhaps the best evidence for the success of the 1911 apology is to be found in the pages of one periodical, where at least six essays published since 1926 contain important references to *The Natural History*.[27] Of all these twentieth-century books and articles that used Dr. John Brickell, only one mentioned Jared Sparks's charge, and the author of that one,[28] having no access to a copy of Lawson, was unable to compare the two books in question.

But they must be compared in order to show how easy it is to give John Brickell credit for something which he did not originate. It is best, perhaps, to begin with the 1911 defense, which can be reduced to three points: because of his "professional" training, Dr. Brickell's *Natural History* is more "systematic" than Lawson's *History* and more replete with information about the medical properties of the flora and fauna described; his work is bigger than Lawson's by one-half, containing, for example, "much more" on social conditions in North Carolina; and the account of his trip to the Indians "is a distinct contribution."

As for the first defense, Dr. Brickell's "system" was hardly original. Lawson, after a preface and an introduction, began with his "Journal of a thousand miles travel among the Indians from South to North Carolina," a section which Brickell omitted—for the time being. But if we start on page 61 of Lawson's *History* and page 1 of *The Natural History*, we find that the two books follow almost exactly the same order, even to the subsections. There are two differences: Brickell added the essay entitled "The Religion, Houses, Raiment, . . . of North Carolina" and waited until the big final section on the red man to include the account of *his* thousand miles travel among the Indians.[29]

Although his table of contents was not original, Dr. Brickell, as the 1911 apology claimed, did include more medical lore than is to be found in Lawson. He often reported old wives' tales, however, as when he said of "Black-mackrel flies," "The powder of these Insects and their Juice cures baldness," and of the moth, "An oil made of them is said to cure Deafness, Warts, and the Leprosy." The original and worthwhile medical information is found in such paragraphs as the one on the "Ipecacuana" and in a four-page subsection on the diseases of North Carolina, from the ague to stomach-ache to whooping cough, all of which universally common diseases the doctor told about in some detail, and for which he prescribed either his favorite remedy or that of the colonists.[30] But most of the time he was not original, finding it convenient simply to transcribe the many medical uses furnished by his predecessor, as shown by the following statement about the virtues of the sassafras root:

The same in Powder, and a Lotion made thereof, is much used by the Savages to mundify old Ulcers, and for several other Uses. (Lawson, p. 96)	. . . the same in Powder, and strong lotions being made thereof, is much used by the Savage Indians, to mundify old Ulcers, and several other uses. (Brickell, p. 76)

In spite of the fact that *The Natural History* is almost entirely unoriginal in its order and seldom original in its medical lore, where its physician-author would be expected to add most, it would seem to contain a great deal of new matter of some sort; for, to consider the second defense of the 1911 preface, it is over half again as long as Lawson's *History*. But on inspection one discovers that Brickell's additions are largely embellishment. For example, by adding nothing of importance, he was able to take Lawson's seventy-two words on the flower of the sassafras and make over one hundred out of them. Another key to the difference in size is found in his account of the "Tyger," which starts with Lawson's facts and then adds from Pliny a long story having nothing to do with North Carolina.[31] Throughout his book he was usually content with Lawson's words or with some sort of adornment, supplying only two original sections of any length. The first of these, the part called "Of the Religion, Houses, . . . ," is twenty-two pages long and contains the "much more" material on social conditions. But even here almost one-fourth is based on Lawson.[32] Another, more original, section about the same length is that which contains information on insects. Whereas Lawson had dismissed them in a few words, Brickell went into detail on such creatures as bees, butterflies, and mosquitoes, all of which, it must be noted, could be found in Europe as well as in America.[33]

But after we have discovered these parts not taken from Lawson, we have still a second problem to deal with in consider-

ing the length of the two books: Since Lawson's trip among the
Indians was recounted in a sixty-page journal and Brickell's
journey required only six in the telling, what happened to the
other fifty-four pages? The answer is that the later writer did
make use of his predecessor's journal by taking from it much
of the information about Indian life—tribes, burial customs,
foods, and sex—and putting it in his last chapter, the "Account
of the Indians of North Carolina," which is considerably longer
than Lawson's chapter with the same title. For example, in order
to describe the feast of the "Waxsaw" Indians at the Harvest of
Corn and to give the name and locations of the Sapona Indians,
the "Toteras," and the "Keyswees," Brickell had to glean his
facts from the journal of Lawson, who had actually traveled
among those tribes.[34]

The third defense advanced by the 1911 preface is that the
"journal" of Dr. Brickell's trip among the Indians, made, we are
told, in 1730, is a "distinct contribution" to history. The six
pages [35] of this account tell how ten white men and two Indian
guides made a remarkably easy journey, saw beautiful scenery,
found abundant game, and had a delightful time. To give an
idea of the idyllic existence, the author told briefly of a typical
night's "camp out" and then added, "It would not be proper to
trouble the Reader with the Adventures of each Day. . . . Let
it suffice to inform them, that after fifteen Days Journey, we
arrived at the foot of the Mountains, having met with no
Human Specie all the way." Lawson, it must be noted, had
traveled in the same direction thirty years before and had encountered numerous Indian tribes and villages. On arriving at
the "Mountains," Brickell's party was discovered by "Iroquois
scouts," whose "King" sent an "Ambassador . . . Painted as
red as Vermillion," to find out if the party was for peace or for
war. Lawson, in similar fashion, had told how, while he was
visiting with the "Waxsaws," the "King" of the Saponas had
sent an "Ambassador . . . painted with Vermillion all over his
Face." The Iroquois "King" entertained his visitors in the
"State House," just as Lawson's Waxsaw "King" had done. Both
Brickell and Lawson slept on "benches" covered with animal

skins, and both were privileged to see dances performed and games played in their honor. The only original fact supplied by Brickell is his insistence on having given copious supplies of rum to the Indians. The best bit of evidence against his having made a trip is the claim that the Indians he visited were Iroquois, who, he said, were "very powerful, and continually at War, wandering all over the Continent betwixt the two Bays of Mexico and St. Lawrence." The Iroquois were not known to go so far south, although their relatives, the Tuscaroras, once occupied a part of North Carolina; but, years before this supposed trip, they had been moved north to increase the Five Nations to six. It would seem then that Dr. Brickell's journey among the Indians was as spurious as were many others of the seventeenth and eighteenth centuries—Couture to the "Island" of California, Lahontan and Hennepin in the Mississippi region, and Chateaubriand in the Gulf Coast country.

Since invented trips were so common among early travel writers, perhaps Dr. Brickell may be forgiven for borrowing his journey from John Lawson. And a very lenient reader might agree with him that his book is a "compendious collection" of facts about North Carolina, even though six-sevenths of the compendium is collected from John Lawson. But probably the most partial of readers should hesitate to approve of Dr. Brickell's being so unimaginative as to adopt many of John Lawson's own experiences, narrating them almost word for word, even retaining the first person pronoun. Here is one example:

Yet I knew an European Man that had a Child or two by one of these Indian Women, and afterwards married a Christian, after which he came to pass away a Night with his Indian Mistress; but she made Answer that she had forgot she ever knew him, and that she never lay with another Woman's Husband, so fell a crying and took up the Child	I knew an *European* Man that lived many Years amongst the Indians, and had a Child by one of their Women, having bought her as they do their Wives, and afterwards married a *Christian*. Sometimes after he came to the *Indian* town, not only to buy Deer-Skins, but likewise to pass away a Night with his former Mistress as usual, but she made

she had by him, and went out of the Cabin [away from him] in great Disorder. (Lawson, p. 199)

answer, *That she then had forgot that she ever knew him, and that she never lay with another Woman's Husband;* so fell a crying, took up the Child she had by him, and went out of the Cabin in great Disorder, although he used all possible means to pacifie her, by offering her presents of several *Toys* and *Rum,* but all to no purpose, for she would never see him afterwards, or be reconciled. (Brickell, p. 299)

The point is that Brickell made use of almost everything in Lawson, sometimes attempting to cover his theft by a slight rearrangement of words or by shifting some bit of information from one part of the book to another; but very often, as in the above instance, he was so bold as to use his source without any pretense at hiding his tracks.

However, Dr. Brickell's lack of originality is not of primary importance; what is important is that his plagiarizing has caused scholars to give him credit for much that was the work of another man. Articles that deal with special phases of early North Carolina history—the inland navigation, the agriculture—have often quoted Brickell when the references should have been to Lawson. One full-length history of pre-Revolutionary North Carolina, while referring on two occasions to something original in Brickell, sometimes ascribed to him facts that had been taken from Lawson, as in the description of the "Yaws"—Lawson's "Pox"—or when telling of Indian superstitions and Indian magic. Another book includes a four-page selection from Brickell almost half of which is found in Lawson.[36] And finally, the latest and best history of North Carolina sometimes gives too much credit to the doctor. Here, for example, is its account of early North Carolina birds:

The whole Carolina region was teeming with birds and wild fowl, especially turkeys in flocks of 500 or more, pheasants, quail, wild geese, ducks, and wild pigeons so numerous that, according to Dr.

John Brickell, they would fly one flock after another for above a quarter of an Hour together, . . .[37]

Now, compare the following passages on wild turkeys and wild pigeons, which show that Lawson, and not Brickell, originated the information:

I have seen about five hundred in a flock . . . (Lawson, p. 156)	You shall see five hundred or more of them in a flock together . . . (Brickell, p. 181)
These pigeons, about Sun-Rise when we were preparing to march on our Journey would fly by us in such vast Flocks that they would be near a Quarter of an Hour before they were all passed by. (Lawson, p. 148)	After Sunrise I have seen them fly, one Flock after another, for above a quarter of an Hour together. (Brickell, p. 186)

Elsewhere in the same history we find this statement: "Lawson and Brickell, contemporary writers, observed that 'marriages were early and frequent, most houses being full of little ones.'" Here is what the two sources say:

The Women are very fruitful, most Houses being full of Little Ones. (Lawson, p. 85)	The Women are very fruitful, most Houses being full of Little Ones (Brickell, p. 31)

Obviously it is not just a matter of agreement between two authors.

The warning of Jared Sparks should be stated again, perhaps in this way: Although historians need not stop using the traveler Dr. John Brickell entirely, they should be very careful in giving him credit for anything, since six-sevenths of what he falsely called a compendium was taken from John Lawson, a first-rate narrator and observer whose reputation would be even greater if it had not suffered because of the overlong life of his various alter egos.

ST. JEAN DE CRÈVECOEUR OR
BENJAMIN FRANKLIN?

Within a few months of the time that the Swiss Jenner and the Englishman Brickell were manufacturing their books, St. Jean de Crèvecoeur was born in Caen, Normandy. This Frenchman served under Montcalm in Canada and then for some twenty years lived in Pennsylvania and New York as a farmer, returning to his native land when the Revolution started. At war's end he was sent back to America as Consul, serving in that capacity until 1790 before being recalled to spend most of the rest of his life in France, where he died in 1813. He was a friend and correspondent of many famous people, among them, Buffon, Franklin, Mme d'Houdetot, the poet Saint-Lambert, and Jefferson. His early fame rested on the English *Letters from an American Farmer,* a volume of essays published in London in 1782 but written while he was a citizen of New York. These he translated and published in France, where for some time he was the most popular of commentators on America. One of the intriguing stories of modern scholarship is that which tells how in the early 1920's more of Crèvecoeur's English essays were discovered in an old trunk in France and given to the world as *Sketches of Eighteenth Century America.* Because of his two volumes in English and his New York citizenship, Crèvecoeur has long been an American classic, justifiably ranking high both in literature and history. But he did follow the then popular practice of adding to his own information by borrowing from other writers, often, as we have seen, attributing his borrowings to the wrong people. At least one of these false statements about sources has caused much trouble.[38]

In 1801, in his last book, the *Voyage dans la haute Pensylvanie et dans l'état de New York,* Crèvecoeur cited Benjamin Franklin three times as a source for information, a fact that is not at all surprising since the two men had known each other from 1782 to 1790 and had corresponded frequently. Of the three passages, however, two were taken from prominent books on America, and the third, though it came from Franklin, was obtained under conditions other than those stated in the *Voyage*. In a discussion of the northwest winter winds that bring such cold weather to the eastern states, Crèvecoeur asserted that, "One day when I asked Dr. Franklin what could be the cause of such a powerful phenomenon, here is what he said to me." But the doctor's supposed reply, an analysis of the origin of the winds in question, turns out to be a close reworking of a passage in Jonathan Carver's *Travels*.[39]

Elsewhere the *Voyage* has a three-page essay on the Gulf Stream, the contents of the essay coming, the author said, from Benjamin Franklin. Crèvecoeur, to show his one-time friendship with the most famous of Americans, prefaced his treatise with the statement, "I have often heard this great man say . . . " What was supposed to have been passed on vocally, however, is simply a translation, sometimes free, often word for word, of a part of Franklin's paper read before the American Philosophical Society at Philadelphia on December 2, 1785,[40] when Crèvecoeur was in Europe. This paper, entitled "Maritime Observations," was translated and published in France in 1787, accompanied by Franklin's chart of the Gulf Stream, drawn at the later date. Crèvecoeur, who could have seen this chart in France, evinced a knowledge of it when he outlined the complete course of the stream, giving information not contained in Franklin's original paper.

These two misstatements about Franklin indicate that the author of the *Voyage*, writing in French for Frenchmen, was inclined to make a display of his friendship with the American most popular in France. The third use of Franklin's name is evidently another attempt at display and is the cause of error in a number of Franklin biographies.

In the second chapter of the first volume of the *Voyage*, Crèvecoeur claimed to have made a journey to Lancaster, Pennsylvania, in 1787 in the company of Benjamin Franklin to attend the ceremonies at the founding of Franklin College. While there, we are told, the aged governor was persuaded to air his views on three subjects: the origins of the North American Indians, the possibility of their being native to the Western Hemisphere, and the newly discovered remains of ancient fortifications and tombs. The discussions of the first two of the three subjects Franklin was alleged to have treated are short and amount to a simple retelling of the then current theories and knowledge concerning the Eskimos, the emigration of the southern Indians from Mexico, and the Bering Strait crossing and eastward migration of the other Indians. For his third topic, ancient fortifications and mounds, the venerable speaker is reported to have said that he would repeat the "reflections which occurred" to him while "reading the papers lately presented to our philosophical society by Generals Varnum and Parsons, and Captains John Hart and Sergeant." But the extemporaneous speech turns out to be a collection of so many facts that even a Franklin would need quite a few notes in his hands to give them. Furthermore, these "reflections," as well as their arrangement, were taken from Gilbert Imlay's *A Topographical Description of the Western Territories of North America,* a compendium published nine years before Crèvecoeur's *Voyage* and one which he no doubt hoped to supplant with his own book.[41]

When he had finished his discourse on the Indians and their antiquities, Franklin is said to have pondered the possibilities to be unearthed in a continuance of such studies. "What a field for reflection!" he is supposed to have mused. "Were it not for my advanced age, I would myself cross the mountains to examine those old military works." One of the first Franklin biographers to accept Crèvecoeur's statement as being authentic concluded his quotation of the speech with the observation that a display of such knowledge at such an advanced age could only be "an argument for the immortality of the soul."[42]

But the support for the argument has not itself been immortal, despite its persistence for over a century. The spurious chapter in the French book was for a long time used by Franklin scholars to help fill the gaps in their treatment of his last years. Half a century after Crèvecoeur wrote it, it was translated by the Duyckinck brothers and inserted in their very popular anthology. From there it was transferred in its entirety to one biography of Franklin and then adopted as an important source of material for other writers.[43] Yet Franklin could not have been in Lancaster on June 5, 1787, since on that day he attended a meeting of the Executive Council in Philadelphia and ate dinner with George Washington.[44] Nor could Crèvecoeur himself have attended the ceremonies at Franklin College because at that time he was on a ship sailing from France to the United States.[45] Although neither of the two men was at Lancaster, Crèvecoeur might have read of the event in the newspapers and assumed that Franklin was present to help in dedicating the college named for him. At any rate, the French writer adopted the time, the place, and the man and invented the speech by using facts from published books.

His reason for telling an untruth was different from that of Samuel Jenner the propagandist. Vanity caused him to display his acquaintance with the famous American friend of France, and—as it did with John Brickell—vanity, urging that he make his book a compendium which would be preferred to all others, caused him to take whatever material he needed and then attempt to hide his theft. But even though their motives may have been somewhat different, the man from Switzerland, the man from England, and the man from France used the same techniques in falsifying their sources, thereby accomplishing an immediate purpose and at the same time bequeathing an untold number of errors to writers and readers of posterity.

TRAVEL CONTROVERSIES

"He abhors to take the lie but not to tell it." [1]

IT IS COMMON KNOWLEDGE that several witnesses to the same crime, to the same accident, to the same scene, several readers of the same book, or several listeners to the same speech will, like the blind men describing the elephant, render judgments and give reports that are sometimes completely at variance with one another. Travelers of the eighteenth century provide many examples of such disagreement. Government embassies, scientific expeditions, missionary activities, colonizing ventures, holiday excursions—all these inspired their participants to compete for the public ear. The books that resulted were good supplements to one another in an age that was becoming more and more aware of the value of comparing authorities. And many travelers—the Sloanes, the Charlevoixs, and the Cooks —actuated by the best principles of the scientist or historian, corrected the errors of visitors who had preceded them. But almost inevitably, whether the reporters went together or separately, there was controversy. Some of the controversialists were seeking revenge for real or imagined persecution or vindication for what were considered false charges made by fellow travelers; some were exploiting the reputation of successful companions who had beaten them into print, or were jealous of those reputations; many were fighting for or against a nation, religion, or philosophy; and a great many give evidence that, as a group, travelers are inclined to be disputatious. More often than not, the disagreements, the charges, and the counter-charges were insignificant, even trifling in importance; but they were also sometimes of grave consequence, ruining or re-establishing reputations, influencing the decisions of courts of law, or leaving the public puzzled as to what the truth really was. And the historian of today, acting both as prosecutor and defense counsel, must conclude that all of the travel contro-versies of the eighteenth century are not possible of perfect solution, that some of them stemmed from errors on both sides, some were the result of honest disagreement, many were colored by something in the background or immediate situation of one or more of the disputants, and some originated only because of blatant falsehood. But in the eighteenth century, "lie" was a charge hurled back and forth among both travelers and travel commentators.

Because of the great popularity of descriptions of the more exotic lands, officers aboard the same ship or ships to the same destination, even ordinary seamen, frequently kept journals in order that on their return from a long voyage they might pub-lish a book, the sale of which would increase their income or bring them fame. One of the most successful of these sailor-narrators was William Dampier, whose experiences included log-wood cutting at Campeachy, running a plantation in Ja-maica, buccaneering from the Caribbean to Cochin China, and circumnavigating the globe more than once. An influence on Swift and a real-life model for Defoe's mariners, such as Cap-tain Singleton and Robert Drury,[2] Dampier in 1691 published *A New Voyage Round the World*, a record of his early exploits written in a fitting style, recording accurate, even scientific, observations, and recounting exciting adventures. The author, an immediate and permanent success, wrote other books and was accepted as the authority on navigation, winds, and geog-raphy. He was patronized by Pepys and Evelyn, became the friend of Sir Hans Sloane and two presidents of the Royal So-ciety, was introduced to Queen Anne by her Prince Consort, and received the captaincy of two ships commissioned by the government, one, the rotten-bottomed *Roebuck,* sailing to northern waters, the other, the equally inadequate *St. George,* starting on a secret mission to plague the Spanish in the South Seas. His last important voyage was made as navigator for Woodes Rogers on a circumnavigation of the globe that ended in the second decade of the century. Dampier's books have always given him a prominent place in the literature of travel: Although he discovered few new lands in the ocean, "he discovered the whole South Seas to his countrymen." [3] A precursor of Banks and Darwin in his concern with natural history, a precursor of Cook and Nelson in his ability at navigation, he was a scientific sailor, ushering in the age of the compass, of exact longitude, and of enlightenment.

But William Dampier had serious faults. He was obviously a poor commander, his quick anger and indecisiveness keeping him constantly at odds with rebellious crews that were not impressed by his reputation among the landsmen. On returning in 1701 from his first voyage as captain, he was court-martialed for marooning his lieutenant. His influence unaffected by the stigma, he was given the *St. George* and a riffraff crew for legalized pirating. After numerous experiences with insubordination, he angered his men so much by failing to capture a Spanish prize off the coast of Mexico that thirty-five of them deserted in a small boat and reached home ahead of their commander, who lost his ship and his commission and ended up in a Dutch jail before returning to England and even greater fame. One of the thirty-five, the mate William Funnell, preceded him in print with a *Voyage round the World: Containing an Account of Captain Dampier's Expedition into the South Seas . . . With his various Adventures, Engagements . . .* (1707). The title page contains no reference to Funnell, and the subtitle indicates clearly that author and publisher were profiting from Dampier's renown even while the book itself attacked him both as a man and a leader, thereby hoping to prove him responsible for the mutiny of the thirty-five men. Although on his return he offered no journal of his own, Dampier was forced to publish a *Vindication of His Voyage to the South Seas in the Ship "St.*

George," which was in turn rebutted with an *Answer to the Vindication,* by midshipman John Welbe, another of the deserters.[4]

Funnell's *Voyage* is actually very readable and trustworthy except in its charges about the conduct of Dampier, whose angry *Vindication* considered the accusations one by one, always providing a different version entirely. Funnell gives one objective for the privateering expedition; Dampier gives another. The mate blames all failures in battle on a weak, unaggressive, even cowardly, captain; the captain blames them on a stupid and frightened crew. The book accuses Dampier of foolishly ordering his men to fire on an Indian canoe that escaped to warn prospective Spanish victims; Dampier says that the unexpected shooting was contrary to his desires. The first witness charges that Dampier and his inferior, Captain Stradling, parted company over a "disagreement"; the answer is, "Whereas Mr. Funnell frequently would insinuate, that I could agree with nobody . . . I say, I Deputed Captain Stradling . . . but never entered into a Dispute. I lent him a spare Top-Mast, his Ship's Crew being sickly, he had always my Chirurgeon." [5]

Welbe went even further than Funnell. He blamed the miscarriage of the venture "wholly on the Want of Courage and Conduct in the Commander." [6] According to him, Dampier was constantly drunk; and during an engagement, unable to encourage his men or give commands, he stood like a frightened boy "behind a good Barricado" on the quarter-deck. At least once Welbe even contradicted Funnell, but the two agreed that the thirty-five men in the barque did not mutiny but were sent away by their commander. Admiral Smyth discredits Funnell completely; Bonner speaks of his "sneers, if not downright lies"; while other judges—Masefield and Wilkinson, for example—find that most of his accusations resulted from an ignorance of his leader's "greater design" or were provoked by Dampier's "overbearing temper" and apparent backwardness in looking for a fight.[7] But Welbe has no defense. His charge of drunkenness is contradicted by all who knew Dampier, and by common agreement the men who ran off in the barque with the *St. George*'s supplies and guns were mutineers. His letters, as well as his *Answer,* prove that the former midshipman would "say almost anything," that "he was a man of little truth and evil temper." [8]

Welbe's story has a sequel. A few years after the exchange with Dampier, in an age of projectors like those satirized in Gulliver's third voyage, the mutinous midshipman, now claiming to be a captain, is discovered proposing schemes for settling Australia. In 1713 he submitted to the government his first unsuccessful plan for colonization, claiming knowledge derived from his experiences with Dampier. Then, in 1716, one year after the death of his former commander, he advanced a second proposal, this time insisting, with the boldness of Hennepin after the death of La Salle, that "from the coast of Peru West to the East Indies is upwards of 2,500 leagues, which to the south of the line is undiscovered to any European, Captain Welbe excepted." [9] Not only did he conveniently forget Dampier's explorations, but in order to enhance his own importance and to claim "firstness," he ignored the many South Sea discoveries of the Dutch, the Portuguese, and the Spanish. And like La Salle, who obtained backing and prestige by bending the Mississippi west to the mines of New Mexico, Welbe sought support for his schemes by claiming that Australia contained great stores of gold and silver which would enrich Britain. Although such a claim was a lie as far as he was concerned, in later centuries it turned out to be the truth. Welbe's proposals to lead ships to Australia failed as completely as had those of Hennepin and Lahontan to head expeditions to North America. But unlike the lies of his French contemporaries, Welbe's did not affect the history of geography because, for one reason, he never set them down in book form for the public to defend or attack but rather submitted them to officials of the state, who turned him down because, one eighteenth-century historian commented, it appeared that "his proposals were made principally with a view to his own relief."

In 1740, a long generation after William Dampier's voyage in the *St. George* ended in public recriminations and accusations of falsehood, Commodore George Anson sailed from England with eight ships and almost 2,000 men to harass the Spaniards and attempt a circumnavigation. He succeeded in going around the world but took almost four years doing it and lost all of his little fleet except the *Centurion.* One of the losses, the storeship *Wager,* was wrecked on a peninsula off the coast of Chile. The success of the *Centurion* was recorded in four books,[10] but the failure of the *Wager* produced still another four [11] and resulted in a controversy both more dramatic and more widely publicized than that of Dampier.

Because it had been separated from Anson's squadron during a storm at night, the *Wager* was completely alone when it hit rocks off southern South America in April of 1741. All but a few drunkards and scavengers among the crew of 130 escaped to the shore, salvaged some supplies from the wreck, built or found makeshift shelter, and lived riotously, dangerously, and mutinously under the nominal command of Captain David Cheap, who at first was partially disabled because of a dislocated shoulder. The best account of the hardships, the thievery, the murders, and the mutiny that followed the wreck is that in the journal kept by Bulkeley, the gunner, and Cummins, the carpenter, who with Lieutenant Bean were leaders in the plot that led to eighty men taking the ship's boat, deserting Captain Cheap, John Byron, Alexander Campbell, and several others, and making a miraculous voyage back through the Strait of Magellan to Brazil, from where the thirty who survived were eventually returned to England in 1743 to face a court-martial. The book by Bulkeley and Cummins was the first of many stories of the adventure, appearing before Cheap, Byron, and their companions were able to make their way north to civilization and help from the enemy Spain, and even before the *Centurion* and Lord Anson returned. Furthermore, all but two [12] of the later stories about the Anson expedition depended for facts, either briefly or at great length, on this first one. And from it sprang the controversy.

Bulkeley and Cummins had two motives in publishing, one —announced in the preface—to clear their "characters, which have been exceedingly blemish'd" by Lieutenant Bean, who arrived first in England, the other—obvious on almost every page—to justify their desertion of Captain Cheap. In their journal the collaborators continually vilified Bean as a coward [13] and described themselves as men of honor, thinking of the good of the whole crew, befriended, trusted, and complimented to the end by the very captain they deserted. According to them, the event that finally caused the men to lose confidence in Cheap and take matters in their own hands was the captain's shooting of a seaman named Cozzens. In their version Cozzens, who had formerly been mistreated by the captain, came to the purser for his ration of wine. The two having words, the purser shot at but missed the seaman. Immediately, "the Captain, and Lieutenant Hamilton, hearing the Discharge of the Pistol, the latter ran out with a Firelock, then called the Captain out of his Tent, telling him that Cozzens was coming to Mutiny; the Captain on this jumped out, asking where the Villain was, clapped a cock'd Pistol to Mr. Cozzen's Cheek, and precipitately shot him, without asking any Questions." [14] After that the captain forced the men to leave their wounded companion on the ground, would permit him no medical care, and harshly refused Bulkeley and Cummins permission to take him to their tent, all of which resulted in the death of Cozzens. It was this event, as recorded by the gunner and carpenter and repeated in the books of certain members of the crew of the *Centurion,* that gave David Cheap the reputation of being a hardhearted murderer, a villain who forced his men to save themselves by making him a prisoner and working out their own salvation.

Three accounts of the wreck of the *Wager,* however, do not make Bulkeley and Cummins the heroes they described themselves to be or agree that Cheap was a murderer. Midshipman Alexander Campbell, who stayed with Cheap and caused a minor controversy by turning Catholic and briefly entering the service of Spain before going home, wrote *The Sequel to Bulkeley and Cummins's Voyage* (1784), which was both an apology for his own actions and an attack on the version by the gunner and carpenter. Although he believed himself to have been unjustly treated by the captain, he absolved Cheap of all blame in the death of Cozzens, which he termed "unfortunate." [15] John Byron, another of those left behind by the eighty deserters, did not bring out his book immediately but waited until 1768, after his own successful circumnavigation as commander of the *Dolphin* had made him famous. Although in the preface he accused Bulkeley and Cummins of telling their story "with the purpose of justifying . . . a direct mutiny," Byron's version of the Cozzens affair, which he did not see, takes a middle course. He remembered the seaman as mild-mannered when not drunk but judged his actions to the captain as "indecent and provoking," while the captain's shot was "rash and hasty." Byron's book, put together long after the event, shows the hand of a ghost writer, since in its account of the Spaniards in Chile it borrowed from earlier writers such as Frézier, and even in its story of Cozzens it frequently employed the very words of Bulkeley and Cummins.[16] It was the official account of the entire Anson expedition, written at least in part by Chaplain Walter, that attempted to exonerate the *Wager*'s captain completely. Here [17] Cheap becomes a leader who did everything to save his men at the time of the wreck, a brave man who refused to give in to the "utterly ungovernable" mutineers or to abandon his plan to rendezvous with Anson at Juan Fernandez. As for Cozzens, he had been "in brawls with most of the officers who had adhered to the Captain's Authority," and the death-dealing shot was the result of Cheap's mistaken but warranted belief that the seaman was mutinying and had fired the pistol which had gone off outside the captain's tent.

As with most such controversies, the truth is hard to arrive at, at least in the matter of the death of Cozzens. But it now seems obvious that Captain Cheap was no murderer. He was perhaps impetuous and nervous because of the trying situation, one in which some of the crew had already deserted and gone off to another camp while many others felt that the captain's authority had ended with the loss of his ship or that his plan to go north among the Spaniards was too dangerous. He and others returned to England to testify against the surviving mutineers, but public sympathy was so aroused by the hazardous voyage they had undergone and by the account of Bulkeley and Cummins that the trial ended with the freedom of all but Lieutenant Bean.

Perhaps not so dramatic as the affair of the *Wager* but nevertheless more influential and certainly more easily judged, was the Dixon-Meares controversy late in the century.[18] During 1787–1788 Captain George Dixon of the *Queen Charlotte* was on the largely unexplored northwest coast of North America in the company of Captain Portlock and the *King George*. While there he encountered John Meares, formerly of the British navy, then commanding ships representing a group of merchants operating out of Canton and attempting to circumvent the fur trade monopoly held by the British South Sea Company and East India Company, both of which had licensed Dixon and Portlock. These two continued on separately to China and Africa and back to England, where each published a *Voyage Round the World*. Meares in 1788–1789 made a second fur-trading visit to Nootka in the American Northwest, where a Spanish commander arrested him for poaching on the rights of Spain. When he was released Meares rushed to England and in 1790 brought out his *Voyages Made in the years 1788 & 1789,* which included "Observations on the Probable Existence of a North-west Passage," and sent a memorial to the government which aroused public opinion against Spain so much that war was talked about. But because her ally France was unable to help, being involved with its Revolution, Spain capitulated, giving up its claim to the northern coast of America and reimbursing Meares for the fur losses he claimed to have sustained. Before the Spanish capitulation, however, an aroused Captain Dixon published a hard-hitting "Remarks on the Voyages of John Meares, Esq." (1790). Meares replied with "An Answer to Mr. George Dixon" (1791) that drew a rebuttal, the most irate of the pieces, called "Further Remarks on the Voyages of John Meares, Esq., in which several important Facts, misrepresented in the said Voyages, relative to Geography and Commerce, are fully substantiated" (1791). The political troubles with Spain having ended at the Nootka Convention, the two men ceased their public debate, which had attracted much attention, for example, the *Critical Review* in January, February, and March of 1791 publishing reviews, summaries, and extended portions of Meares's book and the three controversial pamphlets dealing with it.

Some of the arguments are minor in importance but indicative of the problem. Meares contended that he flew the British flag at Nootka; Dixon, and others, insisted it was the same Portuguese flag under which the Cantonese merchants operated to avoid paying taxes in China. Meares said that he bought land from the Indians in the Northwest; two other Englishmen there said he did not and that the natives called him "Aitaaita," or "Liar." Meares contended that Dixon had mistreated another captain, named Duncan; Duncan unexpectedly returned to England from the Pacific and published a letter defending Dixon and adding damaging facts about his opponent.

Of the major arguments, two were most impressive. In the money settlement with Spain, Meares had asked for $100 for each of the hypothetical furs he had been kept from obtaining; Dixon showed that for all other traders of the preceding decade, from Cook to himself, the average price was $25.00 to $45.00. In fact, Meares had changed the figures on the money involved, doubling the first figure reported to the government and later settling for one-third the original amount. The second charge leveled by Dixon was that Meares not only had pretended to discover certain portions of the American coast discovered already by Cook, Dixon, Portlock, and others, but that in order to support his belief in the existence of a Northwest Passage he had made Cook's River deeper and had changed longitudes and latitudes on real maps and on Juan de Fuca's pretended map to bring the Pacific and Atlantic oceans closer to each other.

Among the controversies of the eighteenth century, that of Dixon and Meares was no doubt one of the most important politically, and it is the easiest to settle satisfactorily now. No one has ever questioned the motives or facts of George Dixon; everyone who has studied the affair, from his contemporaries to modern historians, has condemned Meares as a profiteering adventurer who, in order to attain his ends, would twist the truth in any direction or in any amount. In his own day Captain Vancouver accused him of stating as facts things he did not know, Sir Alexander Mackenzie was "surprised" at some of his geography,[19] and the *Critical Review,* for only one of its adverse conclusions, complained that "in Mr. Meares's map the continent is evidently so narrow as in a moment to excite suspicion." [20] In the twentieth century Professor Manning's *Nootka Sound Controversy* warns the reader to doubt "any important or uncorroborated statement made by Meares," [21] and the most exhaustive scholarly analysis concludes that Meares "endeavoured to magnify his own explorations at the expense of his predecessors; that he made many statements, important and unimportant, without any knowledge of the facts, with a reckless disregard of the truth, or with knowledge of their untruth; that in the discussion of the price of sea-otter skins (which was to him the subject of importance) he has omitted material factors, falsified documents, and made knowingly untrue statements; and that, in consequense, he is not entitled to have credence placed in his unsupported testimoney." [22]

At the time that the Dixon-Meares controversy was brewing at Nootka Sound and fifty years after the events which left the public with an impression of Captain David Cheap as villain of the mutiny of the *Wager,* the most famous mutiny of all time was taking place and inspiring accusations that would create a myth about another captain and make him the archetype of all harsh and niggardly commanders. In 1790 Lieutenant William Bligh [23] miraculously returned to London, having undergone experiences that would destroy men of less ability and perseverance, and published *A Narrative of the Mutiny on H. M. S. Bounty.* The details of that story and of its aftermath are well known: how while the *Bounty* was homeward bound from Tahiti, Acting Lieutenant Fletcher Christian led a revolt, forced Bligh and eighteen others into a twenty-three-foot boat, which they navigated 3,600 miles under his superior leadership, and how Christian sailed back to Tahiti, left the least guilty and least venturesome of the mutineers, and with eight who remained picked up a dozen native women and six native men to end up on Pitcairn Island over one thousand miles away. But the details of the controversy that followed the disappearance of the *Bounty* are not so well known.

When Bligh arrived in England and placed charges against the deserters who had stolen his ship, he immediately became famous, received a promotion and another ship, and left again for the South Seas to finish his assignment of transporting breadfruit trees to the West Indies. While he was gone the mutineers who had chosen to stay at Tahiti were taken into custody and brought back to England, that is, all who did not drown during an unfortunate wreck on the voyage home. Since the government chose to hold the court-martial in Bligh's absence, little or no damaging firsthand evidence was heard against the mutineers, all but three of whom escaped the death sentence. In fact, the public swung over to the side of the men on trial, and the Bligh myth was begun.

It was given much initial impetus by the efforts of two persons. One was a mutineer, boatswain's mate James Morrison, whose journal—much quoted by early commentators such as Sir John Barrow—depicted the cursing, tyrannical, sadistic Bligh of later novels and movies. The other was Fletcher Christian's brother Edward, a professor of law at Cambridge and a prolific author and editor, who had the minutes of the court-martial published with an appendix, which he wrote attempting to prove not only that Fletcher was an unwilling victim of the abuse of William Bligh but that all the men on the *Bounty,* and even those placed in the small boat with Bligh, spoke highly of Fletcher, believed him Bligh's equal as a navigator and commander, and acknowledged that he was one of the few sailors at Tahiti who would have nothing to do with the native women. Back in England by this time, Bligh in 1794 was forced to write "Remarks on the Journal of James Morrison" and "An Answer to Certain Assertions contained in [Edward Christian's] Appendix to a Pamphlet called Minutes of the Proceedings of the Court Martial . . . on Ten Persons charged with Mutiny . . ." In the "Answer" Bligh was able to show that the published minutes were not completely authentic and to furnish sworn affidavits from most of the eighteen men who stayed with him, all of whom contradicted Edward Christian in every important respect, showing that Bligh, in their opinion, was no harsher to Fletcher than to anyone else, that Bligh was his superior, regularly instructing and supervising him, and that the young mate not only had a female consort on Tahiti but one who at the time of the mutiny was bearing his child. In spite of these responses, Fletcher Christian became a sort of Byronic hero, a victim of fate, and a figure about whom many legends grew up. There are at least three versions of his later life, one being that he escaped from Pitcairn Island to live a shadowy existence with relatives in the Lake Country of northern England and to be seen by one of his fellow mutineers, who after being pardoned became a captain in the navy.[24] As one might guess, Fletcher's name was used for a fireside travel account called *Letters from Mr. Fletcher Christian, containing a Narrative of the Transactions . . . before and after the Mutiny, with his subsequent Voyages and Travels in South America* (1796), which would be believed authentic by at least one twentieth-century editor.[25]

The myth of Captain Bligh is hard to bring back to earth, for those scholars who in recent years have tried to be just to his reputation have only partially succeeded in making themselves heard. They have pointed out [26] that his cursing was no worse than that of other commanders, Lord Nelson, for example; that the charges of niggardliness in rationing stemmed from his being the purser as well as the captain; that in spite of any such charges he was able to establish a record for healthy crews— better even than that of his former commander Cook; that he gave up his own cabin to help wet sailors and erected awnings in hot climates to protect them; and that the reputed cruel floggings numbered only seven for the entire voyage, one of which was for desertion, three of which were for mistreating natives, and all of which were according to navy regulations and few in comparison with the punishments on other ships.

Furthermore, it has been shown that the members of the *Bounty* crew were softened and seduced by the long stay at Tahiti before the mutiny, that Fletcher Christian was by no means the only one among them who had become more than attached to particular women on the island, that a few of them had deserted even before the ship sailed, that numerous others had to be rounded up and forced aboard, and that the majority of the mutineers were so enamored of the island they insisted on being left there to face almost certain capture and court-martial. Yet in spite of all these arguments, editors and popular reference books [27] still blame the most famous of mutinies entirely on the commander of the ship, giving no hint that the men and the conditions were at least as responsible as he.

The four sea controversies that have been analyzed were among the most important of the eighteenth century, but they were by no means the only ones. In the 1720's George Shelvocke circumnavigated the globe and published his *Voyage round the World* (1726), which caused one of his officers, William Betagle, to write another account of the voyage "Relating the True historical Facts of the whole Affair; Testifyed by many imployed therein." [28] In June, 1773, while reviewing Hawkesworth's collection of voyages, the *Gentleman's Magazine* is found complaining that the accounts of Anson's and Byron's circumnavigations contradict each other about the island of Tinian; and of the descriptions of King George's Island given by Wallis and Cook, the editor concluded, "Nothing can be more opposite to each other than these two accounts, and yet they are reported by gentlemen whose veracity cannot be called in question." [29] And after the last voyage of Captain Cook, the adventurer John Ledyard, who was with him, beat the official story to press by rewriting another, still earlier, "surreptitious" journal and supplying certain additions, for example, details about Cook's death that make Ledyard's version "differ considerably" from all others.[30] In fact, any voyage of discovery or exploration in the eighteenth century, such as this last one of Cook, was liable to elicit more than one journal—authentic, ghost-written, or fireside—in spite of the government regulation that all state-supported ventures of the kind would be told about in an official report only.

Controversies over land travels were just as numerous and not always inclined to be British, but they were of a different sort and motivated by entirely different reasons. Sometimes they had to do with the authorship of a book. In 1777 after the death of the Duc du Châtelet, the son of Voltaire's mistress and mentor, among his possessions was found a manuscript of a journey to Portugal. A publisher named Buisson and a writer named Bourgoing bought it, rewrote it completely, and published it as Châtelet's, profiting from the name of the Duc and the esteem in which he was held. Then certain people protested that the Duc had never been in Portugal, a fact that Buisson and Bourgoing may not have known. The real author, the Baron de Cormatin, had sent the manuscript to Châtelet, his protector, just before the Duc's death and had himself been thrown into prison about the same time for his part in the wars of the Vendée. Unable to defend himself he had his wife write Bourgoing, who answered that his changes in the manuscript had made it his own but that he would return the original. He did not return it, however, but brought it out again in 1801, this time with his own name on the title page. More correspondence went through the mails, and Cormatin was in the process of recreating the text of his work and showing how it fitted in with his other travels when he too died.[31]

Sometimes a travel writer was condemned for stealing or rewriting when today one can find no reason for the charges. In the 1690's Peter the Great's emissary, a Dane named Everard Ysbrants Ides, headed an embassy to China that required three years for the overland trip through Siberia. In 1697 in Frankfort, and the next year in France and England, appeared a *Journal of the Embassy . . . to China . . . Written by Adam Brant, Secretary of the Embassy*. Then in 1704 in Amsterdam, and two years later in France and England, the "authorized" account of the journey, apparently by Ides himself, was published and has become famous for being one of the chief sources of Defoe's continuation of *Robinson Crusoe*. As with the various versions of any eighteenth-century sea voyage, the two accounts were compared and verdicts were given. One of the most critical of early readers was J.-F. Bernard, who included Ides's journal in a collection of travels [32] and went to the trouble of collating it with that by the "Secretary," adding a footnote every time a discrepancy could be detected and always saying, or implying, that Brant, or Brand, was concocting his story. For example, Bernard was worried because one of the two reporters named a river "Suchina" while the other spelled it "Wergnosuchono." Elsewhere, when Ides called a town "large" and named it "Solowitzjogda," Bernard observed that Brand called it "Lolowitzgotz" and made it "small." [33] All of the complaints are of this sort and all can be explained. It is not surprising that on a journey of such duration, through such strange country where languages were so peculiar, to find two people disagreeing about the spelling of a very difficult name or to discover that they do not always make note of the same town in the same way. Over a period of three years notes could become hard to read, words could be incorrectly written, names could be misunderstood. One could as easily argue that such differences are an indication that both journals are authentic. What may be more important is that the journals agree in substance, Ides's being considerably longer, and that neither seems to borrow from the other. Their authors followed the same route, often not describing the same village or custom, and seeing the same event with different eyes. One can only agree that they supplement each other.[34]

Instead of dealing with authorship or possible theft, a controversy could arise when a traveler's animosity caused him to follow some other traveler and prove him wrong. After fighting for the colonies in the American Revolution, the Marquis de Chastellux visited many of the new states and then returned to France to publish in 1786 an account of America that is justifiably rated high for its historical value. In the same year Brissot de Warville, a lover of liberty and anything American—later to lose his life in the French Revolution—read the book and

wrote a heated "Critical examination" intended to refute its
"opinions on Quakers, on Negroes, on people, and on man." [35]
Then after founding "The Friends of the Blacks" and engaging
in another public debate in which he defended St. Jean de
Crèvecoeur's *Letters from an American Farmer*,[36] he journeyed
to North America to study slavery and the Quakers; and there,
in order to attack Chastellux whenever possible, he followed
the practice of going out of his way to visit the people whom
the marquis had seemed to mistreat in his book. The resulting
account of Brissot's voyage even defended that practice, since his
object was to offer an antidote for the "poison" of the soldier-
aristocrat by exposing "the errors, the lies, the calumnies" which
he had propagated.[37] On examination, the charges frequently
turn out to be rather trivial. Chastellux had said that a certain
Miss Vining of Wilmington, Delaware, was a gossip and a flirt;
after spending two evenings in her company, Brissot admitted
that she was "un peu coquette" but insisted that she never spoke
evil of anyone and comported herself in a manner beyond re-
proach.[38] A more serious charge was that Chastellux had vilified
Colonel Wadsworth of Hartford by recording that in his younger
days he had made several slave-trading voyages to Guinea; Brissot countered the "calumny" by reporting that not only did
Wadsworth hate slavery but that he himself denied ever having
transported slaves.[39] As in this case, most of the more important
accusations against Chastellux were related to his pursuer's very
aggressive concern over slavery and Quakers, for, to Brissot, the
aristocratic marquis did not seem adequately perturbed by the
conditions of the blacks and was not sufficiently an admirer of
the "good Quaker." [40]

Very often the controversy could derive from national bias,
as when Joseph Baretti came to the defense of his native Italy.
Samuel Sharp, an English surgeon traveling for his health, wrote
Letters from Italy (1768) which aroused the irritation of Baretti,
a friend of Dr. Johnson and author of a popular Italian dictionary, and brought on what Fanny Burney called the "book
war." Baretti's *An Account of . . . Italy, with Observations
on the Mistakes of some Travelers . . .* (1768), published in

his native language as well as in English, attacked Sharp for alleged untruths and errors and evoked the Englishman's rejoinder in the same year.[41] The "book war" received much contemporaneous public attention, one periodical contributing this adverse judgment of Baretti, "Nothing can give us stronger proof, that it is more easy to perceive the *contradictions* of another than our own," and favoring the Englishman, "Mr. Baretti has met with a *Rowland for his Oliver;* and may find Mr. Sharp, rather too sharp for him." [42]

Another frequent source for travel controversy was religious disagreement—Protestant opposing Roman Catholic; Récollets, in fact, all non-Jesuits, attacking Jesuits; or the antireligious complaining of the religious viewpoint. Since the influence of this sort of bias is detailed elsewhere in the present book, one need only note the types and extent of the religious debates that went on in voyage literature or revolved about it. Perhaps the longest sustained attack on any single book was that on the *Nouveau voyage d'Italie* (1691), by François Misson, a Huguenot refugee living in England who had toured the Continent in 1687–1688 as tutor to the Earl of Arran. This two-volume work was given high praise by Addison in the preface to his description of the same country; and well past the middle of the century, the mathematician La Lande was providing evidence that it was still considered "indispensable reading for all travellers to Italy." [43] Because of the Protestant Misson's popularity, however, French Catholics, whether travelers or simply commentators, felt obligated to find fault with his picture of Italy and the other countries he visited, especially wherever he made any judgment or observation about religion.

Blainville's *Travels* (1743), for example, followed Misson around almost as much as Brissot's book trailed Chastellux, accusing him of passing on "many Narrations of Things that are trifling, useless, and false." But the evidence that Blainville offered is itself rather trifling, even startling. Misson, he said, told that the Italian people paid for the erection of the church Del Popolo when the Pope actually paid for it. And with Misson's story of an Italian gentleman who fell in a hole and stayed there for sixty hours before clawing his way out, Blainville was quite sarcastic, expending over a page to show that the hole was only a cane's length deep, that it was not just where Misson put it, and that the man himself completely denied the fabrication. Blainville concluded with the question, "Is there, I would ask you, the smallest Probability of truth in this story?" [44]

Not so trifling and nearly always religious were the charges of Père Labat, one of the most voluminous of eighteenth-century authors and editors of travels, who lived in Italy seven years before publishing his account of it. Although he praised Misson's style, Labat showed anger at his statements about the dogma of the Immaculate Conception, derided Misson's short stay in Italy as compared with his own seven-year visit, exclaimed at the Protestant's perpetuating the legend of a Popess Jeanne, and concluded that "it is astonishing how anyone so able as Misson could take so little care to guard against dishonoring himself by writing such false facts." [45] Complaints of this nature, frequently repeated, caused John Pinkerton early in the nineteenth century to say in his bibliography of travels that Misson's *Nouveau voyage* was widely read but replete "with the grossest misrepresentations of the religious state of Italy."

In the twentieth century a French specialist on travels in Holland,[46] after attempting to expose the inaccuracies and incredibilities of an earlier traveler, says that in Misson, "however, he has found his master in the art of presenting without judgment the things he has seen or pretended to see." According to this critic, the *Nouveau voyage* contains "a host of historical stupidities and lies." The one example offered from among the "host" is that Misson described a Dutch fisherman as being eight feet tall, "skinny," and weighing five hundred pounds. If all the praise of Misson and all the complaints about him could be gathered, one would have materials for a small volume, but the complaints would be either unimportant or inspired by religious differences.[47]

A reader of voyage literature must be aware of the possibility of religious controversy and its effects, as in the battle between the Jesuit and Récollet missionaries. Very early in the seventeenth century Champlain brought a number of Récollet priests to New France. This sect welcomed the more political-minded, well-supported Jesuits to Quebec in 1625, only to find themselves barred from that colony seven years later and forced into other areas. Champlain, in the 1619 account of his travels, had praised his Récollet associates highly; but in the later editions someone "studiously cut out the enthusiastic references to the Récollets . . . and awkwardly substituted matter about the Jesuits," who had not been in Canada at the time written about.[48] The controversy thus begun between the two groups continued on to the very end of the century, with much of the Récollet counterattack being built around Père Le Clercq, whose experiences in the New World were recorded in his *Etablissement de la foi* (1691), a book that gave a bitter and satirical review of the Jesuit *Relations*. Le Clercq, his brothers, and his opponents are, of course, vitally important to any student of their period, but Justin Winsor is not the only prominent historian to conclude, "We can scarcely account many of them trustworthy historical authorities, since prejudice and partisanship characterize them for the most part. The contests of the period greatly developed antagonisms." [49]

The Jesuits everywhere were attacked and defended, but especially so was their organization in Argentina, which was considered political as well as religious and which they themselves pictured as utopian. Thomas Falkener, an English Jesuit stationed there in the first half of the eighteenth century, was one who found the Order's accomplishments praiseworthy. From this side, the reader gathers the opinion that the natives of Argentina were being educated and ennobled. But many European travelers, as well as many stay-at-homes, believed that the priests kept their Indian converts in poverty-ridden servitude and ignorance in order to further their own kingdom on earth. This tradition, closely related to the earlier "Tears of the Indians" controversy, deriving from such writers as the Spanish Las Casas and the English Thomas Gage, was the tradition in which Voltaire's *Candide* was written. One of the most influential of later eighteenth-century travelers to see conditions in

Argentina in an anti-Jesuit manner was Bougainville, whose viewpoint was adopted and developed by Diderot and the philosophes.[50]

Travelers could become involved in controversies because of personal, political, national, or religious beliefs, but they also fought over a philosophy or a philosophic concept. And just as the members of the Royal Society or the Academy of Sciences searched the voyage literature for scientific facts, the philosophers who stayed at home raided it for proof of their theories or for evidence to use against rival theories. There is no better example than the great debate over the nature of the New World, a debate which, in part at least, started long before the eighteenth century but which reached its climax after the Comte de Buffon's *Histoire naturelle* (1749–1788) spread the notion that men, animals, and plants of America were smaller, shorter-lived, and fewer in species than those of Europe and that European species degenerated after being brought to America. There were many subsidiary theories, among them that the natives of the Western Hemisphere were weak, impotent, beardless, lacking in creativity, cowardly, and lazy. Buffon's theory— condemned by both Rome and Rousseau—found much support, as from the Scottish historian William Robertson and the Dutch Corneille De Pauw; but it also aroused much opposition, as from the French Dom Pernetty and the American Thomas Jefferson, whose documented and rather indignant reply came in his *Notes on the State of Virginia*. Although most of its defenders were satisfied to quote Buffon, De Pauw supported his *Recherches philosophiques sur les américains* (1768) by referring to dozens of authorities, most of whom were writers of travel books, the evidence from which was carefully selected or twisted to develop a "one-sided picture, written according to a preconceived thesis." [51] For one instance only, even though he had read Frézier and Feüillée, both of whom told in great detail of the fertile soil of South America and the abundant harvest of fruit there, De Pauw still insisted that the soil of all the Americas was poor and that fruit trees flourished only on the island of Juan Fernandez.[52] De Pauw was a man of many controversies, Voltaire, for example, having condescended to disagree with his interpretation of China, but his vitriolic expansion of Buffon's comparatively mild theories helped to make the debate over the New World one of the most inflammatory of the century. In it travelers were not only seized upon as witnesses, but they themselves were frequently so overcome by its heat that some of their reports of what they saw must be judged untrustworthy. One can demonstrate this fact best by tracing a single phase of the controversy through the works of a number of visitors to America, for example, their attitude to the life span of its inhabitants, both Indians and descendants of Europeans.

There was a tradition dating back at least to Elizabethan times that natives of the Americas lived a long life. Laudonnière, on his second trip to Florida, met a man claiming two hundred and fifty years; certain of Hakluyt's voyagers—Vespucci, for example—spoke of Indians one hundred and fifty years old; and others reported ages of one hundred and twenty or one hundred and thirty.[53] This tradition was related to that of the Noble Savage and both existed side by side with the belief that people of the Western Hemisphere were degenerate. John Lawson in his *A New Voyage to Carolina* (1709) was thus able to report, "I had heard (before I knew this new World) that the Natives of America were a short-lived People, which, by all the Observations I could ever make, proves quite contrary; for those who are born here, and in other Colonies, live to as great Ages as any of the Europeans, the Climate being free from Consumption." [54] In 1773, in the same volume in which they fought over the size of the Patagonians, the Buffonian De Pauw and the anti-Buffonian Pernetty came to grips over the ages of Americans, De Pauw asserting that they died young because of their poor climate while Pernetty argued that "they live ordinarily up to eighty and one hundred years," [55] citing as witnesses travelers Lahontan and de Rochefort. French voyagers at the time of the Revolution, aware of the long tradition and of the contemporaneous treatment of it, lined up on opposing sides and gave their evidence.

Among the ardent Buffonites the Abbé Robin reported that in the British colonies the women were beautiful at twenty but at thirty-five or forty "they are wrinkled and decrepit." Furthermore, Robin had examined the tombstones in Boston graveyards and discovered that "the majority of the dead people . . . had scarcely attained fifty years" and that none of them lived beyond sixty-five.[56] He was echoed by Hilliard d'Auberteuil, Chastellux, and Moreau de St. Méry, who was even more extreme, insisting that in North America "ordinarily people die between the ages of thirty-five and forty." F.-M. Bayard is perhaps a more striking witness, since his espousal of Buffon and De Pauw forced his mind to contradict his eyes. After announcing that Buffon was probably more nearly correct than Jefferson, he offered the testimony that not only were American trees and animals less hardy and shorter-lived but that American people reached "puberty and old age sooner than in Europe." All this comes a few pages after the same author had exclaimed over the size and health of the men of Winchester and a few pages before he wrote of seeing thick groves of giant trees and very large chickens.[57]

At the same time these travelers were favoring one side in the controversy, other travelers were opposing them. J.-B. Bossu's popular *Nouveaux voyages dans l'Amérique* (1777), enthusiastically recommended to Emerson by Carlyle, reported an idyllic life for the Noble Savages of middle North America, who were hardy, healthy, and far from being cowardly and impotent; and it told of how these men of nature, aided by a drink made from the marvelous ginseng root, often lived to be a hundred years old.[58] Brissot de Warville not only argued with Chastellux about Negroes and Quakers; he attacked the Buffonites by inspecting the graveyards of Massachusetts—the same ones examined by Robin—and then drew up a table to prove that more Americans than Europeans reached the age of seventy. "Nothing could be more untrue," he said, than the claims of the Abbé Robin. "I have carefully observed women between thirty and fifty years of age, and found most of them plump and of good health." Brissot pointed to nine members of one family with an average life span of eighty years, and then, after listing the ages of Harvard graduates, he came to the vigorous conclusion that "a man's life is much longer in the United States than in the healthiest country of Europe." [59] The travelers who supported Pernetty, Jefferson, and other pro-Americans were themselves supported in turn by such end-of-the-century publications as E. A. W. Zimmerman's *Essai de comparison entre la France et les Etats-Unis* (1797), with its tables to prove the topic sentence, "In Utopia life must be more plentiful and long-lived." [60] It was all part of a controversy that rivaled the slightly younger "periodical war" between British and American writers concerning the prevalence of vulgarity and the success or failure of democracy in the United States, and both controversies quoted or affected the reports of many travelers.

PREJUDICED TRAVELERS

"However I might be disposed to trust his probity,
I dare not trust his prejudice." [1]

ALTHOUGH THE CHIEF CAUSES of travel fabrications, whether
of complete books or short passages, were money and vanity,
prejudice was also a widespread motive for distorting the truth,
both for the voyager who reported the distortions and for the
reader who accepted them. And since it was—and is—a more
subtle motive, the effects of which are often very hard to determine, we need concern ourselves only with its more blatant
examples, some of which have already been noted. Whatever
the reason for the creation of Admiral de Fonte, he was quoted
and advertised by Arthur Dobbs and Benjamin Franklin because they longed so ardently to find a Northwest Passage. Partly
for the same reason, Captain Meares falsified the geography of
the Pacific coast of North America. Family bias, another kind
of vanity, drove Professor Christian to defend his guilty brother
Fletcher and pursue Captain Bligh so relentlessly. And only a
strong prejudice, either for or against the New World or for or
against a philosophic theory, can account for the wide disagreements in travelers' statistics concerning the health and longevity
of Americans.

The eighteenth century was often aware of the prevalence
of this fault among those who recounted their journeys. De
Pauw, himself so biased, sneered at all travelers: "Their prej-

udices travel with them and acquire a sort of authority on crossing the Equinoctial Line or the Tropics." J.-F. Bernard, editor of a collection of voyages (1725), noticed that Lahontan gave his own primitivistic philosophy to the North American Indians while Hennepin went too far in the other direction and made them stupid. And both the French historian Charlevoix and the English geographer Bowen realized that if one group of visitors extolled a place too much another would approach it with high expectations and then leave "bitterly," giving an account at the other extreme.[2]

One prejudice that apparently was not recognized, however, was that which forced travel-book illustrations to conform to the artistic taste of the period. Early in the seventeenth century De Bry and other writers on America who included pictures gave all Indians the appearance of Greek statues. In 1724, the traveler Lafitau, arguing that the red men were similar in many ways to the Greeks, made the supposed similarity even more striking by placing pictures of Indians and Greek heroes side by side, thus helping to prolong a tradition that existed into the next century.[3] The judgment of Frenchmen who went to Egypt in the neoclassical period was "more or less warped by the taste of the times," as proved by their illustrations, which reproduced the Pharaonian statues and lotiform columns of Egypt as if they were in the neo-Hellenic style of the age of Louis XIV and Queen Anne.[4] Current theories could also determine which pieces of foreign art should be approved, as when the "Venus de Medici," spurned by a later period, was rapturously praised by Beckford and Gibbon and a host of eighteenth-century travelers, who, as a group, could also approve of the "Apollo Belvedere" while ignoring Michelangelo's "David." [5]

National prejudice, like that which aroused the Baretti-Sharp controversy over Italy, was much more common than aesthetic bias, as well as more easily recognized at the time. It assumed as many forms as there were nationalities among the travelers. Before 1660 Spain, because of its near monopoly in the New World, received the brunt of the attack from travelers sent in that direction by other countries. The anti-Spanish tradition, already demonstrated in the accounts of La Salle, Defoe, and Coreal, lingered on well into the eighteenth century with such propaganda pieces as the anonymous *The British Sailor's Discovery* (1739), which attempted to prove that Spain's claims to the West Indies were unjustified.

In spite of such famous exceptions as the young Montesquieu and the young Voltaire, who admired England, the image of that nation was often distorted by her visitors who wrote in French. One of the most important of these was Béat de Muralt in his *Lettres sur les anglois et les françois et sur les voiages* (1725), whose otherwise valuable book includes much that is sensational and exaggerated. Muralt insisted far more than necessary on a high rate of suicides in England, a charge repeated by other travelers employing him as a Baedeker. He recounted half a dozen lurid examples of murders committed because of drunkenness and reported that "most" English husbands kept mistresses in the household who "ate at the same table with the wife" and perhaps even "slept in the same bed with her." [6] The domestic English life he described was much like that found in the Restoration drama of twenty-five to sixty-five years earlier, a drama which Muralt knew well. By 1745 the Abbé Leblanc could complain that "most of us like or hate the English without knowing them, some of us following the fashion, others of us listening only to our prejudices." [7] Less than a generation later, however, *L'Observateur français à Londres* was reporting just the opposite, that since the peace ending the Seven Years' War had been signed not only had the French lost all the bias that formerly rendered the word *English* unsavory to them but that the English had also acquired a greater respect for and understanding of the French.[8] While such judgments may have depended little on statistics, they do point to the fact that the climate of opinion within a nation helped to determine the attitude, even the facts, of its travelers to other lands.

The point is further emphasized by noting the German Anglophobia of the last half of the century. There were some calm and objective Germans in England at that time, such as Pastor Wendeborn, who during his twenty-eight years there kept a journal which became a source and a guide for his country-men. But there were others, such as H. M. F. von Watzdorf and Sophie von La Roche, who developed a long-distance love for the land of "liberty," of Richardson, and of Thomson's *Seasons* and who in the 1780's crossed the Channel with eyes blind to anything but the beauties of the English countryside and the nobility of the British people. Such gushing enthusiasm became part of the German *aufklarung* and of European sentimentality in a romantic age.[9]

The eighteenth century, of course, foreshadowed the period of romanticism in many ways, for example, in the tendency to hold up distant lands as models for civilized Europe. One result was that this Age of Reason created the man of the East, repre-sented him as the natural philosopher, and developed the very strong literary tradition of the fictitious foreign observer, not only to satirize European civilization but to display the ideal rational man. Although there were some American Indians and South Sea islanders among these invented natural philosophers, Turks, Persians, and Chinese were popular. Confucius was discovered and Voltaire argued that Hinduism contained most of the elements of Christianity. In such a period the French traveler Sonnerat was able to satisfy his bias and that of his day by describing India as the origin of all thought and religion, claiming that Europeans visited that country because of its sci-ences and philosophy and not, as the seventeenth century had said, because of its wealth.[10]

One of the best illustrations of national prejudice can be found in the British accounts of North America. Before the Revolution they were normally favorable, very often propa-ganda.[11] Long before, for example, Captain John Smith had done more than describe topography and relate his entertaining adventures; he had appealed to his countrymen to emigrate, not only to take advantage of the free, fertile soil of the New World, but to Christianize the natives. This kind of propaganda in-fluenced the later travelers such as John Lawson (1709), or the native commentators such as William Beverley (1705), whose books are on the whole objective but whose enthusiasm showed at times that they hoped to attract settlers. As late as 1773 eulogistic tracts were still appearing, such as the one in Glasgow called "Information concerning the Province of North Carolina addressed to Emigrants from the Highlands and Western Islands of Scotland. By an Impartial Hand." This piece of propaganda was derived largely from Lawson, or Lawson's alter ego, Dr. Brickell, and emphasized only the healthy climate, the ease of making a living, the cheap, hard-working slaves, the productive soil, and the bountiful wildlife.[12] Such lavish attempts at enticement, not always British, can be found in the history of every one of the colonies, as with the Swiss Samuel Jenner's part in the settling of Virginia. Sometimes, however, the traveler in America had no intention of producing propaganda, wanting only to describe something with which he had fallen in love. That was the excuse of Crèvecoeur and the Marquise de la Tour du Pin, both of whom wrote nostalgically of life on an American farm, and of the Scotch Dr. William Douglass, who stayed in Boston in the middle of the century and then published an account that showed "strong prejudices and partialities" for New England, Adam Smith, for example, noting that it was Douglass' "foible to measure the worth of men by his personal friendship for them." [13]

The great periodical war following the Revolution involved most British travelers sent to America. As a group they were openly antipathetic to the vulgar new society that had disgraced the mother country by attaining its freedom. Their antipathy had deep roots, shown in the scorn, for example, that the regulars of the well-trained English army had for the colonial Indian fighter, and in such anecdotes as those told by Captain John Knox, who contemptuously recorded that in any naval engagement the New England sailors fell on their knees, "resigned themselves to Providence," and left the battle to their British allies.[14] After the Revolution an English officer named J. F. D. Smyth, mortified, one historian says, by the "ignominious failure" of his cause, reported harems of beautiful slaves in Maryland and gave political and social interpretations that cannot be trusted, his wishful thinking causing him to prophesy the rapid decline of the new nation. William Cobbett, better known as the irascible Peter Porcupine, settled in Philadelphia in 1796, slandered even the widely loved American Dr. Rush, engaged in controversy with Philip Freneau, who also possessed a poisonous pen, carried back to England the bones of his idol Thomas Paine, and left a reputation that caused Jeremy Bentham to declare "his malevolence and lying beyond contempt." [15]

One of the most biased of the British travelers in the first generation of American independence was Thomas Ashe (1806). Much has been made of his thefts from Carver, Bartram, Crèvecoeur, Catesby, and others who knew the New World better than he, of his sentimental anecdotes that could so easily have been created at the fireside, and of his descriptions of river rapids and Indian mounds that did not exist. But his sneers at Americans themselves made his name anathema to all citizens of the New World. To his supposed correspondent at home he reported:

> The American States through which I have passed are unworthy of your observation. [The inhabitants of the Northeast] are characterized by bigotry, pride, and a malignant hatred to the mother-country. The middle States are less contemptible. . . . The national features here are not strong, and those of different emigrants have not yet composed a face of local deformity: we still see the liberal English, the ostentatious Scotch, the warmhearted Irish, the penurious Dutch, the proud German, the solemn Spanish, the gaudy Italian, and the profligate French. What kind of character is hereafter to arise from an amalgamation of such discordant materials, I am at a loss to conjecture.

One is immediately reminded of Ashe's contemporary Crèvecoeur and his very optimistic analysis of the new "melting pot" society. Ashe went on:

> For the southern States nature has done much, but man little. Society is here in a shameful degeneracy: an additional proof of the pernicious tendency of those detestable principles of political licentiousness, . . . doctrines here found by experience, to make men turbulent citizens, abandoned Christians, inconstant husbands, unnatural fathers, and treacherous friends.

Such animosity, coupled with unacknowledged borrowings and many curious but entertaining adventures, forced even a British periodical unfriendly to America to believe that Ashe was "engrafting incredible stories on authentic facts." By 1819 Washington Irving, a relatively calm judge in a heated debate, was able to give five reasons for the bias of British visitors like Smyth, Cobbett, and Ashe: jealousy; the lack of comfortable inns and carriages; the fact that only the worst class of English travelers did the writing; disappointed avarice because of ill success in business; and their own antidemocratic environment.[16]

A book's bias for or against a nation was not always the fault of the traveler whose name appeared on the title page, since opinions could be added or altered by an editor or a translator. Not only could a prudish Englishwoman cover up the overexposed African flesh in Le Vaillant's illustrations, complaining meanwhile of French lack of decency; if William Beverley described a Virginia frog so big that "six French-Men might have made a comfortable Meal of its Carcase," a patriotic French translator could easily change the one word "French-Men" to "people." [17] Or the pro-American London publisher of Crèvecoeur's first edition of *Letters from an American Farmer* (1782) could select twelve letters for the book that would exclude any which recounted the hardships of the American farmer or the horrors of frontier Indian warfare, thereby forcing more than a dozen such letters into an attic trunk, from which they would be rescued and published only in the twentieth century.

Prejudice for one's nation, in spite of its importance, was hardly so universal or so deep as prejudice for or against a religion. Professor Frantz, citing three Englishmen in particular, concludes that the Protestant British travelers of the early eighteenth century "repeatedly vilified and damned Catholicism. . . . Into the various parts of the world they carried their own religious beliefs, which invariably distorted perspective." Daniel Denton (1670), for example, was able to display pro-Christian evidence that God aided the English settlers and punished the pagan Indians, while the normally objective John Lawson

(1709) showed what sounded like anti-Calvinism by reporting a Carolina tribe which did "not believe that God punishes any person, either in this life, or that to come." [18]

One of the wittiest of biased Englishmen was Ned Ward, whose *A Trip to New England* (1699?) showed no mercy on the Puritans of Boston.[19] There he found four churches and four ministers, "one a Scholar, the Second a Gentleman, the Third a Dunce, and the Fourth a Clown." To Ward the staid Bostonians were hypocrites:

[They] seem very Religious, showing many outward and visible Signs of an inward and Spiritual Grace: But tho' they wear in their Faces the Innocence of Doves, you will find them in their Dealings, as Subtile as Serpents. Interest is their Faith, Money their God, and Large Possessions the only Heaven they covet.

The Anglican visitor sneered at the doctrine of Saints:

Election, Commencement, and Training-days, are their only Holy-days; they keep no Saints-Days, nor will they allow the Apostles to be Saints, yet they assume that sacred dignity to themselves; and say in the Title Page of their Psalm-Book, "Printed for the Edification of the Saints in Old and New-England."

And he made merry over their Calvinistic belief in natural depravity, their severity against adultery, and their notorious blue laws:

They have been very severe against Adultery, which they Punish'd with Death; yet, notwithstanding the Harshness of their Law, the Women are of such noble Souls, and undaunted Resolutions, that they will run the hazard of being Hang'd, rather than not be reveng'd on Matrimony, or forbear to discover the Corruption of their own Natures.

If you Kiss a Woman in Publick, tho' offer'd as a Curteous Salutation . . . both shall be Whip'd or Fin'd. It's an excellent Law to make Lovers in Privat make much of their time, since open Lip-Lechery is so dearly purchas'd. But the good humor'd Lasses, to make you amends, will Kiss the kinder in a Corner.

Ward concluded:

The Gravity and Piety of their looks, are of great Service to these American Christians [in business dealings, since] it makes strangers that come amongst them, give Credit to their Words, . . . Many of the Leading Puritans may (without Injustice) be thus Characteris'd. They are Saints without Religion, Traders without Honesty, Christians without Charity, Magistrates without Mercy, Subjects without Loyalty, Neighbours without Amity, Faithless Friends, Implacable Enemys, and Rich Men without Money.

The allegations of the English Anglican were alliterative but hardly objective.

French travelers were often as ready to condemn Catholicism as the Protestant English were. As we have seen, the Huguenot Misson was at least expected to attack the religion that drove him from his native land, and the fireside creator of François Coreal, although claiming to be a good Catholic, loaded his books with stories of conniving, grasping, hypocritical representatives of the Church who were supposed to be keeping the natives of South and Central America in subjection.[20] Late in the century Fleuriot's *Voyage de Figaro en Espagne* (1785), which irritated the "true" Figaro so much, reported slanderously of the convent of Escalessas, "This monastery for young women, which formerly served as a seraglio for the kings, infante, and grandees of Spain, is still famous for the amorous intrigues of these brides of God, who very often, it is said, produce children who are not His." Nicholas Massias, writing in the freethinking period after the French Revolution, claimed to have found the fathers of those illegitimate babies; the Spanish "bastards," he said "are nearly all children of monks." [21] In addition to being anti-Catholic, the books of Fleuriot and Massias are melodramatic and sentimental, belonging far out on the left in the spectrum of travel lies.

There were, of course, French travelers, especially those many members of the clergy, who were ready to defend vigorously a belief in God or their nation's religion. Even a mathematician and scientist such as Father Feüillée (1714, 1725) might claim that on the banks of a river in Chile he discovered stones every one of which was in the shape of a cross and any one of which, when broken, would with all its parts form other crosses. Such a phenomenon, he attested, proves "the Empire of Jesus Christ over all the souls of earth." One eighteenth-century editor, Bernard, would question such evidence by "letting the judicious reader judge it." Another editor, Delisle de Sales, would be just as ready, however, to discount Pernetty's statement that the natives of Brazil worshipped no god. It is "impossible" for a whole tribe or nation not to worship a deity, Delisle said, and he refused to believe such a report because "nature is more sacred to me than human witnesses." [22]

The religious bias of the travelers and readers of England, and frequently of other nations, was very often directed at the Jesuits, whose greatest power lasted through the seventeenth century and at least until the Pope abolished their Society temporarily in 1773. It was the Victorian writer Macaulay who is reported to have coined the expression, "Liars by a double right, as travellers and as Jesuits," but the judgment of eighteenth-century Englishmen was equally harsh. Early in the period Joseph Addison reproached the entire order for adapting "all Christianity to temporal and political views," and in 1769 the French Jesuits were accused by a writer in the *American Magazine, or General Repository* of "having two powerful motives for deviating from the truth . . . zeal for the credit and reputation of their missions, and French vain glory." [23] But there were strong critics in France too. From the Récollet fathers of the seventeenth century, to the Baron Lahontan, who held the "pious" Jesuit churchmen responsible for all the troubles between the French and the Indians,[24] to Voltaire and the Encyclopédistes, writers of that country worked to *"écraser"* the Society of Jesus until it was outlawed there in 1764. Nevertheless, the Jesuits left an astounding mark on history, not only as missionaries but as scientists and politicians, and their "Letters," written from every part of the less civilized world, recorded events, advances, and customs that history could not do without.

And after every new edition of these letters, edited first by Father Charles Le Gobien and later by J.-D. Du Halde, there were approving reviews in Paris periodicals, summarizing the separate pieces and seldom reproaching the authors.[25] In London praise for the letters was not so unqualified, however. In fact, in his edition John Lockman (1743) announced that he had found it necessary to expunge certain miraculous incidents as being "quite insipid or ridiculous to most English Readers; and indeed to all Persons of Understanding and Taste." Emanuel Bowen, employing the fathers throughout his geography, nevertheless complained of their contradictions and of the influence of their zeal for conversion on their facts about pagan lands.[26]

Before Du Halde had brought out the last of the letters in 1776, Corneille De Pauw, while basing whole volumes on them, continually attacked the Jesuit reports as a "tissue of lies," concentrating on those from China. He delighted in discovering their incredibilities, such as stories that told of gold ducks swimming on mercury or of lamps that burned human fat; and he exposed their "lies" by comparing, for example, Jesuit Père Le Comte's account of Nanking with that of the unattached traveler Nieuhof.[27] But De Pauw was regarded as an extremist, who obviously selected from travel accounts the facts that tended to prove his own theories.

The twentieth century has republished the letters and learned much from them, but it has often been inclined to agree with De Pauw's condemnation, if not with his own very biased methods. Lawrence Wroth, speaking of the letters from Canada, notes their contradictions as well as the alterations they underwent to rid them of any information not congenial to the Church in general and to the order in particular.[28] Virgile Pinot shows clearly that the papers from the Orient which Le Gobien and Du Halde edited "were not published in their original state." For example, the letter of Père Parrenin was made up of observations from a number of his pieces molded with four pages by the editor himself, who put into the missionary's mouth the statement—very amicable to eighteenth-century orientalism—that in China "there is no war as in Europe, nor plagues, nor wide-spread illnesses." Even more reprehensible, Pinot charges, was the practice the two editors followed of omitting any passage that militated against their biases, as when they excised young Pére de Premare's long account of the superstitions of the Chinese and their lack of a clear knowledge of a supreme being, or when they refused to include Pére d'Entrecolles' adverse criticism of the Chinese school system and lack of morality. Obviously the omitted passages would have made it harder for the Age of Enlightenment to praise so strongly the philosophic Easterner. Pinot concludes that the edited letters and Du Halde's *Description de la Chine* were "apologies" for Christianity, for the Society of Jesus, and for the popular thesis that China was a land of reason where no drunkenness, no debauchery, and no ignorance, superstition, or magic were permitted.[29]

Not only did writers and editors of voyage literature help create the Oriental natural philosopher; they helped to cement the myth of the Noble Savage. We have long ago been convinced of the early origin of this myth,[30] which had "arrived" in literature by 1600. By that time Montaigne and other philosophers, wishing to attack a too-sophisticated European civilization, borrowed hints from travelers in order to contrast the corruptions of Europe with the simplicity and health of the New World, a contrast that these early voyagers—Columbus, Raleigh, and Drake among them—did not make, even though they sometimes emphasized the beauty, self-sufficiency, and happiness of the Indians. The Noble Savage was thus largely a fireside creation and, as a result, assumed many forms, depending on the nation, the time, and the literary school of the man of letters involved. From Montaigne to Rousseau, however, the greater emphasis was not on the ideal life of a distant Indian, or South Sea Islander, or even Oriental, but rather on the evils and faults of life in a pretended civilization. For example, Montaigne's famous "Of Cannibals," so often misunderstood, does not laud the Western man-eater so much as, by ironic indirection, it condemns the European who has such subtle ways of eating his fellow man. And Rousseau's even more famous "Discourse on Inequality" is not so much an expression of primitivism as it is a plea for his kind of progress.[31] It was the Age of Romanticism—the Chateaubriands and the Wordsworths—that sentimentalized the savage and sought more than other periods to escape to the banks of the Ohio, to the shores of Tahiti, or simply to the farm of Michael. Throughout his career, then, the Noble Savage was a pawn for any polemicist. He was the victim of cruel Spaniards in America, according to the enemies not only of Spain but of injustice and Catholicism. He was the "artificial savage" of a court primitivist like Dryden. He was the foil of pessimists like Hobbes and theorists like Buffon. And he was a chief support of anti-Buffonites like Pernetty. "If," H. N. Fairchild says, "Oroonoko is the Noble Savage of heroic romance, and the old Houyhnhnm is the Noble Savage of misanthropic satire, Friday is the Noble Savage of early eighteenth century 'common sense.' " [32]

In such a climate travelers could seldom avoid prejudgment or exaggeration for the sake of a thesis. Among the English and American commentators on the New World, what else could cause Robert Beverley (1705) to defend so vehemently Indian chastity, beauty, and virtue, a defense that he toned down considerably in later editions; or John Lawson (1709) to insist, "They have learnt several Vices of the Europeans, but not one Vertue as I know of," an extreme opinion often repeated, as by the New Yorker Cadwallader Colden (1727); or William Bartram (1791) to sentimentalize a band of Cherokee maidens picking strawberries near the Tennessee River? [33]

And among French voyagers the same climate would let someone as early as Lahontan (1703) meet Indians who could not be tempted to visit such a place as Europe, where "the property of goods . . . is the only source of all the disorders that perplex" society; or cause Adanson (1757) to see among the Senegalese "a perfect image of pure nature" where one "seemed to contemplate the world in its primitive state"; or produce a Bossu (1768) who during six years in America learned that Indian women had only horror for the licentious European lady and who "never saw a misshapen man or woman, as in the Old World"; or help Le Vaillant (1790) blame all the misery and evil of the Hottentots on the cupidity, treachery, tobacco, and brandy of their civilized conquerors. With James Fenimore Cooper, travelers and travel editors were "fully aware of the importance of writing what the world thinks rather than what is true." [34]

To be sure, these voyagers, and many like them, were ready to describe a Noble Savage already described to them, but one cannot measure their own great influence on philosophy and literature. It may be that, as often said, Rousseau found his pawn in Tacitus' history of the Germania, but he cannot have failed to profit from Lahontan's scorn of property or from Coreal in concluding that "sexual vice is the fruit of sophistication." Lawson's "Self-interest and the public good prompted the native Carolinians to benevolence," [35] sounds like a quotation from Shaftesbury's *Characteristics,* published two years later. Chateaubriand borrowed Lafitau's parallel between the American Indian and the Homeric Greek, and Wordsworth reproduced Bartram's blushing Cherokee maidens. It may be true, however, that if the travelers had not existed the theorists would have reached the desired conclusions anyway, or if it had been necessary readers would have distorted or misread the voyage literature, just as Hawkesworth distorted Captain Cook or Rousseau misread Coreal.

One of the best ways to demonstrate the influence of the prejudices of eighteenth-century travelers is to inspect their widespread use of a literary device that we can call the Adario motif, after Lahontan's Huron who carried on such a versatile argument in that traveler's *Dialogues between the Author and a Discerning Savage Who Has Done Some Traveling* (1703–1705). By setting himself up as a rather naïve foil, Lahontan was able to extract from his savage a withering attack on the Catholic religion, European laws, and the acquisition of property. Adario was an actual name among the northern Hurons; [36] but after the employment of a native philosopher had become a commonplace in literature, Thomas Ashe almost exactly one hundred years later used the same name for an invented southern Indian, a once "Noble Shawnee" who had been corrupted by the white man's weapons, smallpox, and liquor.

In spite of the popular opinion that its "point of departure" seems to be given by Lahontan,[37] the Adario commonplace is

ancient. In Eastern literature there were countless such dialogues in the Upanishads, like that between Krishna and Ar-
juna which proves that a warrior's duty is to kill; and in Western literature Lucian's "Dialogues of the Gods" and "Dialogues
of the Dead" are only the best examples of the same phenomenon. Closer to the method of the travelers, however, was that of
the second-century Greek Pausanias, who took information from
local guidebooks and put it into the mouths of natives.[38] Obviously such a motif was peculiarly adaptable to voyage literature and to imitation voyages of whatever kind, for by 1700
the pretended conversation with a savage had become a tradition among Europeans journeying to newly opened continents or to fictional Utopias. One respected historian of ideas,
in fact, asserts that "since the discovery of America, there is not
a single account which does not contain a scene of this sort." [39]
It was true for other parts of the world also. A generation before
Lahontan a narrative of West Barbary by Lancelot Addison
(1674) attacked hypocritical Christianity by employing a Moor,
who, like Adario after him, could not be deceived because he
had "unluckily" been in England.[40] Such sentiments—religious,
political, or philosophical—placed in the mouth of an imaginary savage comprised one important similarity between the
real travelers, like Lancelot Addison and Lahontan, and the authors of extraordinary voyages.[41] Foigny's Jacques Sadeur (1670),
for example, learned most about the fictional Sevarites and their
deism by talking with an old Sevarite; and Swift's Lemuel
Gulliver met two stubborn antagonists in the King of Brob-
dingnag and the wise Houyhnhnm.

Throughout the eighteenth century, authentic travelers and
commentators continued to impose their own biases on the public by attributing them to native speakers. Defoe's Drury (1729)
conversed with a Madagascar prince who called the Christian
heritage "old women's stories"; and John Marshall (1668–1672),
preceding his translation of the *Shri Bhagavata Purana*, inserted a long dialogue that he claimed to have had with a Brah-
min, who preached more Thomism than Hinduism. The romantic Bossu (1768) told of a young "Akanca" Indian, handsome

and talented, who not only lectured his white friends on their prudery in matters of exposing the human body but composed a long poem, in alexandrines, which he addressed to "Manon," a beautiful European whose body he had been restrained from exposing. Sometimes in following the Adario tradition the traveler did not restrict himself to conversations with invented savages. F.-M. Bayard (1797) provided a farmer-philosopher, said to have been on Washington's staff, to retell dramatically the events leading up to the American Revolution, and Crève-coeur (1801) employed a fictitious aide to General Bouquet for an account of the Indian wars.[42]

But the distinctive form of the Adario motif was that which involved the native polemicist instructing the visitor from so-phisticated Europe, and it was that motif which philosophers and novelists adapted to their use—from Coree's *The Visions of Government* (1684), a dramatization of monarchial beliefs by means of a conversation between a Roman Catholic priest and "a poor Indian Savage"; to the Hurons of Voltaire and Rousseau; to Bage's novel *Hermsprong* (1796), in which the hero's mother comes out loser in an exchange of myths with Great Beaver; to Diderot's wise old Tahitian reworked from Bougainville. Such a widespread use of a device popularized by travelers is con-vincing evidence not only that they often had to be read with caution but that the eighteenth century often was aware that they were prone to supplement truth with fiction.

XI

MORE SINNED AGAINST THAN SINNING

Le vrai n'est pas toujours le vraisemblable.[1]

BEFORE THE EIGHTEENTH CENTURY, voyage literature had produced so many exaggerations and inventions that although the Age of Reason depended heavily for geographical, scientific, and other facts on its travelers, it sometimes mistreated their reports or unjustifiably accused them of dishonesty. Nearly always, however, such unfairness was, in part at least, induced by the traveler himself. La Salle's very capable lieutenant, Tonty, was one victim of mistreatment. His accounts of discoveries and adventures in America after La Salle's death were sent to Paris and so completely and imaginatively rewritten by someone there that historians have rejected the resulting book as "a legend full of geographical contradictions, of confused dates, and manifest fiction." Tonty himself complained bitterly but unavailingly in a letter written in 1700: "I am very sorry to see that a relation to which much has been added is published under my name. The reports I sent have not been followed point by point. It is very hard to pass for a liar." [2] Another experienced and honest traveler mistreated, even rejected, by his superiors was Captain Middleton, who in the 1740's was sent by Arthur Dobbs to investigate possible entrances to the Northwest Passage and then on his return was subjected to indignities because Dobbs and the prejudiced public refused to believe his relation of failure.[3] But Tonty and Middleton were somewhat unusual in that in no way were they responsible for the unfair treatment accorded their reports. Furthermore, they were neither so influential on history nor so widely attacked and then vindicated as were two other travelers, the German John Lederer, who arrived in America about 1668, and the Scotsman James Bruce, who went to Abyssinia one hundred years later.

Lederer and Bruce were alike in many ways. Both were scholars of a sort, knew much about medicine, and could speak or read several languages. The short German and the tall Scotsman could endure great hardship; they dared to penetrate areas in which Europeans normally met death; and they had determination, pushing on when others faltered or failed. Neither of them, however, was in sympathy with the philosophy of reporting expressed in the very middle of the eighteenth century by the Earl of Chesterfield when he told his son, "Had I seen anything so very extraordinary as to be almost incredible I would keep it to myself, rather than by telling it give anybody room to doubt, for one minute, of my veracity." At least, both returned from their journeys to tell truth stranger than fiction, even though, like all travelers, both were inclined to some exaggeration of that truth. Intrepid travelers have always been not only fearless but more than ordinarily aggressive and self-confident, and Lederer and Bruce were by no means exceptions to the rule, for their personalities tended to arouse opposition, even antagonism. Consequently, because of their personal characteristics and the external conditions involved, both were at first disbelieved by many people, even sneered at. But in both cases vindication began in their own lifetimes, and later scholarship, in spite of many expressions of doubt, has restored their reputations.

JOHN LEDERER IN AMERICA

John Lederer's American career began in Jamestown, Virginia.[4] Although he knew German, French, and Italian well and wrote Latin, he spoke English poorly. When Governor William Berkeley, an agent for the Hudson Bay Company, selected him to explore the interior of Virginia for a pass to the fur regions of the West and to the "Indian" Ocean, he carried out his commission by making three expeditions within a year and a half. The first, in the spring of 1669, took him and three Indians up the Pamunkey River to the Blue Ridge, where he climbed one peak, found no pass, reported seeing the Atlantic Ocean to the east, and returned because of bad weather and failure. The second expedition was made farther south in the summer of 1670, and this time the explorer was accompanied by five Indians and twenty whites, including a Major Harris, who had made a short war trip west in 1656. Within a few days, however, Major Harris and all the party except one Indian decided to go back, leaving Lederer and his one companion to push on to visit native tribes, listen to marvelous tales, and cross uncharted country before returning with enthusiastic suggestions. No doubt as a result of this enthusiasm, the third expedition began almost immediately, included a Colonel Catlett, nine troopers, and five Indians, and again reached the crest of the Blue Ridge only to return because from there nothing could be seen but more mountains.

Lederer became so unpopular during this time that he left Virginia and went to Maryland, perhaps partly because of personal debts, more probably because his explorations were financed by tax money that the public felt should have been used for something else. In Maryland Sir William Talbot, Secretary of the colony and nephew of Lord Baltimore, received him warmly, read the Latin journal of his three expeditions, and translated it into English as the *Discoveries of John Lederer,* published in 1672. Sir William's foreword speaks of the resentment that greeted the explorer at the end of this third journey: "He was look'd on as so great insolence that our traveller at his return, instead of welcome and applause, met nothing but affronts and reproaches." After he applied for naturalization papers in Maryland in 1671 and led a large fur-trading party west from the borders of that colony in the same year, Lederer's American career was lost in history until he reappeared in 1674 in Connecticut as a physician, leaving there early the following year, perhaps for Europe but stopping off at Barbados, where he disappeared again, this time for good.

Although the traveler was gone, the twenty-seven-page journal, in spite of its author's Virginia reputation, had wide influence and has kept his name alive.[5] For example, Lederer's information and the map he drew affected over thirty maps by the middle of the eighteenth century.[6] However, when the late nineteenth century began to reprint the journal, Lederer's reputation was again attacked, the only real charge being directed at his account of the second expedition. Cyrus Thomas, writing in the *American Anthropologist,* doubted Lederer's story of what happened after Major Harris turned back; in 1915 Captain S. A. Ashe, after studying the geographical facts of the *Discoveries,* concluded that "the physical conditions prove that a large part of Lederer's narrative is the product of his imagination"; and E. G. Cox's bibliography of travels quoted Thomas and others to the effect that Lederer's tales of "marvels" caused him to be driven out of Virginia.[7] Perhaps the most heavily documented charge was leveled by C. W. Alvord and L. Bidgood, who, nevertheless, reprinted the *Discoveries* completely.[8]

Although these two editors believed that "most" of Lederer's "striking untruths" were not lies "but the misconceptions of a European, new to the country, or merely the harmless exaggerations, natural to a certain type of mind," they characterized him as "the Hennepin, or better as the Lahontan of English exploration" and charged that "in the matter of his alleged journey into the Carolinas—the latter part of his second expedition—he undoubtedly made a deliberate but clumsy attempt to deceive." Concerning this much-discussed second exploring trip, Lederer's journal relates how he and his companion, after the other members of the party had gone, pushed on to a number of Indian villages, the fourth of which was inhabited by the Saras, or Samas, who lived on the Yadkin River. It is then, according to Alvord and Bidgood, that the account becomes most unbelievable, as Lederer narrated how he found a tribe of Indians on the shore of a great lake with a "brackish"

taste, which he called "Ushery." "How far this lake tends west-
erly," he said, "or where it ends, I could neither learn or guess."
The Usheries told him some entertaining stories about Indians on the other side of the water, who in time of war forced
their women to stand behind them and shoot arrows at the
approaching enemy warriors, who had silver hatchets and pea-
cock feathers, and who knew of bearded men two and one-half
days journey to the southwest. Finally, Lederer concluded this
part of the journal, he left Lake Ushery and traveled north and
east, across sandy and barren country, to end up back in Virginia in mid-July. Although Alvord and Bidgood found misconceptions and exaggerations in the accounts of all three expeditions, they were most amused at the story of the second:
"It makes pleasant reading: Silver tomahawks, Amazonian Indian women, peacocks, lakes 'ten leagues broad,' and barren
sandy deserts two weeks' journey in width, when located in the
Carolina piedmont sound like the tales of Baron Munchausen."
These editors, like so many others, concluded that even though
Lederer's book was of great historical and ethnological value,
"no certainty can be evolved from the mass of palpable falsehood" to be found in the one part.

Such charges have not always gone unchallenged. Among the
early defenders of the *Discoveries* were the North Carolina
historian Hawks, who, in spite of his friendly attitude, misread
Lederer's geography, and the German Ratterman, who moved
Lake Ushery all the way down to Florida.[9] However, Lederer
has been most thoroughly vindicated only in the 1930's and
1940's. The minor charges have been easily cleared up. His
claim of seeing the Atlantic from the Blue Ridge has been explained as a mirage seen also by many other people. His willingness to believe Indian reports that an arm of the western ocean
extended almost to the Appalachians was no doubt the result
of studying maps that reproduced the guess of Verrazano made
in 1524. And the "Amazons" were perhaps only the result of
Indian derision of enemies. But the major charges have not been
so satisfactorily resolved. Much more attention has necessarily

been devoted to the Lake Ushery and to the sandy region of North Carolina that Lederer seemed to say required twelve days to cross.

The favorite explanation for the lake is that Lederer saw either the Catawba or the Yadkin River in flood, swollen because of debris and filling up some valley, the opposite side of which, as the explorer said, was obscured by mist or fog. And his acceptance of the temporary body of water as a huge lake could have been conditioned by the many maps of the time that showed such a lake in the southeastern part of what is now the United States. This tradition was begun in the sixteenth century, and by Lederer's time the maps showed not only a lake in the Piedmont section but a swamp over two hundred miles long to the north and a barren, sandy region to the east called usually the "Arenosa desert." All of these standard, but incorrect, geographical facts Lederer experienced to some degree, as W. P. Cumming, one of Lederer's defenders, has so carefully shown.[10] But even Cumming found a tendency to credulousness and exaggeration in the *Discoveries,* especially in the description of the "desert," which he resolved thus: "Nor are there sandy barrens in the state of North Carolina where one can go for twelve days in a *north-easterly* direction without crossing rivers. He probably did cross a section of the sand-hill section of North Carolina during the heat of July; he may have been told it extended a considerable distance southward from where he crossed. Also in retrospect it would be easy to exaggerate the proportion of the return journey spent in that region and the extent of its aridity." [11] Actually the existence of the lake, estimated to be thirty miles broad at one point, is the harder to believe, for Lederer's journal does not contend that he spent twelve days crossing a "desert." On the contrary, it says that the North Carolina stream beds were dry from lack of rain, that he found "shady oaks" covering "standing pools," that he traveled twelve days before finding a *flowing* river. His version of lake and desert, however, whether completely contrived or whether completely innocent and in part indebted to the mistakes of his predecessors, was accepted as corroboration of the current maps, and "traveler and cartographer contributed to the development of the errors." [12]

One of the most determined defenses of Lederer was made in 1939 by Lyman Carrier, who apparently did not know of Cumming's article of the year before. Carrier spoke of the *Discoveries* as "probably the most misunderstood piece of literature in all Virginia history," contended that its author's reputation had "suffered from both his friends and his enemies," and collated Lederer's journal with journals of two other expeditions made into Carolina within four years after his return. The collation was successful in proving the veracity of Lederer's account of all the Indians and all the geography up to and including his visit with the Saras on the Yadkin. After that, Lederer's route took him over territory not covered by the other travelers. However, the later journals tell, as the Usheries did, of bearded Spaniards who had contact with the Cherokees to the west and who had metal implements that could have been described as silver tomahawks. If the many facts that can be checked are true, Carrier concluded wisely, why should not the others be considered the result of honest reporting.

So far the last word in exonerating Lederer has been spoken by Dieter Cunz in his history of the Maryland Germans. Not only does Cunz agree in every respect with Carrier's analysis of the three expeditions, but he also adds much to the story of Lederer's later life, showing how highly the citizens of Connecticut esteemed their learned "physician" and "friend" and how sorry they were to see him leave America. Two letters written in September and November of 1674 praised his "Learning and Experience" and expressed the hope that he would remain in the colony as a doctor because he was so capable and so universally liked. Another letter, written to John Winthrop in December of the same year, spoke of the German's "singular and rich endowments" and regretted his decision not to stay. This evidence from Connecticut, like that from Maryland, makes it even harder to think of Lederer's journal as in any way a record of travels that did not take place.

However, the defense has not always shown that the journal, in spite of its authenticity, contains many passages that hazard guesses, emphasize possibilities, or offer suggestions which must have inspired the reader with visions of opportunity. It contains much in addition to the accounts of the three expeditions, for example, a section called "Instructions to such as shall march upon Discoveries into the North-America." Although this set of instructions is actually very practical, it is also much like another set that implied its author's own readiness to lead such a party, that one written a few years later by Lahontan. Another section, "Touching Trade with Indians," not only urged large groups of men to go on trading trips to protect wealth but spoke of "some pieces of silver unwrought I purchased my self of the Usheries, for no other end than to justifie this account I give of my second expedition, which had not determined [ended] at Ushery, were I accompanied with half a score resolute youths that would have stuck to me in a further discovery toward the Spanish mines." Still another section, while it asserted the error of those who believed North America to be only "eight or ten days journey over," offered the conclusion, gathered from talks with the Indians, that the western ocean extended an arm to the Appalachians. And in the narrative of his second expedition Lederer told of the "hard cakes of white salt" he found among the Sara Indians, even though he did not know whether the salt came from the ocean or from pits; but he did say with confidence, "Many other rich commodities and minerals there are undoubtedly in these parts." It is possible that Sir William Talbot, like so many translators and editors of travels, was partly responsible for the journal's excessive optimism, for in the introduction to his translation of the *Discoveries* we find him telling Lord Shaftesbury, who with the help of John Locke and others was at that time working on plans for America, "My Lord, From this discourse it is clear that the long looked-for discovery of the Indian Sea does nearly approach." But whether the guilty one was Lederer or his patron-translator, the sin was hardly mortal, for every visitor to the Virginia-Carolina area, from John Smith to John Lawson, urged, with perhaps more enthusiasm than necessary, the really great potentialities of the land. Dr. John Lederer was hardly more inclined to propaganda than others; and it seems obvious now that while he may have made certain assumptions and perhaps misunderstood certain information supplied by the Indians, he was not only a venturesome but an honest man who, unlike Hennepin and Lahontan, actually performed all the journeys he wrote about.

JAMES BRUCE IN ABYSSINIA

Even more unfairly treated, especially in his own day, was James Bruce, perhaps the most widely read but also the most severely maligned traveler to come out of the British Isles. Born in 1730, Bruce early in life showed a penchant for exploring, making an extended visit in 1755 to the Roman ruins in North Africa and continuing on to Asia Minor and the Mediterranean islands. Then after a period of preparation in languages and medicine, backed by the British government, which he had served as Consul for Algiers from 1763 to 1765, equipped with expensive scientific apparatus, and accompanied by a Greek servant named Michael, he set out in 1768 on a trip that was to last five years and bring him both honor and notoriety. He went down the Red Sea, charting the coast on the way, struck inland at Massawa, visited certain towns and cities such as Thebes and Axum, and eventually reached Gondar, the capital of Abyssinia, now Ethiopia. His skill in medicine as well as his athletic ability and commanding appearance soon made him a favorite with the ruler, who assisted him in the attempt to achieve his primary objective of finding the source of the Nile. This excursion he made in 1770, following the Blue Nile to its beginnings near the village of Geesh and then descending that branch of the river to its junction with the White Nile. Largely because of the bloody internecine wars in Abyssinia, Bruce, after experiencing great danger, left the country and made a harrowing escape across the Egyptian deserts to Cairo, returning to Europe in 1773 with manuscript notes and drawings and with the belief that he was the first person to find the sources of the Nile. This belief, which not only failed to acknowledge the sixteenth-century claims of the Portuguese missionaries Lobo and Paez but was unaware that the White Nile would later be accepted as the longer and more important branch, was one of many reasons why Bruce's entire experience was often questioned by the eighteenth century.

At first, however, he was received enthusiastically. In Paris he presented Louis XV with some rare seeds, donated a copy of the Abyssinian "Prophecies of Enoch" to the Royal Library, displayed detailed drawings of African cities, and became a friend of the Comte de Buffon, most noted of eighteenth-century natural historians. In England Bruce was given even more attention. On September 8, 1774, the *London Chronicle* ran a long and very favorable account of his adventures, especially of his discovery of the sources of the Nile and of the wars he engaged in or witnessed. And on the first day of the following month the same paper, still favorable, added a number of stories brought back and narrated by Bruce.[13] The featured story, one that raised many eyebrows and caused some tongues to classify this account of Abyssinia with a certain description of Formosa and another of Lilliput, told with entire credulousness and much enthusiasm that the favorite food of the Abyssinians was raw flesh cut from a live cow and that the best butcher in their country was the one who could slice longest without killing the animal. Publicity such as this not only brought Bruce invitations to many fashionable drawing rooms but caused him to be the butt of jokes in those circles to which he was not invited.

Elderly Dr. Johnson met him soon after the arrival back in England, but not until after the newspapers had publicized the most incredible of the Abyssinian experiences, and came away doubting. On April 1, 1775, Boswell reported that Johnson had been in the company of Bruce, "whose extraordinary travels had been much the subject of conversation. But," added Boswell, "I found that he had not listened to him with that full confidence without which there is little satisfaction in the society of travellers." And in 1789, five years after Johnson's death, the *Gentleman's Magazine* reported that when he "first conversed with Mr. Bruce, the Abyssinian traveller, he was very much inclined to believe he had been there; but that he had afterwards altered his opinion." [14] Such a statement, in such a respected periodical, must have been quite damaging to Bruce's reputation because Dr. Johnson was considered to be an authority on Abyssinia, his first literary effort having been a translation of Father Lobo's account of that country, and one of his best-known books having been called *Rasselas, Prince of Abyssinia.*

Even more damaging as a critic was Horace Walpole, an omniverous reader of travel books, who had many a laugh at the expense of the lanky Scottish explorer. On July 10, 1774, he wrote to Horace Mann, "Africa is, indeed, coming into fashion. There is just returned a Mr. Bruce, who has lived three years in the court of Abyssinia and breakfasted every morning with the Maids of Honor on live oxen. . . . We shall have Negro butchers and French cooks will be laid aside." And on August 10, in a letter to George Selwyn, he was praying for a strength of character that would force him to pay a visit to that friend, a strength of character as strong, he said, as that of "Hercules or Mr. Bruce. But pray do not give me live beef for supper." Such jokes about "Abyssinian Bruce," coupled with anecdotes and puns, consumed much space in the correspondence of the Prince of Letter Writers. His most extended reference to the explorer was in a letter to the Reverend William Mason, on February 29, 1776. Here he spoke quite sarcastically of the term *intrepid traveller* applied to Bruce by Dr. Burney, the famous historian of music and father of Fanny Burney the novelist, thought the doctor was making a mistake to use Bruce's drawings of Abyssinian musical instruments, angrily accused the Scotsman of telling many "lies," and concluded with this story:

> It is unfortunate that Mr. Bruce does not possess another secret reckoned very essential to intrepid travellers—a good memory. Last spring he dined at Mr. Crawford's. George Selwyn was one of the company. After relating the story of the bramble, and several other curious particulars, somebody asked Mr. Bruce if the Abyssinians had any musical instruments? 'Musical instruments!' said he, and paused—'yes, I think I remember one—lyre.'

George Selwyn whispered his neighbor, 'I am sure there is one less since he came out of the country.' There are now six instruments there [in the material submitted to Dr. Burney].

And then Walpole urged his correspondent, "Remember this is only for your own private eye; I do not desire to be engaged in a controversy or a duel."

The plea for secrecy with which Horace Walpole ended his letter was obviously inspired by the reputation which Bruce was acquiring because of his ability to defend himself, both verbally and physically, from the attacks of the unbelievers. Like most travelers he thrived on the attention his narratives evoked, but the irritability and dubiousness caused by his egotism and the marvelous nature of his exploits made him easily offended. His sensitivity in the matter seems to be reflected in the published version of his travels, written years later. Here he told of an incident that happened in Abyssinia in which the king of that country expressed disbelief at his visitor's claim of being able to shoot a tallow candle through a warrior's shield, a claim also arousing something more than doubt in England. Bruce reported that he proved his boast but only after saying to the king, "I would not wish to remain a moment longer under so disagreeable an imputation as that of lying, an infamous one in *my* country, whatever it may be in this." [15] The same book shows that he had been made even touchier on the subject of the Abyssinian diet of raw, live flesh, for in it he reported with bitter contempt, "When I first mentioned this in England, . . . I was told by my friends it was not believed. I asked the reason of this unbelief, and was answered, that people who had never been out of their own country, and others well acquainted with the manners of the world, for they had traveled as far as France, had agreed the thing was impossible, and therefore it was so." [16] Then, in answer to his friends' suggestions that he drop the claim because of the public unbelief, Bruce announced with determination, "To represent as truth a thing I know to be a falsehood, not to avow a truth which I know I ought to declare; the one is fraud, the other cowardice, . . . and I pledge myself never to retract the fact here advanced, that the Abyssinians do feed in common upon live flesh, and that I myself have, for several years, been partaker of that disagreeable and beastly diet."

However, Bruce's sensitivity and his ability to defend himself are reflected most dramatically not in his own words but in the story of a dinner party which he attended while house guest at a country estate. When another guest jokingly remarked on the impossibility of natives of Abyssinia eating raw meat, Bruce, the story goes, "said not a word, but leaving the room, shortly returned from the kitchen with a piece of raw beef-steak, peppered and salted in the Abyssinian fashion. 'You will eat that, sir, or fight me,' he said. When the gentleman had eaten up the raw flesh . . . , Bruce calmly observed, 'Now, sir, you will never again say it is *impossible.*'" [17] The story was even more entertaining to the eighteenth century, and more influential, when people recalled Bruce's extraordinary athletic prowess and his almost giantlike stature. It also explains why Horace Walpole was so careful to swear his correspondent to secrecy.

The Scotsman's readiness to fight made his stories more notorious and gave his critics greater incentive to ridicule his adventures, the live-meat diet always attracting most attention. Upon his return to Europe Bruce had told of two incidents in particular involving that custom, and then in the huge, five-volume edition of his *Travels to Discover the Source of the Nile,* published in London and Edinburgh in 1790, he recounted those same stories. One told of how three soldiers who were driving a captured cow before them stopped by a riverside, threw the poor animal to the ground, cut off and ate two large steaks from the buttocks, pinned the hide back over the wound, which they covered with a mud plaster, and then drove their captive on to camp "to furnish them with a fuller meal when they should meet their companions in the evening." [18] The other story described in great detail a typical Abyssinian noon banquet. After the table was set and the company seated, Bruce said:

A cow or bull, one or more as the company is numerous, is brought close to the door, and his feet strongly tied. The skin that hangs down under his chin and throat, which I think we call the dewlap in England, is cut only so deep as to arrive at the fat, of which it totally consists, and by the separation of a few small blood-vessels, six or seven drops of blood only fall upon the ground. They have no stone, bench, nor altar upon which these cruel assassins lay the animal's head in this operation. I should beg his pardon indeed for calling him an assassin, as he is not so merciful as to aim at the life, but on the contrary, to keep the beast alive till he be totally eat up. Having satisfied the Mosaical law, according to his conception, by pouring these six or seven drops upon the ground, two or more of them fall to work; on the back of the beast, and on each side of the spine they cut skin-deep; then putting their fingers between the flesh and the skin, they begin to strip the hide of the animal half way down his ribs, and so on to the buttock, cutting the skin wherever it hinders them commodiously to strip the poor animal bare. All the flesh on the buttocks is cut off then, and in solid, square pieces, without bones, or much effusion of blood; and the prodigious noise the animal makes is a signal for the company to sit down to table. . . .

The company are so ranged that one man sits between two women; the man with his long knife cuts a thin piece, which would be thought a good beefsteak in England, while you see the motion of the fibres yet perfectly distinct, and alive in the flesh. No man in Abyssinia, of any fashion whatever, feeds himself, or touches his own meat. The women take the steak and cut it lengthways like strings, about the thickness of your little finger, then crossways into square pieces, something smaller than dice. This they lay upon a piece of the teff bread, strongly powdered with black pepper, or Cayenne pepper, and fissile-salt, they then wrap it up in the teff bread like a cartridge.

In the mean time, the man having put up his knife, with each hand resting upon his neighbour's knee, his body stooping, his head low and forward, and mouth open very like an idiot, turns to the one whose cartridge is first ready, who stuffs the whole of it into his mouth, which is so full that he is in constant danger of being choked. This is a mark of grandeur. The greater the man would seem to be, the larger piece he takes in his mouth; and the more noise he makes in chewing it, the more polite he is thought to be. They have, indeed, a proverb that says, 'Beggars and thieves only eat small pieces, or without making a noise.' Having dispatched this morsel, which he does very expeditiously, his next female neighbour holds forth another cartridge, which goes the same way, and so on till he is satisfied. . . . A great deal of mirth and joke goes round, very seldom with any mixture of acrimoney or ill-humour.

All this time, the unfortunate victim at the door is bleeding indeed, but bleeding little. As long as they can cut off the flesh from his bones, they do not meddle with the thighs, or the parts where the great arteries are. At last they fall upon the thighs likewise; and soon after the animal, bleeding to death, becomes so tough that the cannibals, who have the rest of it to eat, find very hard work to separate the flesh from the bones with their teeth like dogs.[19]

Johnson, Walpole and his circle, and the anonymous dinner guest who ate his words were not the only ones to throw up their hands at such stories. Bruce was burlesqued on the stage as Macfable, a narrator of tall tales, and lampooned by such witty versifiers as Dr. John Wolcot, who once wrote under his famous pseudonym of "Peter Pindar,"

> Nor have I been where men (what loss alas!)
> Kill half a cow, then send the rest to grass.[20]

But the most popular of the satires directed at the Scotsman was *The Adventures of Baron Munchausen.*

Rudolph Erich Raspe, whose name is the only one now connected with certainty to the writing of that book, was another of the notorious adventurers of the eighteenth century. Scholar, linguist, scientist, mining engineer, poet, librarian, coin expert, editor, and hoaxer, he stole coins placed in his keeping by the Landgrave of Hesse and in 1775 or 1776, at the peak of the interest aroused by Bruce's return, fled to London. There he was befriended by Horace Walpole, wrote at least five of the first six books of *The Adventures of Baron Munchausen,* which was added to in edition after edition by various hack writers, and finally died in Ireland in 1794 after being foiled in an attempt to convince a Scotch landowner that there was gold on his property. From the beginning Raspe's Munchausen was popularly recognized as "a mouthpiece for ridiculing travellers' tall-tales, or indeed anything that shocked the incredulity of the age." [21] And the traveler to Abyssinia was a favorite target throughout the long life of the Baron.

Perhaps Horace Walpole had nothing to do with the satire directed at Bruce through the character invented by Raspe and developed by his unknown successors, but the two men were friends during the years Walpole was so irritated at Bruce and before the first edition of *Munchausen* in 1785. Furthermore, a favorite source of humor in that book seemed to be one of the Abyssinian adventures which Walpole made most fun of.[22] On his homeward trek across deserts Bruce, sick and out of food, had been told of a deer being eaten by a pack of hyenas. Taking his blunderbuss he slipped up on the festivities and shot into the middle of all the noses. Two hyenas were killed outright, two others died twenty yards away, and all the rest fled. The adventure may have, in part at least, inspired those accounts of amazing marksmanship found especially in the early chapters of *The Adventures of Baron Munchausen*.

This book continued its satire in the expanded editions that came out after Bruce's *Travels* was published in 1790, one of the later chapters beginning, "All that I have related before is gospel; and if there be anyone so hardy as to deny it, I am ready to fight him with any weapon he pleases. Yes, . . . I will condemn him to swallow this decanter, glass and all, perhaps and filled with kerren-wasser." Then followed a ridiculous treatment of Bruce's vanity, his angry withdrawal to Scotland because of so much public disbelief in him, and his adventures in Africa, especially the live-meat-eating and the claims of having so frequently dined with the ladies of the court at Gondar. Finally, in 1792 a book called *A Sequel to the Adventures of Baron Munchausen* was dedicated to "Mr. Bruce the Abyssinian Traveller, as the Baron conceives that it may be some service to him, previous to his making another journey into Abyssinia. But if this advice does not delight Mr. Bruce, the Baron is willing to fight him on any terms he pleases." [23]

The newspaper reports, the public charges and defenses, the parlor witticisms, Bruce's notorious sensitivity, and the popular reading material of the day—all these made a chief literary and historical event of the 1790 publication in both London and Edinburgh of *Travels to Discover the Source of the Nile*. The year before, Bruce's doubters had added to the public's impatience to read the book by resurrecting Dr. Johnson's translation of Father Lobo's seventeenth-century travels to

Abyssinia and publishing them, it was generally believed, in order to have a volume by which to test Bruce's veracity. One reviewer of Lobo, writing in the *Gentleman's Magazine,* said, "It is universally known that doubts have been entertained, whether Mr. Bruce was ever in Abyssinia. The Baron de Tott, speaking of the sources of the Nile, says, 'A Traveller named Bruce, it is said, has pretended to have discovered them. I saw at Cairo the servant who was his guide and companion during the journey, who assured me that he had not known of any such discovery.' " [24] But the *Gentleman's Magazine,* with a history of prejudice for Dr. Johnson, their one-time contributor, did not represent the majority opinion among periodicals.

In fact, when Bruce's *Travels* appeared, the press was very favorable. Both the *London Chronicle* and the *Critical Review,* for example, published long articles that extended through five issues in one periodical and seven in the other. The reviewers quoted many pages, flattered the author's style, aggressiveness, and detailed information, and reported that this "entertaining book" had raised public curiosity to "an uncommon pitch." [25] The *Critical Review* believed Bruce to be more reliable than Lobo and defended the story of Abyssinians eating live raw flesh by saying that it was "sufficiently supported by other travelers." Meanwhile, the opposition was not completely silenced. In November of the same year the *Gentleman's Magazine* published a letter from Italy claiming that Bruce lied about doing his own drawings; but in December, trying to be fair about the whole matter, it printed a letter signed "W." that said Robert Drury's *History of Madagascar* confirmed Bruce by giving accounts of natives cutting steaks from live animals. But almost immediately, in the "Supplement for the Year 1790," the same magazine contained a refuting letter from "D. H.," who had checked all of Drury and found him to have eaten steaks only from dead animals. The generally favorable reception of Bruce in Britain was echoed in France when, in 1791, the *Travels* was translated and reviewed, receiving two notices, for example, in the *Journal des Sçavans.*

Within his own lifetime Bruce was accused of having told

many lies. The eating of raw meat, especially from live cows, the hyena episode, the originality of his drawings, the Abyssinian "lyre," the shooting of the tallow candle through a shield —all these were doubted, and some people went so far as to say that Bruce had not even been to Abyssinia. In addition, he was thought to have lied about the dreadful ravages of the "Tsaltsalya" insect, about the geography of the Red Sea, about having extracted four gallons of water from each of two dead camels on the desert, and about the King of Abyssinia's killing a general and his son because during a battle the king's robe was pulled off by a bramble. Some of the charges about Bruce's lack of veracity were defended from the very beginning. Not only did Dr. Burney insist on using the drawings of an African harp and not only did the *Critical Review* and the reader of *Robert Drury* attempt to corroborate the eating of live meat; but within a very few months after Bruce's death in 1794, the *Gentleman's Magazine* contained a heated letter [26] verifying the fact that he could have taken water from dead camels. This letter quoted from Dr. Russel's *Natural History of Aleppo* and cited numerous other authorities to prove that the expedient was often resorted to on the desert. Another defense, written by someone in government circles, perhaps the Hon. Daines Barrington, had to do with the more serious question of whether Bruce had even been to Abyssinia. Specifically it countered the charge made in 1785 by Baron de Tott, a traveler who had also been satirized by Baron Munchausen, that Bruce's servant Michael knew nothing of the expedition to trace the Nile to its source. This anonymous defense received much attention, being reproduced, for example, in a 1798 American edition of Bruce's *Travels*.[27] The battle over Bruce's truthfulness abated somewhat in the closing years of the eighteenth century, but it was revived during the first two decades of the next, becoming even more violent because of the issuance of two new editions of the *Travels* and because other Englishmen went to Abyssinia.

Shortly after the new century began, George Mountnorris, Viscount Valentia, later to become prominent in British African affairs, spent four years in North Africa and India and in 1809 published an account [28] that often took issue with Bruce, for example, with his description of the Red Sea. The most important criticism in this book, however, was derived not from Lord Valentia himself but from his man Henry Salt, who with companions was sent into the interior of Abyssinia to follow in the footsteps of Bruce. Salt returned, after leaving one companion named Pearce, but without finding any major error in Bruce's narration. However, he did make many petty charges about such details as the accuracy of Bruce's description of towns, monuments, and birds, and he often spoke of Bruce's "want of veracity." Some years later Salt went back to Abyssinia, found his friend Pearce, and spent some time before returning to England to publish his own story in 1814 [29] and receive appointment as Consul General to Cairo. Although in his second account Salt continued his attack on Bruce, in general he corroborated his predecessor. Without mentioning the Scotch explorer, he repeated a story told by Pearce of watching soldiers cut steaks from a live cow in exactly the same manner described by Bruce, and Salt himself witnessed more than one huge banquet at which raw "quivering" flesh was served. However, he asserted that Mr. Bruce was "decidedly mistaken" in claiming that the Abyssinian custom was to keep the cow alive as long as possible. Neither he nor Mr. Pearce had ever witnessed it or heard of it, he said.[30] In spite of these disagreements and Bruce's "vanity," Salt was now able to praise the Scotsman very highly as a person and as a writer, concluding that "no man can more truly admire his courage, his perseverance, his sagacity, or his genius more than myself." [31]

While Lord Valentia and Henry Salt were keeping alive the tradition of the unbelievers, during the same period there were many travelers and other writers who worked hard at clearing Bruce's reputation. Alexander Murray edited a new edition of the *Travels* in 1805 and wrote a biography in 1808 that praised Bruce as a scholar in history, science, and linguistics. Dr. Edward Clarke went to North Africa, discovered that Bruce's charts of the Red Sea, condemned in England, were constantly being used by British military officers, compared Salt's two versions of Abyssinia with Bruce's in order to point out that the later man verified the earlier in every important respect, and found a learned and religious Abyssinian dean in Cairo who, on being questioned surreptitiously, verified even Bruce's live-meat-eating. Dr. Clarke, whose eleven-volume *Travels* went through four editions by 1824, concluded that "there has not been an example, in the annals of literature of more unfair and disgraceful hostility than that which an intolerant and invidious party levelled . . . at the writings of Bruce." [32] This extended defense in a very popular book became widely known. The *Scots Magazine* of December, 1819, extracted it for republication, and in 1830 Sir Francis Head expanded it for his biography of Bruce. In between those dates the *North American Review*, writing two years after it had deplored the long life of the lies told by Hennepin and Lahontan, spoke of Bruce as one "whose reputation as an authority has, contrary to that of some travellers, increased with the increasing knowledge obtained of the countries which he visited." [33]

And that reputation continued to grow. For over a hundred years after Clarke's successful defense, Abyssinia was one of the African countries most popular with travelers, and everyone who went there, without exception, used Bruce's account as a sort of Baedeker, praising him for accuracy and thoroughness. Nevertheless, all of them tested his live-meat story, and all of them found it true in every respect save one—that the Abyssinians kept the cow alive as long as possible. One traveler, whose description of a typical feast was even bloodier and more revolting than Bruce's, had the animal's head "nearly severed from the body . . . and no sooner is the breath out of the carcass, than the rare and quivering flesh is handed to the banquet." [34] Another traveler had the "warm and quivering" meat served "almost before the death struggle is over." [35] In fact, while no one but Bruce and Henry Salt's friend Pearce ever reported seeing meat cut from a living cow, all the travelers since their time have agreed that the favorite way of eating beef in Abyssinia was to cut it so nearly alive that it was "quivering" when served; and more than one visitor to that country has either thought it possible that Bruce was right for his time or that he was the victim of an honest error, one that could easily have been made.[36]

Now that the issue of the Abyssinian diet has been settled more or less to everyone's satisfaction, the *Travels to Discover the Source of the Nile* has become accepted as a classic. The latest and best book on Abyssinia quotes it constantly, calls one chapter "The Coming of James Bruce," and devotes still another entirely to Bruce's exploits and scholarship.[37] The *Columbia Encyclopedia* in 1947 listed two sources for its article on Ethiopia, one being James Bruce; and the *Encyclopædia Britannica* ranks him at the head of perhaps a dozen authorities who have written about that country. His final vindication is the greatest example of the truth of a statement made fifteen years before he returned from Africa, "Many relations of travellers have been slighted as fabulous, till more frequent voyages have confirmed their veracity." Ironically, that statement was made by Dr. Samuel Johnson,[38] one of the men most responsible for the eighteenth-century doubts about the veracity of James Bruce.

CHAPTER

XII

THE VOYAGE ENDS:
The Methods and Effects
of Travel Liars

"Seek the reasons that writers may have for deceiving themselves, for deceiving you. Be critical: Otherwise it will come
to pass that people will give to the truth and to the lie the
same degree of authority." [1]

DR. JOHNSON AND HORACE WALPOLE thought that "Abyssinian Bruce" was a liar. And in spite of the obvious influence
for objectivity and truth exerted by the Royal Society and other
academies of science, there was reason why any traveler of the
eighteenth century might be suspected. Voyage literature was
popular; it had an incalculable influence. In an age of enlightenment readers were dependent on it, not only for facts about a
world that was growing both larger and very interesting, but
for entertainment—the adventurous, the exotic, the marvelous.
An intelligent reader might soon learn, however, that pleasure
is sometimes an overly seductive companion for the kind of
profit expected from travel books and that, as a result, the information in them was often too curious, too unoriginal, or too
entertaining. At the same time, the critical reader would be
aware of the absolute necessity of studying the travelers.

Voyage literature was indeed popular between 1660 and 1800.

At the very beginning of that period one Frenchman noted that the reading taste of his nation had changed, romances having fallen from fashion while "voyages have come into credit and now hold first place both at court and in the city." Some three generations later Hawkesworth was reportedly given £6,000 for editing a collection of travels, while Henry Fielding received only £1,000 for what is perhaps the best novel of the entire period. By the end of the century a bibliographer was convinced that "never have there appeared so many voyages" to be read not only by the "ordinary" person but to be studied by "naturalists and geographers, artists and archeologists, even by political scientists, economists, and moral philosophers." [2]

The popularity of this literature with the savant as well as with the ordinary reader caused its influence to be inestimable. Some historians find that influence greatest in the imaginative and poetic arts, from the Elizabethan period of Shakespeare and his fellows who have been called "the children and inheritors of the voyagers," to Jonathan Swift and his confession to Stella that he was immersed in travel books, to the period of Romanticism, when the parqueted "Road to Xanadu" was paved with those same books. They were the inspiration for the thousand Robinsoniads; for the fantastic voyage, such as Cyrano's to the moon; for the *conte philosophique,* such as *Candide;* and for the sea novel, like that of Smollett and Cooper.[3] And they attracted emulation from the creative writers, four of the five great eighteenth-century English novelists, for example, from Defoe to Sterne, writing accounts of their own trips.

But the influence went beyond belles-lettres. In a period when tolerance, democracy, and relativity became important, no thinker or historian could do without the voyagers, who taught that each nation had a distinctive, even appropriate, way of life. They inspired studies in comparative religion, comparative natural history, and comparative government. Although their great wealth of illustrative material has sometimes caused historians to decry their lack of "ideas," [4] the ratio of original thinkers among them was no doubt as high as it was for any class of writers. At the beginning of the period, long before Montes-

quieu's theory of climate in the *Esprit des Lois,* the traveler
Chardin was pointing out that "the climate of each nation is always . . . the chief cause of the inclinations and customs of its
inhabitants." And at the end of the period, Crèvecoeur was
analyzing the same three stages in the development of the
American frontier that F. J. Turner was to make so famous
nearly a century later.[5]

To understand fully the effect that travel literature had, one
needs to remember that such an influence could not have been
static, that it had to change with the pressures exerted on it. In
the decades after 1660 the Royal Society's interest in natural
science began to be reflected in the reports of voyagers, both
British and continental, some of whom responded to the "Directions" given them by Robert Boyle and labored at being
"auxiliaries" of science.[6] The best travel writers—Dampier and
Bruce in Britain, Careri in Italy, Wendeborn of Germany,
Chardin, Frézier, and the Jesuits of France—inspired imitation
both in style and subject matter. Louis XIV and Colbert pushed
exploration, and consequently produced reports, by men sent
out *"par ordre du roi,"* thus attracting competitive explorations
and reports from the rival England. The South Sea Bubble, the
Louisiana schemes of John Law, the flight of the Huguenots, the
periodic government-supported circumnavigations, the fluctu-
ations in literary taste, and the wars fought between France and
England, from the Indies to Gibraltar to India, or between
Britain and her colonies, or within a country such as Poland—
all these were factors in determining the direction a traveler
might take at a particular time, the kind of objects he chose to
observe, the cast of his mind, the organization of his book, and
the style in which he wrote it.[7]

One way to demonstrate this dynamic quality in travel writing
is to consider the phenomenal rise of the sentimental journey
after 1765, brought about not only by Laurence Sterne but by
Rousseau's *Confessions* and by the whole school of sentimentality—the *Comédie larmoyante,* the "graveyard" poems, and
novels such as *Clarissa* and *La Nouvelle Héloïse.* After
Sterne commiserated with a forlorn Maria or wept over a dead

ass on a highway in France, after Rousseau cried nostalgically
into Lake Leman, Germans like Bretschneider could be overly
emotional about the English landscape. Crèvecoeur could exploit, perhaps invent, a dreadful scene in which a Carolina slave
was shut up in a cage, hung from a tree in the forest, and left
to be maddened by flies and eaten by birds. The adventurer
Cagliostro could tell of his tearful parting with two Swiss sisters
both of whom he loved, of sentimental love affairs that exploited
sex but kept the heroine virtuous. Or the Russian Radischev, in
order to attack his government for permitting legal prostitution,
could fabricate a funeral in which a father jumped on his son's
coffin as it lay in the grave and begged the onlookers to cover
him too since he had caused the son's death by giving him
syphilis contracted from a government-supported prostitute.[8]
Sentimentalists such as these comprise only one of the groups
of travelers who did not always follow the "Directions" of the
Royal Society. All voyagers, then, were not Dampiers or Sloanes
observing minutely and recording carefully.[9]

The eighteenth century was quite aware that in spite of its
dependence on travel accounts they had to be handled with care
and compared with one another. Such an awareness was one
reason for the success of the great collections of voyages published in that period, the editors of which were trusted to do the
comparing and selecting. One of the most critical of these editors
was J.-F. Bernard (1725). Although he gave the public a number
of travels in the north which he defended as examples of reliable
reporting, his last volume contains a documented attack on the
kind of writer he had tried to avoid. After paraphrasing all of
Boyle's "Directions for traveling usefully" of two generations
earlier, Bernard added advice of his own and then revealed frequent disagreements among travelers to the same spot, unacceptable stories of marvels, and distortions of the truth, referring
not only to his French countrymen for evidence but to British
and Dutch voyagers as well. He inveighed against incredible
serpents, trees with live leaves, and plants with marvelous cura-
tive powers, noted that Chardin vouched for the totally false
description of the tomb of Persepolis given by Jan Struys, and

accused Gueudeville and Chappuzeau of rewriting parts of Lahontan and Tavernier. "The world of the travelers," he concluded, is filled with exaggerations and "an infinity of falsehoods" in order to make the authors "appear worthy in the eyes of the reader." [10]

Editors of travel accounts were not the only discerning critics. Condemnation did not cease with seventeenth-century writers such as Sir Thomas Browne and his "Inquiry into vulgar errors" or Père Le Comte in *China of Today* (1699), who generously blamed most travel deceptions on the fact that their authors were themselves deceived first, a complaint that echoed through the century.[11] The philosopher Shaftesbury studied the voyagers but fretted over their lack of truth. A bitter American expressed the sentiments of his countrymen by saying, "We object to a man like Thomas Ashe, because he was a plain liar, not because he finds fault with us." And Laurence Sterne berated Smollett thus: "The learned Smelfungus travelled from Boulogne to Paris, from Paris to Rome, but he set out with the spleen and the jaundice, and every object he passed by was discolored and distorted. He wrote an account of them but 'twas nothing but the account of his miserable feelings." [12] Time has partially agreed with this judgment, while realizing that its author was hardly to be exonerated himself. The difference is that Sterne's *Sentimental Journey* was jovial in its distortions; Smollett's *Travels* was vindictive. Just as striking as the frequency with which travelers were charged with dishonesty and prejudice was the hesitant acceptance of all voyage literature, readers of that day and scholars ever since feeling compelled to be cautious and use such expressions as "an air of honesty," "apparently true." [13]

This caution was reflected in the periodicals, in particular, the *Gentleman's Magazine,* which was always more than ready to expose, condemn, or taunt the travelers it reviewed. Although it sometimes succumbed to their errors, as with the story of the tall Patagonians, the *Gentleman's Magazine* of the same decade persecuted Bruce, attacked the Baron de Tott, and found Dr. Hasselquist's account of Egypt unreliable, sneering at the "learned" doctor's pills made of "snuff of candles and German soap," prescribed for colic, and his "tea cup full of clove water" before going to bed, prescribed for childless couples. Of Hassel-quist's story of how Egyptian women hatched chicken eggs by holding them for days in their armpits, the reviewer wondered sarcastically why "it is worth their while to be idle so long, merely to hatch eggs." The same periodical announced boldly that Lady Craven "never wrote a line" of the travel letters pub-lished under her name and cast doubt on the authenticity of Lady Millar's sentimental journey, while being resigned to the fact that the gullible public would make its sale profitable. Even Samuel Ireland's account of his travels on the Continent was charged with incredibilities, among them a stork with a wooden leg and the introduction of virtuous innocence into the brothels of Holland.[14]

Such charges were burlesqued in the stories invented about the reception of *Gulliver's Travels*. Although in reality Swift's fantastic voyage deceived no one, at the time of its publication in 1726 there were claims that certain simple souls took it literally. The author's friend, Dr. John Arbuthnot, told him of a ship captain who knew Gulliver but was sure that Gulliver lived in Wapping and not Redriff, as the account claimed. Swift countered this joke with another about an Irish bishop who said that *Gulliver's Travels* was full of improbable lies, and for his part, he hardly believed a word of it.[15]

That travelers were eyed askance is proved not only by the hesitant acceptance accorded them, but ironically, by the great necessity they all—truthful and untruthful—felt to profess their innocence, as if they had been caught in a company of shady characters. The apology, often coupled with denunciation of less honest voyagers, usually came in a preface. John Lawson, who claimed "a faithful account . . . wherein I have laid down everything with Impartiality and Truth," was much safer with this contention than was Dr. Brickell, who stole it as well as the book that followed. All of the authors who recorded the history of the *Wager,* whether as eyewitness or by plundering their predecessors, began with a boast about objectivity and a quarrel with the genus *traveler,* and all of their prefaces could have been written by the same hand. Sometimes, as with Ides, the Russian ambassador who crossed Siberia, the apology and assault were reserved for the conclusion.

Gulliver's Travels parodied both methods. In the opening letter to "His Cousin Sympson" Gulliver asserts his honesty even while scorning the "miserable animals" who might "presume to think that I am so far degenerated as to defend my veracity. Yahoo as I am, it is well known through all Houyhnhnmland, that by the instructions and example of my illustrious master, I was able in the compass of two years (although I confess with the utmost difficulty) to remove that infernal habit of lying, shuffling, deceiving and equivocating, so deeply rooted in the very souls of all my species, especially the Europeans." Swift's last chapter is an even longer burlesque, both of the lack of truthfulness in travelers and the persecution complex that possessed them. There, with a straight face, Gulliver denounced the "fabulous accounts" disproved by his own eyes, lamented "the credulity of mankind so impudently abused," and proudly asseverated, "I imposed on myself as a maxim, never to be swerved from, that I would *strictly adhere to truth.*"

The deceitful travelers imitated their more nearly authentic brethren by professing truth and attacking one another, but they also had methods and characteristics that were unique. One of the chief complaints directed at them from earlier times was their willingness to quote an outmoded authority such as Pliny or to record hearsay, legend, old wives' tales, and tall tales, a fault that lingered on through the eighteenth century, as with Dr. Brickell and Dr. Hasselquist. Although a new age was ushered in by the Royal Society and other scientific academies, the thirst for accuracy and objectivity which they fostered backfired a thousand times when voyagers, imbued with a real or supposed desire to be thorough about the lands they had visited or pretended to visit, read other travelers or geographers and then shamelessly plagiarized them. Even Commodore John Byron, who had been to Chile as a young ensign, felt obliged to fill out his weak memories by borrowing, without acknowledgment, or letting some ghost writer borrow for him, passages from Frézier.[16] Very frequently the deceivers exaggerated—the height of a waterfall, the size of a frog, the age of a person; or they invented—a tribe of Indians, a trip down a river, an Adario; or they deliberately transferred something from one place to another—radical European ideas credited to savage tribes, Roman customs moved to Nice. Invention could go still farther, for, like Wilhelm Meister, there was a whole host of travelers— from Leguat and Drury to Carver and Anbury—who could say with more or less truth, "My journal is none of mine! . . . it was patched together by a friend's help out of many books." [17] Sometimes the "friend" was more than helpful, as with Psalmanazer's George Innes, the Jesuits' Du Halde, or Captain Cook's Hawkesworth. One practice pursued by at least the more cautious sinners was that of covering their tracks as much as possible by attacking, misquoting, plagiarizing, or contradicting a dead person, as Crèvecoeur did with Franklin, or a foreign book, as the inventor of Coreal did with the *Atlas Geographus*. In fact, the fabricators knew that their work would acquire an aura of respectability if they occasionally referred to real and accepted travelers or other authorities, perhaps to disagree with them audaciously, as Misson belabored his source Corneille or Defoe teased the geographer Moll, whom he could hardly have done without. Swift burlesqued every one of these devices of the travel deceiver. The humorous misuse of authority, for example, is reflected in Gulliver's reference to "Cousin Dampier," dead and unable to defend himself, and in his ironic defense of his veracity by quoting the Greek Sinon, one of the notorious liars of antiquity, and attributing the quotation to the *Aeneid*. All of these methods, when used by skillful writers widely read in voyage literature, produced partly or wholly fabricated books that have left a deep imprint on history.

Their influence has been assessed in every chapter of the present work. Travel lies affected national politics from the beginning of the eighteenth century, when Hennepin, Lahontan, and La Salle aroused the courts of England and France, to the end of the century when Maldonado caused nations to send ships to the Pacific and Meares brought on the Nootka Sound controversy between Britain and Spain. Travel lies have contorted history by bequeathing John Lawson's work to William Byrd and to Dr. Brickell, by confusing the biographers of Franklin, or by forcing error on dozens of editors, one of whom by a quirk of fate—not without many suspicions and some discoveries— edited three travel books, two of which, *Leguat* and *Drury*, were completely fireside and one of which, *Benyowski*, was only in part authentic.[18]

Because of the rapid progress in discovery and exploration the travel lies told about geography were not so long-lasting as they were effective. The very exaggerated heights of Niagara and the Aswan cataract on the Nile lived out most of the century, however; and for decades an unbelievable number of maps kept alive the *"Rivière longue,"* its apocryphal tribes of Indians, and the various Northwest Passages.

The sea novel and other types of fiction owe much to voyage accounts, whether true or false, but literary figures in general were affected by travel deceptions. Not only did Swift parody them; they inspired many humorous lines among wits such as Voltaire and Horace Walpole and many poetic lines among the Romanticists. Not only did Schiller employ an Indian death song which Carver, or Carver's editor, had taken from Lahontan, another deceiver; the young Chateaubriand, himself a deceiver, succumbed to untrustworthy travelers while writing *Les Natchez*.

Voyagers, publishers, and editors combined to make money from spurious, or partly spurious, travel accounts, but such books have always spurred on the publishing and business worlds. Not only did the discoveries of Northwest Passages and tall Patagonians keep presses busy; the French publisher of the first version of Byron's circumnavigation was so impressed with the possibilities of the giants that he printed an entirely false title on the spine, *Histoire des Patagones*, thereby exploiting the fewer than ten pages of his book that dealt with that notorious exaggeration. La Salle's stories and maps enticed investors, and de Fonte and Maldonado persuaded businessmen, as well as governments, of at least four nations to back ventures to the

Pacific. One effect of travel deceptions on recent business can be found in the sales catalogues of outstanding bookstores. In 1960 such a catalogue offered the honest Captain Dixon's first edition, in two volumes, at £15, while at the same time asking over four times as much for the one-volume first edition of his opponent, the lying Captain Meares. The same catalogue wanted £130 for Hennepin's pretended discovery of the mouth of the Mississippi.[19]

Theologians and philosophers depended heavily on voyage literature and, as a result, often fell victim to its less trustworthy segment. The religious controversies of the age provided travelers with a biased viewpoint, and they in turn supplied theorists with biased evidence. The moral and political philosophers— from Temple, Locke, and Shaftesbury, to Bayle and Montesquieu, to the Romanticists—employed the testimony of the travelers. Of the historically important philosophers, Rousseau was most often deceived by them, in spite of the fact that in *Emile* he charged, "I have passed my life in reading the accounts that Travellers give, and have not met with two that have given me the same idea of the same people." [20] He complained of their "lies and their bad faith" and then took from them what he needed, not only from the more reliable Charlevoix and Lafitau but from the very unreliable Lahontan and the useless Le Beau and Coreal.

The "Directions" for travelers published by the Royal Society in 1666, added to almost immediately by Boyle, and republished in the collections of Churchill and Bernard, seemed to give most impetus to the collecting of facts about natural history, but it was in that field of thought that travel deceptions were most abundant and perhaps most effective. One must, of course, be especially careful to distinguish between the lie and the tall tale when he investigates the accounts of plants and animals. The Swedish scientist Pehr Kalm (1753–1761) was the victim of a tall tale when he relayed the homespun naturalist John Bartram's story of how bears of North America killed cows. "When a bear catches a Cow," Kalm recorded seriously, "he kills her in the following manner: he bites a hole into the hide, and blows with

all his power into it, till the animal swells excessively and dies;
for the air expands greatly between the flesh and the hide." [21] It
has been suggested that one reason travelers like Kalm were so
often victimized by such stories was the persistence, the scientific
curiosity of the travelers in searching for facts.[22]

Yet when the tall tales are set aside one still finds a great many
false reports about nature that were not always lies of ignorance.
Few of these were in botany; most concerned animal life, as
with Coreal's oversize manati or Misson's fabricated bird, the
Erythromachus Leguati. The Englishman Weld reported a
mosquito that could bite through Washington's thickest book.
Bossu, in the Mississippi country, recorded that alligators with
bullet holes in their hides, hibernating in the mud, gave growth
to little elms and willows whose seeds had dropped into the
pits. Maillet, in Egypt, reported an incredible hippopotamus
and fish that looked like women, with two arms and two hands.
Rusoe d'Eres, on a fantastic trip down a mythical Red River that
began at Lake Superior, saw monkeys in America. William
Bartram told of frogs eighteen inches long, while Dumont in
Louisiana saw them two feet long weighing thirty-seven pounds,
increased to fifty-seven by De Pauw, who had a thesis to prove.
And Labat, one of the most dependable of travelers, had a story
of a man who tied his canoe to a sleeping turtle and then let it
drag him two nights and days until it became tired enough to
be killed. Snake stories were unlimited in number: one snake
was so big that while it slept three men mistook it for a log and
sat down on it; another, in order to pursue its prey more swiftly,
joined its head and tail and rolled on the ground like a wheel;
and at least three travelers to different parts of the world
vouched for the existence of a kind of snake that when cut
completely in two could rejoin the parts. Marvelous cures from
nature were advocated seriously by travelers other than Dr.
Hasselquist in Egypt. Dr. Brickell passed on many such prescrip-
tions, all of which he did not steal from Lawson. The goss-
hawk's dung, he said, "is exceedingly hot, and being drank fasting
in wine, is said to cause conception." The water of certain rivers
was potent too, since Bossu knew that "seven or eight women

who had been childless at Mobile became mothers after they and their husbands, removing to New Orleans, drank the waters of the Mississippi." [23]

With so many false facts about natural history being brought back by travelers, sedentary scientists could not help but err in making compilations or improvising theories. Paul Dudley, writing in the *Philosophical Transactions*, was deceived (1723) about the powers of rattlesnakes, accepted as true (1725) a report that whales "making love" stand straight up with heads out of the water, and was only "doubtful" that North American Indians killed whales by straddling their backs and plugging up their spouts till they strangled. Sir Hans Sloane repeated unreliable stories of sharks, even though he was sometimes skeptical about them; and Funnell's footless bird of paradise became Linnaeus' *Paridisea apoda*. Maupertuis fashioned a beautiful theory about dwarfs and giants. "If," he said, "there is truth in what the travelers tell us about the Strait of Magellan and the lands of the far North, the races of giants and dwarves settled there either because of the fitness of the climate or, what is more likely, because . . . they were driven to those regions by other men, who feared the giants or scorned the pigmies. . . . The dwarves retired to the North Pole, the giants to the South." [24] Wider acquaintance with voyage literature would have informed Maupertuis that there were also tribes of "pigmies" along the Strait of Magellan and both tall men and tiny men in the equatorial regions.

The Comte de Buffon's *Histoire naturelle* (1749–1788), in thirty-one volumes, was the most impressive work of its kind in the century, receiving five editions during the author's lifetime. Although Buffon was a scientist himself and made the Jardin des Plantes in Paris the outstanding such collection of Europe, in his scientific encyclopedia he was forced to employ the travelers for data about species in the lands he had not visited. And because of his thoroughness, he was led by unreliable sources into making many mistakes. On a single page he quoted Misson's manufactured *Leguat* twice, once to the effect that an entire nation in Java could see well in the dark but could not stand daylight and so long as the sun was shining went about with heads down and eyes closed waiting for nightfall. Careri and Struys, both real, but sometimes untrustworthy, travelers, were cited as evidence that men in Formosa, Mindoro, and the Philippine Islands had tails; Buffon did think Struys's estimate of the length of the tails in Formosa was somewhat exaggerated, however. From voyage literature the scientist arrived at a hesitating belief in nine-foot Patagonians but refused unequivocally to accept pigmies, a stand that should have been reversed. His theory that "a beaver has a scaly tail, because he eats fish" seems to have no source in travels to North America; but one commentator, while refuting dozens of misconceptions about beavers, wondered "much" that Buffon did not himself have a tail "for the same reason." [25]

One section of eighteen pages in the *Histoire naturelle* [26] cites ten travelers, some more than once. Every one of the ten has much truth, no doubt, but at each of them suspicion or certainty of falsehood has been directed. One was Defoe's Captain Roberts, another Misson's François Leguat. One was Paul Lucas, the most popular and most deceitful of the Frenchmen who went to Egypt; another was the Baron Lahontan. One, Tavernier, was said by Bernard to have had a ghost writer; another, Struys, was justifiably attacked by Chardin as being inclined to invention. A seventh, Bosman,[27] was much more addicted to chortling over salacious sex stories out of Africa than to recording correct natural history. The remaining three, Frézier, Careri, and Misson with his journey to Italy, were among the most respected of travelers, but all three were sometimes accused of errors, even lies.

Travelers of the eighteenth century, then, not only unfolded for Europe the picture of the expanding world; they caused that picture to be discolored and distorted in each of its parts, from government to natural history. But the backgrounds were not always shaded properly either, certain myths becoming part of life because the voyage literature started them or lent them support. The savage was more noble than he actually was, or too much like Homer's heroes. The Oriental was too moral and too rational. The Western Hemisphere was either too degenerate or too attractive. And Russia not only was seen as a land with lions, tigers, and wild bulls like those of Africa; for a century this poorest of countries, continually struggling along without funds and inventing ruses to get money, was looked upon as one where the treasures of the czar were the greatest in all Europe.[28] To show these distortions in the image of the eighteenth-century world has been the chief objective of our present study, but certain derivative lessons can be suggested.

One is that no estimate of the effects and methods of travel writers in this period can be satisfactory if they are considered on a national basis only. Sir William Temple resorted to foreign voyagers more than he did to the English, and in a discussion of morals John Locke referred to four travelers, not one of whom was a countryman of his.[29] All editors of the big collections crossed national boundaries, imitating and plundering one another. Defoe knew the Russian ambassador Ides and the French buccaneers as well as he knew Dampier and Rogers. The creator of Coreal depended more on the English *Atlas Geographus* than on native authorities. And because of Britain's ruling that withheld all accounts of long voyages until the authorized one could be issued, continental readers were sometimes given the news first in journals that were smuggled across the Channel. There is no literature more international than voyage literature.

Another derivative lesson is that the search for sources is under certain conditions not only rewarding but necessary. It is necessary when it proves that some travelers are not to be trusted because they did not narrate their own experiences, when it helps to determine the methods and the canon of such a realistic fictionizer as Defoe, when it leads to a correction of history, or when it helps a bibliographer place a book or a librarian to catalogue it.

One might also agree that encyclopedias and other reference works would be doing their readers a service by exposing the fraudulent voyagers or assessing the degree of their reliability. Instead, the general practice seems to be that when a travel writer is found to be a fake he is dropped from the reference work, no matter what his ability or his influence. Such an editorial procedure, it can be argued, only aids the myth to live on. The *Encyclopædia Britannica*, for example, formerly carried articles on Leguat and Drury as real travelers, but when they were shown to be fireside fabrications the two were omitted from all later editions. As a result, there is now no quick way of finding out about these inventions, one of which was reissued by the Hakluyt Society because of its supposed value to natural history, the other of which was for two centuries rated as the best description of Madagascar, and neither of which when pulled from the library shelves exposes itself editorially.

Nor is it satisfactory to call such books "Voyages, Imaginary," as in the Library of Congress system. They were inventions, it is true, like the obviously fantastic voyages of Gulliver, but their object was to deceive, in the way that Gulliver's contemporary, the inventor of Captain William Symson, deceived his readers. And as authentic voyages they lived their lives, often as effectively and almost as enduringly as "Cousin" Dampier and other real travelers, more than a few of whom obtained part of their success by employing the methods of the master deceivers and recording false facts or taking true facts from other travelers and working them into a false framework, thereby not only "giving to the truth and the lie the same degree of authority" but forcing enlightened readers such as Swift, Walpole, and Dr. Johnson to be skeptical about all voyage literature.

NOTES

CHAPTER I: THE VOYAGE BEGINS

1. Lord Chesterfield, Letter to his son, January 8, O.S., 1750.

2. See note 48, chap. v.

3. Etienne Rey, *Eloge du Mensonge* (Paris: 1925), p. 27.

4. "One writer," in *Encyclopedia of Religion and Ethics*, VIII, (1951), 220 ff.; Samuel Johnson in *Life of Johnson*, in 1781; Corneille de Pauw, *Recherches philosophiques sur les Américains* (Berlin: 1770), VIII, 8 [Here de Pauw is replying to Dom Pernetty]; and "a recent scholar," in Philip Babcock Gove, *The Imaginary Voyage in Prose Fiction* (New York: 1941), p. 16.

5. Quoted in Paul Hazard, *La Crise de la conscience européene, 1680–1715* (Paris: 1935), p. 245.

6. XI, 647, as quoted in NED, VI, 647.

7. (1818), I, 187, as quoted in NED, VI, 251.

8. (London: 1785), chap. x.

9. Fielding, in preface to *Journal of a Voyage to Lisbon; The Adventurer*, no. 50, April 28, 1753; and Atkinson, as quoted in Gove, p. 16.

10. Rey, p. 11.

11. J. P. Brissot de Warville, *Nouveau voyage dans les Etats–Unis* (Paris: 1791), pp. xxix–xxxi.

12. Edmund Hickeringill, "The History of Priestcraft," in *Works* (London: 1721), I, 17, as quoted in NED, VI, 251.

13. George P. Winship, "Travellers and Explorers, 1583–1763," CHAL, I (New York: 1943), 7.

14. Diderot, "Voyageur," *Encyclopédie ou dictionnaire raisonné*, nouvelle éd. (Genève: 1778); De Pauw, *Recherches philosophiques*, I, 10 ff., II, 24, 45, III, 8; for Locke see Michael Kraus, "Literary Relations between Europe and America in the Eighteenth Century," *William and Mary Quarterly*, 3rd S., I (1944), 210–234; for Adams see his introduction to *Modern Voyages*, 2 vols. (Dublin: 1790), or the French translation of 1800.

15. Rey, pp. 19, 57.

16. *Ibid.*, p. 49.

17. Jean Baptiste Bossu, *Nouveaux voyages dans l'Amérique septentrionale* (Amsterdam: 1777), p. 195.

18. *L'Amérique et le rêve exotique dans la littérature française au XVIIᵉ et au XVIIIᵉ siècle* (Paris: 1934), p. vi. First printed in 1913.

CHAPTER II: THE PATAGONIAN GIANTS

1. Carlyle, speaking of Frederick the Great; as quoted in NED, VI, 256.

2. *Terra Australis Cognita* (Edinburgh: 1766–1768), I, 370.

3. *Magellan's Voyage around the World,* edited by James Alexander Robinson (Cleveland: 1906), I, 49 ff. The information on Magellan's voyage given herein is taken from Robinson's edition; from Lord Stanley's 1874 Hakluyt Society edition; and from James Burney, *A Chronological History of the Discoveries in the South Seas* . . . (London: 1817), I, 16 ff.

4. *Braza = braccia*(?), a cubit, or arm's length. Stanley, p. 51, avoids reference to breasts and simply translates Pigafetta as saying that the women "are very sufficiently large."

5. The "Genoese pilot," in Stanley, pp. 1 ff.; the "Portuguese, companion of Odoardo [Duarte] Barbosa," in Stanley, pp. 30–32; and Francisca Alba, in Stanley, pp. 211 ff.

6. The information about Drake given herein is taken from *The World Encompassed by Sir Francis Drake,* collated with an unpublished MS of Francis Fletcher . . . with appendices and introduction by W. S. W. Vaux (London: 1854); *New Light on Drake* . . . Discovered, translated, and annotated by Mrs. Zelia Nuttall (London: 1914); and *Sir Francis Drake's Voyage round the World,* edited by Henry R. Wagner (San Francisco: 1926).

7. Burney, II, 4.

8. *Narratives of the Voyages to the Straits of Magellan,* translated and edited, with notes and introduction by Clements R. Markham for the Hakluyt Society (London: 1895), p. 136.

9. *The Voyages and Works of John Davis,* edited by Admiral Sir Albert H. Markham for the Hakluyt Society (London: 1880), p. xlvii.

10. For this and the following references to Knivet's journal, see *Hakluytus posthumus, or Purchas, his Pilgrimes* . . . (Glasgow: 1905–1907), XVI, 185–186, 265–266.

11. See Burney, II, 190, 203, 211, 215; *The East and West Indian Mirror, being an account of Joris Van Speilbergen's Voyage around the World (1614–1617);* and the *Australian Navigations of Jacob Le Maire,* translated with notes and introduction by J. A. J. de Villiers of the British Museum (The Hakluyt Society, 1906), p. 39.

12. *The Relation of a wonderful voiage made by William Cornelison Schouten* (London: 1619). Original edition at Amsterdam, 1617, in Dutch and French.

13. For example, the 1619 DeBry, Latin edition, appendix xi; the Amsterdam, French edition of 1617, pp. 14–15; and the 1619 Latin edition —not DeBry's—the frontispiece. For some five other references in Elizabethan times to the giants of Patagonia, see Robert R. Cawley, *The Voyagers and Elizabethan Drama* (Boston: 1938), pp. 378–379.

14. Leonardo de Argensola, *Histoire de la conquête des Isles Moluques par les Espagnols, par les Portugais et par les Hollandois, traduite de l'espagnol d'Argensola* (Amsterdam: 1706), Book I, Vol. I, p. 35; Book III, Vol. I, pp. 255–258; and Book III, Vol. I, p. 218.

15. *Relation du voyage de la mer du Sud aux côtes du Chily et Perou, 1712, 1713, et 1714* (Paris: 1716).

16. (Paris: 1845), III, 331–332.

17. *Les Oeuvres* (Dresden: 1753), p. 334.

18. I, 140 ff.

19. *Navigantium atque itinerantium bibliotheca* (London: 1744), I, 7. This and the 1764 edition were redone by Dr. John Campbell.

20. XXXVI, 245. *The London Magazine,* XXXV, 323, had the same report but said "great stature" for "eight feet and a half high," while the *Scots Magazine,* XXVIII, 329, spoke of "nine feet" and added "but the report concerning the stature of the inhabitants was afterwards said to be fictitious."

21. XXXVI, 291.

22. XX, 46.

23. XX (August 2, 1766), 121. This letter was reprinted in other publications, for example, the *London Magazine,* XXXV (August, 1766), 428–430.

24. See note 26.

25. The *London Chronicle,* XXI (April 11, and April 14, 1767), 252. The *Gentleman's Magazine,* XXXVII (April, 1767), 147–151, tells of the public concern as to the identity of the anonymous author.

26. See the *London Chronicle* and the *Gentleman's Magazine* on the dates given in the previous notes.

27. C, 506.

28. P. 132.

29. Pp. 105 ff.

30. *Histoire d'un voyage aux Isles Malouines; Fait en 1763–1764.*

31. *Ibid.,* pp. 106, 140.

32. XXI (June 13, 1767), 567–568.

33. September 8, 1766, p. 571; and April 27, 1767, pp. 261–262.

34. CII (January, 1768), 40–41.

35. XVII, 75.

36. The *London Chronicle,* XXIV (July 5, 1768), 15. See also the *Gentleman's Magazine,* XXXVIII (July, 1768), 321–322.

37. April, 1769, pp. 106–111.

38. May 26, 1768.

39. See also the *London Chronicle,* XXI (June 13, 1767), 567; and the *London Magazine,* XXXVI (July, 1767), 343–344.

40. *Viage al Estrecho de Magallanes por el Capitan Pedro Sarmiento de Gamboa en los años 1579 y 1580* (Madrid: 1768).

41. The *Gentleman's Magazine,* XXXVIII (May, 1768), 236.

42. See *Mercure de France,* December, 1766, pp. 123–124.

43. See *Journal des Sçavans,* CVII (November, 1773), 761.

44. II, 772–773.

45. (Berlin: 1770), III, 88–89.

46. XL, 64.

47. I, 27–29.

48. I, 374.

49. See the *Massachusetts Magazine,* II (November, 1790), 654–656.

50. (London: 1871), pp. 57 ff.

51. Quoted in P. E. Launois and Pierre Roy, *Etudes biologiques sur les géants* (Paris: 1904), p. 24.

52. *Viage al Pais de los Tehuel-Ches* (Buenos Aires: 1879), p. 79.

53. See, for example, *Handbook of South American Indians,* Smithsonian Institution, Bureau of American Ethnology, Bulletin 143, VI (Washington: 1946–1950), 57–69.

CHAPTER III: FALSE TOPOGRAPHY

1. Swift, "On Poetry, a Rhapsody."

2. Quoted in Pierre Margry, *Découvertes et établissements des Français* . . . (Paris: 1879–1888), II, 259–260; and in Jean Delanglez, *Hennepin's "Description of Louisiana"* (Chicago: 1941), p. 86.

3. See *Father Louis Hennepin's Description of Louisiana,* translated by Marion E. Cross and introduction by Grace Lee Nute (University of Minnesota Press, 1938), p. 19, for one example.

4. *Ibid.*

5. *Ibid.,* pp. 78–79.

6. *Ibid.,* p. 45.

7. *Cartier to Frontenac* (New York: 1894), pp. 278–279. See *Description,* translated by Cross, p. 22, for a map that shows the location of the supposed mission.

8. See Francis Parkman, *La Salle and the Discovery of the Great West* (Boston: 1901), pp. 125, 248 ff., for one classic treatment of what the historian called Hennepin's "gross exaggerations." For other eyewitness accounts of Niagara, read Charles Mason Dow, *Anthology and Bibliography of Niagara Falls* (Albany: 1921), 2 vols. For the 600-feet report see, for example, "The New Discovery," in *Transactions of the American Antiquarian Society,* I (1820), 168. Although the height of Niagara Falls may vary slightly, *Webster's Geographical Dictionary* gives 158 feet for the Canadian Fall and 167 feet for the American Fall.

9. For the best treatment see Jean Delanglez, "Hennepin's Voyage to the Gulf of Mexico," *Mid-America,* XXI (1939), 32–81. For a summarizing essay and an excellent bibliography, see A. H. Greenly, "Father Louis Hennepin: His Travels and His Books," *The Papers of the Bibliographical Society of America,* LI (First Quarter, 1957), 38–60.

10. *La Salle and the Discovery of the Great West,* p. 230.

11. Information about these various editions is to be found in Delanglez, "Hennepin's *Description of Louisiana:* A Critical Essay," *Mid-America,* XXIII (1941), 32 ff., and in Greenly. The American abridgement is not included by Delanglez and is found in *The American Antiquarian Society Transactions* (see note 8).

12. See the preface to P. de Charlevoix, *Histoire et description générale de la Nouvelle France* (Paris: 1744), p. iii; and Kalm's letter to John Bartram, in *John Bartram's Observations* . . . (London: 1751).

13. Jules Baron de Saint Genois des Mottes, *Les Voyageurs belges du XIIIᵉ au XVIIIᵉ siècle* (Brussels: 1852), as quoted in "Hennepin," *La Grande encyclopédie*.

14. II, 622 ff.

15. *The North American Review*, XLVIII (January, 1839), 78–81, XLIX (July, 1839), 258–262, attacked Hennepin while *The United States Magazine*, V (April, 1839), 394–405, defended him. See Ralph Leslie Rusk, *The Literature of the Middle Western Frontier* (New York: 1926), I, 81.

16. *Voyages and Travels*, Maggs Bros., Ltd., Catalogue no. 842, Item 2312.

17. See note 3.

18. See note 2.

19. Parkman, pp. 110 ff.; for more recent treatments, see Frances Gaither, *The Fatal River; the Life and Death of La Salle* (New York: 1931), pp. 201 ff.; Henry Folmer, *Franco-Spanish Rivalry in North America, 1524–1763* (Glendale, California: 1953), pp. 144 ff.

20. Margry, II, 288 ff. Quoted also in Jean Delanglez, "The Cartography of the Mississippi," *Mid-America*, XXI (January, 1949), 29–30.

21. For a full treatment of the question, see Delanglez, *The Cartography of the Mississippi, Some La Salle Journeys* (Chicago: 1938); Delanglez, "Franquelin, Mapmaker," *Mid-America*, XXV (1943), 29–74; and Folmer, p. 150.

22. Delanglez, "Franquelin, Mapmaker," p. 61.

23. This 1688 map is in Gaither, opposite p. 198. For the 1684 map, see illustrations following p. 100 of the present book; *Narrative and Critical History of America*, edited by Justin Winsor (Boston and New York: 1884), IV, 228; R. G. Thwaites, *Jesuit Relations*, LXIII, frontispiece.

24. *La Salle* (New York: 1931), pp. 185–192.

25. Pp. 197 ff.

26. "The Cartography of the Mississippi," p. 41.

27. Most of this evidence is provided in *ibid*.

28. P. 340.

29. The journal was bought in France by Francis Parkman and given to J. D. G. Shea, who edited and published it in 1858. Another edition, by Jean Delanglez, was brought out in Chicago in 1938. Father Delanglez has studied this journal and the two subsequent versions, all attributed to Jean Cavelier, in an attempt to discover reasons for their differences and obvious misstatements of fact. See his "The Authorship of the Journal of Jean Cavelier," *Mid-America*, XXV (1943), 220–223. Lahontan's letter is included in the 1938 edition, p. 41. For Parkman's judgment see his *La Salle and the Great West*, p. 408. De Villiers is quoted by Delanglez in the 1938 edition, p. 27.

30. For Lahontan's biography see *Un Outre-Mer au XVIIᵉ siècle, Voyages au Canada Du Baron de la Hontan, Publiés avec une Introduction et des Notes*, edited by François de Nion (Paris: 1900); Gilbert Chinard's intro-

duction to Baron de Lahontan, *Dialogues curieux entre l'auteur et un sauvage de bon sens qui a voyagé, et Mémoires de l'Amérique Septentrionale* (Baltimore: 1931); J. Edmond Roy, *Le Baron de Lahontan, Mémoires de la société Royale du Canada* (1895), XII, 63–192; and, especially, the introduction by Gustave Lanctot, editor of *New Documents by Lahontan,* The Oakes Collection (1940). See also the excellent bibliography by A. H. Greenly, "Lahontan: An Essay and Bibliography," *The Papers of the Bibliographical Society of America,* XLVIII (Fourth Quarter, 1954), 334–389.

31. See Lanctot, note 28.

32. Chinard's introduction to *Dialogues curieux,* gives a full account of the early editions in The Hague and in London. Also see Greenly.

33. All quotations from and references to the content of Letter Sixteen are taken from the English translation found in John Pinkerton, *Voyages and Travels* (London: 1814), XIII, 306–323.

34. For those unacquainted with the legends of the great Southwest—New Spain—we recommend the books of J. Frank Dobie and Paul Horgan; and the important bibliography, H. R. Wagner, *The Spanish Southwest, 1542–1794,* 2 vols.

35. J. Long, "Travels of an Indian Interpreter and Trader," *Early Western Travels, 1748–1846,* edited by Reuben Gold Thwaites (Cleveland: 1904), pp. 168 ff.

36. Carver, *Travels through the Interior Parts of North America* (Philadelphia: 1796), pp. 160–161; and Crèvecoeur, *Lettres d'un cultivateur américain* (Paris: 1787), II, 46. Carver's *Travels* first appeared in London in 1778.

37. Pinkerton, XIII, 296.

38. For these statistics see Lanctot, pp. 17–19; and Chinard's introduction to *Dialogues curieux,* p. 19, who quotes and adds to Roy.

39. Bowen, II, part 2, 622; D. Fenning and J. Collyer, *A New System of Geography* (London: 1771), II, 645.

40. In a review of Schoolcraft's *Narrative Journal,* N.S., XV (July, 1822), 228. See note 8 for present official statistics on the Falls.

41. For some of this information on the eighteenth-century influence of Lahontan's geography, see Nellis M. Crouse, *In Quest of the Western Ocean* (New York: 1928), pp. 318–320, 332, 345, 347; H. R. Wagner, *The Cartography of the Northwest Coast of America* (Berkeley: 1937), I, 140 ff.

42. *North American Review,* II (January, 1816), 149.

43. *Lahontan's Voyages,* edited with an introduction and notes by Stephen Leacock (Ottawa: 1932), p. 192. Leacock and Nion (note 30) believed that Lahontan was speaking of either the St. Pierre or the Minnesota River.

44. IV, 262.

45. *Count Frontenac and New France Under Louis XIV* (Boston: 1877), p. 105.

46. Delanglez, "The Voyages of Tonti," *Mid-America,* XXVI (October, 1944), 281.

47. See *ibid.*, where Father Delanglez waxes merry over the picture of the lone man, the tiny canoe, the furious paddling, and the 15,000-mile round trip.

48. (Paris: 1885), Map no. 28. See *ibid.*

49. J. B. Brebner, *The Explorers of North America, 1492–1806* (Garden City, New York: 1955), p. 315. This book was first published in 1933.

CHAPTER IV: MORE FALSE TOPOGRAPHY

1. The *Examiner*, no. 14.

2. *Proceedings of the American Antiquarian Society*, N.S., XLI (April 15–October 21, 1931), 190–196. For other reprintings see the *London Chronicle*, July 19–21, 1768; and Burney, II, 184 ff.

3. Burney, III, 184 ff.; Winsor, VIII, 110; Crouse, pp. 418 ff.; Wagner, "Apocryphal Voyages" [see note 2, above], pp. 196 ff.; and Lawrence C. Wroth, "The Early Cartography of the Pacific," *The Papers of the Bibliographical Society of America*, XXXVIII, no. 2 (1944), 224–225. These five writers, especially Wagner, have contributed much to the present discussion of de Fonte.

4. For an account of Peñalosa, see chap. vii.

5. For one history of a search for the Northwest Passage, see Crouse.

6. Gary S. Dunbar, "Assessment of Virginia's Natural Qualities by Explorers and Early Settlers," *Virginia in History and Tradition* (Longwood College, Farmville, Virginia: 1958), pp. 65–85.

7. For the most widely disseminated of these, see the story of de Fuca and Lok in chap. vii.

8. Crouse, pp. 421–425, gives an account of the Dobbs–Middleton story. For more details, especially on Swaine and on Dobbs's final acts in the affair, see Wagner, "Apocryphal Voyages," p. 203, and *Cartography*, I, 158–159; and for the latest treatments, Wroth, pp. 223–227, and the sources cited in notes 20 and 24 below.

9. *A New System of Geography*, II, 784 ff.

10. Wagner, *Cartography*, I, 3.

11. For example, John Dee, who in 1575 or 1576 drew a map with four false water routes through North America. This particular map, rediscovered and made famous in 1928, contains the signature of Sir Humphrey Gilbert, who at that time was propagandizing the search for a Northwest Passage. "It is just such a sketch," H. R. Wagner concludes, "as might have been presented to a council . . . which had under consideration the forthcoming voyage of Frobisher" [*Cartography*, I, 79].

12. *Gentleman's Magazine*, XXIV (March, 1754), 124.

13. Burney, III, 191.

14. *Ibid.*, p. 192.

15. *Histoire de l'Académie des Sciences* (Paris: 1750), p. 152, as quoted by Burney, III, 192.

16. A review of *Voyages et découvertes faites par les Russes le long des*

côtes de la mer Glaciale . . . (Amsterdam: 1766), 2 vols. This work was a translation from the German original, published by the Academy of Sciences at Petersburg.

17. XXIV (March, April, 1754), 123-128, 166-167. The "adverse criticism" mentioned in the next sentence was by the Russian historian G. F. Muller and had been published in France the year before. See Wroth, p. 224.

18. Wagner, *Cartography*, I, 160.

19. *Gentleman's Magazine*, XXIV (December, 1754), 542-543.

20. For the story of Swaine, long a puzzle to scholars, see Bertha Solis-Cohen, "Bibliographical Notes," *The Proceedings of the Bibliographical Society of America*, XXXVII (Fourth Quarter, 1943), 308; Howard N. Eavenson, *Map Maker and Indian Traders* (University of Pittsburgh Press, 1949); and Eavenson, *Swaine and Drage, A Sequel to Map Maker and Indian Traders* (University of Pittsburgh Press, 1950). For Franklin's approval of Dobbs, see the letter to William Strahan, *The Papers of Franklin*, edited by Leonard W. Labaree (New Haven: 1959), II, 409-412. Franklin eventually received at least some of Middleton's arguments, which apparently never influenced his theories about a Northwest Passage [see *ibid.*, III, 13-14].

21. Letter to Jean Baptiste Le Roy (A.P.S.), April 20, 1772.

22. "Benjamin Franklin Defends Northwest Passage Navigation, with an Introduction by Bertha Solis-Cohen," *Princeton University Library Chronicle*, XIX, no. 1 (1957-1958), 15-34. But compare the introduction to this letter with Percy G. Adams, "Benjamin Franklin's Defense of the de Fonte Hoax," *The Princeton University Library Chronicle*, XXII, no. 3 (Spring, 1961), 133-141.

23. See *Magnalia Christi Americana* (1820), II, 297. In 1668 a book was published in London called *The Great Probability of a North West Passage: Deduced from Observations on the Letter of Admiral De Fonte.* This book, formerly attributed to Thomas Jefferys, who drew the maps for it, employed arguments about Shapley and Gibbons similar to the unpublished ones of Franklin but drew its parallels with the French pirate story from Cotton, instead of Increase, Mather. Crouse, p. 420, says of the 1668 *Probability*, "With the aid of a little imagination Jefferys distorts the incidents mentioned by Mather to make them bear out de Fonte's story, though the discrepancies are so great as to render the attempt obvious." Bertha Solis-Cohen, "Bibliographical Notes," *The Papers of the Bibliographical Society of America*, XXXIX (Fourth Quarter, 1945), 319-320, and Eavenson, *Map Maker and Indian Traders*, p. 47, have suggested, with excellent evidence, that Charles Swaine was the real author of the *Probability*. Franklin may have had some connection with it, as he was in London at the time it was going to press.

24. [Charles Swaine], *An Account of a Voyage For the Discovery of a North-West Passage by Hudson's Streights* (London: 1748), II, 304-318; Henry Ellis, *A Voyage to Hudson's Bay . . . For Discovering a North West Passage* (London: 1748); and the *Gentleman's Magazine* (April, 1754).

25. Maldonado's fictitious voyage has often been written about, the

latest and best treatment being that of Professor Wagner in his "Apocryphal Voyages." However, Professor Wagner, while clearing up nearly everything about the matter, included his own translation of a part of the document referred to by Buache when an excellent translation of the entire document had already been made by Sir John Barrow for his *A Chronological History of Voyages into the Arctic Regions* (London: 1818), appendix ii, pp. 24–48. Furthermore, of those who have treated Maldonado none has spoken of the important connection between him and Quiros [see note 28, below]. In addition to Wagner, one should refer to Burney, V, 165–173; Martin Fernandez Navarrete, *Examen historico-critico de los viajes y descubrimientos apocrifos del capitan Lorenzo Ferrer Maldonado*, XV (Madrid: 1881).

26. "Comentarios de la embajarda . . . ," not published until 1782, at the end of Don Eugenio Llaguno, *Historia del gran Tamorlan*. All that Don Garcia said about the projector is quoted in Navarrete, XV, 77–81.

27. *Bibliotheca Hispana Nova* (Rome: 1672), I, 2.

28. See *The Voyages of Pedro Fernandez de Quiros, 1595 to 1606*, translated and edited by Sir Clements Markham (London: 1904), p. xxxi.

29. *Ibid.*

30. One of which, according to Wagner, "Apocryphal Voyages," is found, with the drawings and maps, in Munoz's "Collection now in Madrid in the Real Academia de la Historia," Vol. XXVIII.

31. Duque de Almodovar del Rio, *Historia politica de los establicimientos ultramarinos* . . . (Madrid: 1784–1790), V, 584–589. Almodovar did not, as a number of historians claim, reproduce the *Relation*.

32. *Isla de Leon. Y.D.C.G.M.* (Madrid: 1798), in two parts, one a Spanish translation of Buache, the other, Zevallos's refutation.

33. *Viaggio dal Mare Atlantico al Pacifico . . . Tradotto da un Manoscritto Spagnuolo inedito da Carlo Amoretti* (Milan: 1811); *Voyage . . .* (Plaisance: 1912).

34. See note 25 for full bibliographical details.

35. Navarrete, Colson, and Wagner.

36. See Navarrete, p. 92, and Amoretti, 1812, p. 31.

37. Crouse, pp. 14–19.

38. See note 1 above.

CHAPTER V: FIRESIDE TRAVELERS,
BEFORE DEFOE

1. Daniel Defoe, *The Complete English Gentleman* (London: 1890), p. 225.

2. There were such fireside travelers in earlier periods, the Italian Benzoni, for example, who was not content with his own real life in South America and robbed other writers of adventures and facts for his sixteenth-century *Historia del mondo nuovo*. See Josephus Nelson Larned, *The Literature of American History* (Boston: 1902), Item 763, for a brief summary of this traveler's borrowings.

3. Quoted in J. G. Droysen, *Geschichte der Preussischen Politik*, 2nd ed. (Leipzig: 1876–1878), IV, 103–104; and in W. D. Robson-Scott, *German Travellers in England, 1400–1800* (Oxford: 1953), p. 126.

4. Robson-Scott, pp. 126 ff. For the original travel books, see *Mémoires de Charles Louis Baron de Pöllnitz, contenant les observations qu'il a faites dans ses voyages, . . .* (Liège: 1734), 3 vols.; and *Nouveaux voyages* (Amsterdam: 1737).

5. *The Memoirs and Travels of Mauritius Augustus, Count de Benyowski, in Siberia, Kamchatka, . . . and Formosa,* introduction by Captain Pasfield Oliver (London: 1890), p. 29.

6. LXIX (May, 1790), 533–545.

7. LX, part 2 (August, 1790), 725–727.

8. See note 5.

9. For the following facts, see *ibid.* and *La Grande encyclopédie*, VI, 184.

10. *Travels* (London: 1781), p. 222.

11. See E. G. Bourne, "The Travels of Jonathan Carver," *American Historical Review*, XI (1906), 287–302. Bourne has not only gathered a list of authorities who knew of Carver's falsifications, but he has added his own evidence to show that little in the *Travels* could be Carver's own.

12. Louise P. Kellogg, "The Mission of Jonathan Carver," *Wisconsin Magazine of History,* XII (1928), 127–145.

13. *The Literary History of the American Revolution* (New York: 1897), I, 150.

14. J. Bédier, *Etudes critiques* (Paris: 1903), pp. 127 ff.

15. "Notes sur le voyage de Chateaubriand en Amérique," *Modern Philology,* IV, no. 2 (November 10, 1915), 269–349. Chinard and Bédier provide long lists of articles and books that have treated Chateaubriand's *Voyage.*

16. For example, the Chevalier d'Arvieux, Gemelli Careri, and Claude Le Beau. The *Mémoires* (1735) of d'Arvieux, who went to Egypt, were edited over three decades after his death by Père Labat, a famous voyager himself. The author, or the editor, included, as eyewitness accounts, many descriptions and incidents taken from Jean de Thevenot's 1664 book on Egypt, which was read and rifled by travelers to that country perhaps as much as visitors to Italy used Misson. [See J. M. Carré, *Les Voyageurs et écrivains français en Egypte* (Paris: 1932), I, 19; and Pierre Martino, *L'Orient dans la littérature française au XVIIe et au XVIIIe siècle* (Paris: 1906), pp. 228–230.] Gemelli Careri's six-volume *Giro del Mondo* (1699–1700), justifiably one of the most popular such books, both with the general reader and with scientists such as Buffon, sometimes included false information, such as the report that on the Philippines there were men with tails; and H. R. Wagner, *Cartography,* I, 94, 139, has shown how hard it is to believe that Careri actually saw California, the coast of which he described as if he were sitting in front of maps printed one hundred years before his time. Le Beau went to North America and then published his *Voyage curieux et nouveau parmi les sauvages de l'Amérique Septentrionale* (Amsterdam: 1738), 2 vols., which Justin Winsor called "semi-historical"

because it mixed so much fancy with information, some of which may have been his own but much of which is taken from other travel liars, among them Hennepin and Lahontan.

17. For the comparison of the published book and Ringrose's own manuscript in the British Museum, see Clennell Wilkinson, *Dampier's Voyages and Discoveries* (London: 1929), pp. 65 ff.; and William Dampier, *A New Voyage Round the World*, introduction by Sir Albert Gray (London: 1927), pp. xxi ff.

18. Translated by Elizabeth Helme (London: 1790), p. x.

19. Compare (Paris: 1790), II, 3, with translation by Helme, II, 3. Many other, longer, omissions can be found. Another London edition of the same year is much more faithful.

20. John Wilke satisfied his anti-Scottish prejudice by publishing in *The North Briton* a contemptuous account of Scotland that purported to give contemporary conditions there. [See *The North Briton*, no. 13.] The description, by James Howells, was published in 1649. A German translator created a marvel by insisting untruthfully that J. B. le Blond's *Voyage aux Antilles, 1767–1802*, told of mermen in Domenica. Le Blond's original work was published in 1813, the German translation in 1818. [See James R. Masterson, "Traveller's Tales of Colonial Natural History," *Journal of American Folklore*, XIX (January–March, 1948), 55.]

21. See Carré, I, 60. Maillet's two-volume *Description de l'Egypte,* was published in Paris in 1735 and in La Haye in 1740.

22. Louis Lohr Martz, *The Later Career of Tobias Smollett* (New Haven and London: 1942), p. 31. For most of these facts about Smollett I am indebted to Mr. Martz and to George M. Kahrl, *Tobias Smollett, Traveler-Novelist* (Chicago: 1945).

23. *Compendium*, VI, 123, as quoted in Martz, p. 46.

24. Martz, p. 32.

25. The words of Thomas Seccombe, "Smelfungus Goes South," *Cornhill Magazine*, N.S., XI (1901), 195, as quoted in Martz, p. 46.

26. The following information about Foigny and Tyssot can be found in Geoffroy Atkinson, *The Extraordinary Voyage in French Literature from 1700 to 1720* (Paris: 1922), pp. 15 ff., 67 ff. For Vairasse see Atkinson, pp. 19 ff. and Emanuel von der Mühl, *Denis Vairasse et son Histoire des Sévarambes* (Paris: 1938).

27. See Benjamin M. Woodbridge, *Gatien de Courtilz, Sieur de Verger. Etude sur un précurseur du roman réaliste en France* (Baltimore and Paris: 1925).

28. E. A. Baker, *The History of the English Novel* (London: 1924–1939), III, 179.

29. For the facts of Psalmanazar's life see his *Memoirs* (London: 1765); Robert Bracey, *Eighteenth Century Studies* (Oxford: 1925); Rosamond Bayne-Powell, *Travellers in Eighteenth-Century England* (London: 1951), pp. 192–194; A. L. Maycock, "The Amazing Story of George Psalmanasar," *Blackwoods,* CCXXXV (1934), 797–808; Sir John Haskins, *Life of Samuel Johnson, LLd.* (London: 1787); and, most particularly, *Boswell's Life of*

Johnson, edited by George Birkbeck Hill (Oxford: 1887). The publisher's advertisement to the posthumous *Memoirs* says, "we do not question to say, He was a Frenchman."

30. For example, du Tertre's *Histoire générale des Antilles* (Paris: 1667), 2 vols., has the same three selections translated into the Carib language.

31. A name which, the author explained, was borrowed from "Shalmeneser," II Kings 17:3. See *An Historical and Geographical Description of Formosa* (London: 1704), pp. 133 ff.

32. Quoted by Hill, III, 449.

33. John Ogilby, *America* (London: 1671), p. 248; and Gemelli Careri, in Awnsham and John Churchill, *A Collection of Voyages . . .* (London: 1704), IV, 520. Careri's *Giro del Mondo* was first published in Naples, in 6 vols., in 1699–1700.

34. Bracey, p. 79.

35. E. G. Cox, *A Reference Guide to the Literature of Travel* (Seattle: 1935), II, 476.

36. Hill, I, 359, and 359–360n.

37. Psalmanazar's last days as a writer in need are briefly described in Melford's Letter of June 10 in Smollett's *Humphrey Clinker*.

38. II, 251. The confession is repeated, often in the same words, in *The Modern Part of an Universal History* (London: 1759), VIII, 60, for which Psalmanazar wrote a number of sections [see Hill, I, 443].

39. *Boswell's Life*, edited by Hill, IV, 274.

40. *Memoirs*, p. 5.

41. Letter to William Mason, February 17, 1777.

42. R. Foulché-Delbosc, in introduction to *Madame D'Aulnoy, Travels in Spain* (London: 1930), p. i.

43. Quoted in notes to *ibid.*, p. 403.

44. *Queens of Old Spain* (London: 1911), p. 419, as quoted in *ibid.*, p. 420.

45. For the complete exposure of her two books on Spain, see *Madame d'Aulnoy, Relation de Voyage d'Espagne, avec une introduction et des notes par R. Foulché Delbosc* (Paris: 1926). For the British translation see note 42, above.

46. "Mme d'Aulnoy n'aurait-elle pas été en Espagne," *Revue de littérature comparée*, VII (1927), 724–736.

47. II, 113.

48. Among them was the creator of Captain William Symson and his *A New Voyage to the East-Indies . . . to Suratte, and . . . the Maldivy-Islands* (1715), one of the few English predecessors of Defoe's classics so far identified. This volume reworked Pyrard de Laval's 1611 account of the Maldive Islands, abridgements of which were to be found in Purchas and Harris (1705), and, more particularly, John Ovington's *Voyage to Suratt* (1696), which itself had drawn freely and without acknowledgment on previous travelers to India. The nonexistent Captain Symson has not had the broad influence of some other such fabrications, but he went through three editions in seventeen years and was taken seriously by at least one modern editor [Captain Pasfield Oliver in the Hakluyt edition of

Leguat (London: 1891), II, 183n.] Furthermore, shortly after his first print-ing he was the inspiration for Gulliver's "Captain Sympson" and provided the one passage that Swift took directly from a travel book to incorporate in *Gulliver's Travels*. See R. W. Frantz, "Gulliver's 'Cousin Sympson,'" *Huntington Library Quarterly*, I (1938), 329 ff.; and—for Ovington and Pyrard de Laval—Cox, I, 279–280, I, 290; and E. F. Oaten, *European Travellers in India* (London: 1899), pp. 248–249, who elaborates on Oving-ton's shortcomings.

49. See Atkinson, *Extraordinary Voyage*, pp. 143–144, for a bibliography. The present section on Leguat is indebted to Mr. Atkinson, pp. 35–65, 113–135; to Captain Pasfield Oliver [note 48]; to Gove, pp. 208–210; and to the 1707 review of *Leguat* [note 50].

50. XLV (December, 1707), 603–623. See p. 605 and, for an English translation, Oliver, pp. xxvi–xxvii.

51. Thomas Sauzier, *Un Projet de républic à l'isle d'Eden (l'île Bourbon) en 1689* (Paris: 1887), p. 23.

52. Bruzen de la Martinière, but not in his *Introductionis universam geographiam* (Amsterdam: 1729) as Oliver, whose footnote is incomplete (p. xxvi), implies, but in the *Dictionnaire géographique* (Paris: 1768), I, viii, as pointed out by Gove, p. 209.

53. Jean B. B. Eyries, compiler of *Abrégé des voyages modernes* (Paris: 1819), Vol. XIII, according to Oliver, I, xxiv–xxv.

54. See note 51, above. Gove, p. 210, cites earlier evidence to show that there was always a strong belief in the authenticity of *Leguat*.

55. P. xxxiv. Atkinson, *Extraordinary Voyage*, p. 42, forgot these quoted reservations when he claimed that not until 1894 did Oliver have any suspicion of the apocryphal nature of the *Voyage*.

56. Hakluyt edition, I, 74.

57. See Atkinson, *Extraordinary Voyage*, pp. 115–118, for the evidence.

58. Alfred Newton, *A Dictionary of Birds* (London: 1893–1896), p. 217.

59. Edited by S. P. Harmer and A. E. Shipley (10 vols.; London: 1895–1909), IX, 330.

60. See Oliver's note, I, 81; *A Dictionary of Birds*, p. 218; and *Cambridge Natural History*, p. 251.

61. See "Rodriguez," 11th edition.

62. Gove, p. 110.

CHAPTER VI: FIRESIDE TRAVELERS, DEFOE AND AFTER

1. Parson Adams, in Henry Fielding, *Joseph Andrews*, chap. xvii.

2. See George A. Aitken, "Defoe's Library," *Athenaeum* (June 1, 1895), 706–707, for a discussion of the impossibility of ascertaining from the sales catalogue just which books Defoe owned, since the catalogue also is for the library of Dr. Philip Farewell.

3. See note 1 of chap. iv and, for almost the same words, the last page of the preface to *A General History of the Pyrates*.

4. See John Robert Moore, *Defoe in the Pillory and Other Studies* (Bloomington: 1939), p. 135.

5. For the evidence for Defoe's authorship, see *ibid.*, pp. 126–189.

6. *Ibid.*

7. *Ibid.*, p. 134. For other discussions of this side of Defoe, read James Sutherland, *Defoe* (London: 1937), p. 244; and Rudolph G. Stamm, "Daniel Defoe: An Artist in the Puritan Tradition," *Philological Quarterly*, XV, no. 3 (July, 1936), 225–246.

8. William P. Trent, *Daniel Defoe, How to Know Him* (Indianapolis; 1916), p. 130.

9. Sir Thomas Wright, *The Life of Daniel Defoe* (London: 1931), p. 260.

10. Quoted in Sutherland, p. 243.

11. Moore, *Defoe in the Pillory*, p. 90.

12. See C. E. Burch, "British Criticism of Defoe as a Novelist, 1719–1860," *Englische Studien*, LXVII (1932), 178–198.

13. "Studies in the Narrative Method of Defoe," *University of Illinois Studies in Language and Literature*, IX, no. 1 (February, 1924).

14. W. H. Bonner, *Captain William Dampier, Buccaneer-Author* (Stanford and London: 1934), p. 69.

15. Quoted by Baker, III, 173, from "On Talking Falsily."

16. See Walter Wilson, *Memoir of the Life and Times of Daniel De Foe* (London: 1830), III, 509.

17. For the evidence on *Captain Carleton* see Secord, pp. 165 ff.; Moore, *Defoe in the Pillory;* Moore "Evidence for Defoe's Authorship of *The Memoirs of Captain Carleton,*" MLN, LV (1940), 430–431; and various reviewers of Secord.

18. Cyril Hughes Hartmann, *The Memoirs of Captain Carleton* (London: 1929).

19. For a discussion of *Captain Roberts,* see Paul Dottin, *Daniel DeFoe et ses romans* (Paris: 1924), pp. 774 ff.; and Moore, *Defoe in the Pillory,* pp. 169–177, who does not seem to have read Dottin's evidence from the *Daily Journal* that in 1728 a real Captain Roberts arrived on his ship the *Providence* from the very part of the world in which Defoe had placed him.

20. *Robinson Crusoe,* edited by Henry Kingsley (London: 1868), p. xxx. For a full discussion of the sources for *Captain Singleton,* see Secord, pp. 112–165, who continued and corrected the work of William Minto, *Macmillan's Magazine,* XXXVIII (October, 1878), 459 ff. See also Dottin, pp. 617 ff.

21. James M'Queen, "Captain Speke's Discovery of the Source of the Nile," in Richard F. Burton, *The Nile Basin* (London: 1864), pp. 184 ff., as quoted in Gove, p. 169n.

22. April 31, 1705. See Luttrell's *Brief Relation,* V, 542–543, as quoted in Moore, *Defoe in the Pillory,* p. 111.

23. *Madagascar; or Robert Drury's Journal,* edited by Captain Pasfield Oliver (London: 1890), I, 28–30. See Captain Oliver's note, p. 308, and the last few pages of the journal for more information about Mackett, his bringing Drury home in 1717, and his subsequent sailing ventures.

24. XVII, 250.

25. In his *Defoe in the Pillory* and *Defoe's Sources for "Robert Drury's Journal"* (Bloomington: 1943). See also two articles in *Notes and Queries* by him in 1943 and 1945. There are two other articles, by A. W. Secord, one in *Notes and Queries* for 1945 and another in JEGP, XLIV (1945), 66–73.

26. *Defoe's Sources,* p. 11.

27. For the vocabulary itself see the 1890 edition, pp. 319–336; and for discussions of it see the Rev. J. Richardson in the same book, pp. 316–319; Moore, *Defoe in the Pillory,* pp. 108–109; and *Defoe's Sources,* pp. 74–79.

28. See Moore, *Defoe's Sources,* pp. 52–53.

29. *Ibid.,* pp. 37 ff.

30. *Ibid.,* pp. 29 ff.

31. Moore, *Defoe in the Pillory,* p. 105.

32. Moore, *Defoe's Sources,* pp. 16–18.

33. *Ibid.,* p. 85.

34. For a discussion of Defoe's part in the South Sea Bubble, see Dottin, pp. 751 ff. See also W. B. Ewald, *The Masks of Jonathan Swift* (Oxford: 1954), who blames it on "such projectors as Defoe," while Arthur E. Case, *Four Essays on Gulliver's Travels* (Princeton: 1945), pp. 88–89, seems to blame it all on Defoe.

35. For this summary of Defoe's mannerisms, I am indebted most to Professor Moore's convincing and interesting discussions in his two books on Defoe's sources.

36. *Colonel Jack,* edited by Aitken (London: 1900), II, 157.

37. Cox, II, 267, is confused about Coreal, spelling his name Correal, listing the Amsterdam edition as being in two volumes, and omitting both the Paris edition and the Brussels reprint. Sabin says there was a 1738 Amsterdam edition, but no one else seems to have seen it. All references hereinafter to Coreal will be to the first volume of the Paris, two-volume edition.

38. Among those who have said so is Chinard, *L'Amérique,* pp. 347, 351, 353.

39. II, (July–September, 1722), 1–17, 3–18.

40. *Dictionnaire historique* (La Haye: 1758–1759), II, 197.

41. See, for example, the *Bibliotheca historica* (Lipsiae: 1782–1804), III, 241–242. See also Pinkerton, XVII, 208, and Boucher de la Richarderie, *Bibliographie universelle des voyages,* (Paris: 1808), V, 504–505, 6 vols.

42. (1846), I, 31.

43. Joseph Thomas (4th ed.; Philadelphia: 1915), I, 716; and the *New Century* (New York: 1954), I, 1087.

44. Coreal, p. 7; *Atlas Geographus,* V, 574. The author of the present book is responsible for any translation of Coreal used herein.

45. Coreal, p. 55; *Atlas,* p. 652; Rogers, *A Cruising Voyage round the World* (London: 1712), p. 327; *The Compleat Geographer* (London: 1709), II, 260; Careri, in Churchill (London: 1704), IV, 508.

46. Coreal, pp. 173–180; *Atlas,* pp. 260–262.

47. Coreal, pp. 11–12; *Atlas,* pp. 564–568.

48. Coreal, pp. 23–46; *Atlas,* pp. 676–682.

49. "L'Amérique," *Description de tout l'univers* (Amsterdam: 1700), p. 17.

50. P. 95.

51. Coreal, pp. 81–82; *Atlas,* p. 546.

52. Coreal, p. 4; *Atlas,* pp. 39, 501.

53. For the evidence on Leguat, see Atkinson, *Extraordinary Voyage,* pp. 115–118; for Defoe's use of the device, see Moore, *Defoe's Sources,* pp. 50–51.

54. Coreal, p. 326; Père Louis Feüillée, *Journal des Observations physiques, mathématiques et botaniques . . . sur les côtes orientales de l'Amérique Meridionale* (Paris: 1714–1725), II, 590–592.

55. Pp. 312, 316.

56. Coreal, pp. 313–316; Frézier, *A Voyage to the South Seas, and along the Coasts of Chili and Peru In the Years 1712, 1713, and 1714* (London: 1717), pp. 253–254 (first edition at Paris, 1716). For the charts see Coreal, pp. 304–305, 324–325; Frézier, pp. 194–195, 206–207; Feüillée, I, 498–499. Others of Coreal's charts can be found in Froger and Careri.

57. For the *colibri,* see Coreal, p. 180, and the *Atlas,* pp. 268, 540.

58. Coreal, p. 65; *Atlas,* pp. 520, 617.

59. Coreal, pp. 81–82; *Atlas,* p. 546.

60. Coreal, p. 305; *Atlas,* p. 230.

61. For example, see Gueudeville, *Atlas Historique* (Paris: 1705–1720), VI, 135; or Frézier, p. 218, whose population figures are hopelessly confused.

62. P. 70. As a cure for syphilis, Guaiac was written about before 1600, with jokes being made then about the West Indies supplying both the disease and the cure. See, for example, Cawley, pp. 313–314.

63. P. 20.

64. P. 148.

65. P. 437. This scene is a dramatizing of the reputed forcing of saint-idol worship on the Indians of Central America, a strong tradition stemming especially from Thomas Gage in the middle seventeenth century. See, for example, *Thomas Gage's Travels in the New World,* edited with an introduction by J. Eric S. Thompson (Norman, Oklahoma: 1958), pp. 237–240.

66. P. 71.

67. Pp. 143–144.

68. For these three, see Edward O. Seeber, "The Authenticity of *The Voyage of Richard Castleman,* 1726," *The Papers of the Bibliographical Society of America,* XXXVII (Third Quarter, 1943), 261–275; Whitfield J. Bell, Jr., "Thomas Anbury's *Travels through America:* A Note on Eighteenth-Century Plagiarism," *The Papers of the Bibliographical Society of America,* XXXVII (First Quarter, 1943), 23–37; and Robson-Scott, pp. 175–176.

69. See Cox, I, 198, and *Biographie Universelle,* edited by J. F. and L. G. Michaud (Vives: 1842–1865), VIII, 46. Pinkerton's *Bibliography* (1814) warned the public about Chantreau, but Lowndes recommended his "original information."

70. For more precise details see Percy G. Adams, "Notes on Crèvecoeur," *American Literature*, XX, no. 3 (November, 1948), 327–333.

71. For the exposure and the defense see the present writer's articles in *The French-American Review* (July–September, 1949), pp. 115–134; in *Pennsylvania History*, XIV, no. 4 (October, 1947), 273–280; in *American Literature*, XX, no. 3 (November, 1948), 327–333, and XXV, no. 2 (May, 1953), 152–169; and in the introduction to Crèvecoeur, *Eighteenth-Century Travels in Pennsylvania and New York*, translated and edited by Percy G. Adams (Lexington, Kentucky: 1961).

72. For example, in 1801 there also occurred the amusing but short-lived incident of the many travel volumes attributed to three different writers, all of whom turned out to be the same person who "succeeded for a short time in deceiving geographers and publishers in three countries." [Gove, p. 401] Gove fills up three pages with the bibliography of this fireside traveler.

73. J. Scott Keltrie, "Fictitious Travel and Phantom Lands," *Harper's Monthly Magazine*, CXV (1907), 186.

CHAPTER VII: FANTASTIC MEMORIES

1. *The Tempest*, I, ii, 99.

2. This information about Ingram and his influence is taken from "The Relation of David Ingram," transcribed in full in *The Magazine of American History*, IX (March, 1883), 200–209; from B. F. De Costa, "Ingram's Journey through North America, 1567–1569," in the same issue of the same magazine; from Brebner, pp. 142–143, 168–177; from William H. Durham and Stanley M. Pargellis, *Complaint and Reform in England, 1436–1714* (New York: 1938), pp. 293 ff.; and from Franklin T. McCann, *English Discovery of America to 1585* (New York: 1952), pp. 180–182. For a recent defense of Ingram, read Emmett De Golyer, *The Journey of Three Englishmen across Texas* (El Paso: 1947).

3. By De Costa (see note 2) and by P. C. G. Weston in London, 1856.

4. Brebner, p. 143.

5. The oft-repeated story of de Fuca is to be found in its completest form in Wagner, "Apocryphal Voyages," pp. 184 ff.; Crouse, pp. 107 ff., 311, 347, 348; and, for the original documents by Michael Lok, Samuel Purchas, *His Pilgrimage* (London: 1625), III, 849 ff.

6. See introduction to Alexander Henry, *Travels and Adventures in Canada and the Indian Territories between the years 1760 and 1776*, edited by James Bain (Boston: 1901).

7. Crouse, *In Quest of the Western Ocean*, p. 116.

8. Wagner, "Apocryphal Voyages," p. 190.

9. More information about Peñalosa may be found in Wagner, pp. 201–202; Gaither, pp. 194–196; Delanglez, *Some La Salle Journeys*; Folmer, pp. 137–167. There are also two books: C. Fernandez Duro, *Don Diego Penalosa* (Madrid: 1882), and John G. Shea, *The Expedition of Don Diego Dionisio de Penalosa* (New York: 1882).

10. Wagner, "Apocryphal Voyages," p. 201.

11. Gaither, p. 196.

12. For all this information on Pénicaut, see Elizabeth McCann, "Péni-caut and His Chronicle of Early Louisiana," *Mid-America,* XXIII (October, 1941), 288–305.

13. *Ibid.,* p. 288.

14. *Ibid.*

15. In his *Histoire et description générale de la Nouvelle-France* (1744).

16. *Découvertes et établissements des Français* (Paris: 1876–1878), V, 375–586.

17. For example, Peter J. Hamilton, *Colonial Mobile* (Cambridge: 1910).

18. Abbé Coyer, *Oeuvres complètes* (Paris: 1783), II, 462.

19. For Pernetty and the *Chronicle,* see chap. ii. Also, for only one example, see the *Journal Encyclopédique* (July, 1767), pp. 85–94.

20. F. A. Kirkpatrick, *The Story of Exploration and Adventure,* edited by Sir Percy Sykes (London: 1949c), III, 747.

CHAPTER VIII: PECULIAR PLAGIARISMS

1. From *The Praise of Folly.*

2. This account of the Jenner–Byrd affair is a reworking of the present author's article, "The Real Author of *William Byrd's Natural History of Virginia,*" *American Literature,* XXVIII, no. 2 (May, 1956) 211–220.

3. He became "President," however, shortly before he died, some six years after the signing of the purchase contract. See Louis B. Wright and Marion Tinling, introduction to *The Secret Diary of William Byrd, 1709–1712* (Richmond: 1941), p. x; or P. A. Bruce, *The Virginia Plutarch* (Chapel Hill: 1929), I, 151.

4. Edited and translated from the German by Richmond Croom Beatty and William J. Mulloy (Richmond: 1940). The translations given above and taken from the German are found in the introduction to this book, p. xxiv and p. xxv. For the information about Byrd's land ventures I am indebted to Mr. Beatty's introduction and to his book, *William Byrd of Westover* (Boston and New York: 1932), pp. 213 ff.

5. For example, see *The Literary History of the United States,* edited by Spiller, *et al.* (New York: 1948), III, 429; and *The Literature of the American People,* edited by A. H. Quinn (New York: 1951), pp. 995–996.

6. Jay B. Hubbell, in a review of *William Byrd's Natural History of Virginia,* in *American Literature,* XIII (May, 1941), 186. But this review does praise the editors for recognizing the importance of the *Neu-gefundenes Eden.*

7. First published as *A New Voyage to Carolina,* apparently in 1709, in John Stevens, *A New Collection of Voyages and Travels* (London: 1708, 1711), Lawson's book was republished separately in 1709 and, as *The History of Carolina,* again in 1714 and 1718. It was translated into German in 1712, this edition being reissued in 1722. The latest edition, that of Francis L. Harriss, is called *Lawson's History of North Carolina* (Richmond: 1937). Hereinafter, all references to Lawson are to the 1937 edition.

8. See Jenner, p. 60, and Lawson, p. 144. Among other commentators treating this subject were Beverley, Chastellux, Crévecoeur, and Barbé-Marbois, all of whom correctly related the sizes of the two birds.

9. Jenner, p. 83; Lawson, p. 171.

10. Boyd edition, p. 314.

11. First published in London in 1705 and republished in 1722, this book was very popular on the Continent, with four French issues by 1718. The present study makes use of the edition by Louis B. Wright (Chapel Hill: 1947).

12. Jenner also took from Beverley information on Indian corn [see Jenner, p. 20; Beverley, pp. 143–144; and Lawson, p. 76] and the cherry tree [see Jenner, p. 34, and Beverley, pp. 129–130]. Still other natural history facts taken from Beverley have to do with the various kinds of berries more suitable to Virginia than to Carolina and with the amusing but harmful effects of the Jamestown weed, a story that even the propagandist could not resist [see Jenner, pp. 38–39, and Beverley, pp. 131, 137–139].

13. Introduction to *William Byrd's Natural History of Virginia,* p. xxvi.

14. Compare, for example, Jenner, pp. 1–3, with Lawson, pp. 80–90; Jenner, pp. 7–8, with Beverley, pp. 120–121; Jenner, pp. 87–88, with Lawson, p. 205; and Jenner, pp. 92–93, with Beverley, p. 230.

15. As the editors of what is called *William Byrd's Natural History of Virginia* point out, pp. xxvi, 6–17.

16. The following account of Brickell's hoax is a reworking of Percy G. Adams, "John Lawson's Alter-Ego—Dr. John Brickell," *The North Carolina Historical Review,* XXXIV, no. 3 (July, 1957), 313–327.

17. Some biographical information is to be found in the preface to the 1911 Raleigh edition, edited by J. Bryan Grimes. Hereinafter references to Brickell will be to this edition. Apparently the only contemporaneous notice of the book was one in the *Journal des Sciences* for April, 1739.

18. Published in London in two volumes. In the treatment of Virginia, Carolina, Georgia, and Florida, Brickell is often quoted and referred to.

19. Michaux's work was translated into English as *The North American Sylva* (Philadelphia: 1817), 3 vols., and went through many editions. For the use of Brickell, see I, 157, and II, 222.

20. N.s., IV (July, 1821), 102.

21. *North American Review,* n.s., XIV (October, 1826), 288–289n. Sparks was incorrect in his opinion that Lawson's book was rare. See note 7.

22. C. M. Andrews, *The Colonial Period of American History* (New York: 1934), III, 258; and G. G. Johnson, *Ante-Bellum North Carolina* (Chapel Hill: 1937).

23. II, 103.

24. Masterson, *Journal of American Folklore,* XIX (January–March, April–June, 1948), 51–67, 174–188.

25. H. T. Lefler (Chapel Hill: 1948), pp. 61–65.

26. H. T. Lefler and A. R. Newsome, *North Carolina, The History of a Southern State* (Chapel Hill: 1954).

27. See the *North Carolina Historical Review:* W. Neil Franklin, "Agri-

culture in Colonial North Carolina," III (October, 1926), 539–575; Charles Christopher Crittenden, "Inland Navigation, in North Carolina," VIII (April, 1931), 145–155; Douglas L. Rights, "The Buffalo in North Carolina," IX (July, 1932), 242–250; Julia Cherry Spruill, "Virginia and Carolina Homes before the Revolution," XII (October, 1935), 320–341; Spruill, "Southern Housewives before the Revolution," XIII (January, 1936), 25–47; Alonzo Thomas Dill, "History of Eighteenth Century New Bern," XXII–XXIII, in 8 parts (January, 1945—October, 1946); Wendell H. Stephenson, "John Spencer Bassett as a Historian of the South," XXV (July, 1948), 289–318.

28. Franklin [see note 27, above].

29. The two tables of contents:

Preface [Lawson]		Preface [Brickell]	
Introduction			
Journal of a thousand miles . . .	(1–61)		
A Description of North Carolina	(61–75)	[No title in Brickell, but the contents fit the corresponding title in Lawson]	(1–14)
A Description of the Corn of Carolina	(75–80)	The Corn of North Carolina	(14–27)
The Present State of Carolina	(80–90)	The Present State of Carolina	(27–35)
		The Religion, Houses, Raiment, . . .	(35–57)
Of the Vegetables of Carolina	(90–118)	The Vegetables of North Carolina	(57–107)
The Beasts of Carolina	(118–140)	Of the Beasts	(107–171)
Birds of Carolina	(140–159)	Of the Birds	(171–215)
The Fish . . .	(159–172)	Of the Fish of North Carolina	(215–251)
The Present State of Carolina	(172–179)	Further Observations on the Present State of North Carolina	(251–277)
An Account of the Indians of North Carolina	(179–260)	An Account of the Indians of North Carolina	(277–409)

30. P. 160. For the "flies" see p. 160. For the "Ipecacuana" see p. 21; this plant, not mentioned by Lawson, was one of the many North American substitutes for the tropical "Ipecacuanha." For the diseases see pp. 46–50.

31. Pp. 114–115.

32. After reading Brickell's twenty-two pages, compare Lawson, pp. 14, 82–90.

33. Brickell, pp. 153–171; Lawson, p. 139. For a few other original passages see Brickell, pp. 215–220, and Lawson, pp. 162–163; Brickell, p. 178; Brickell, pp. 187–188, and Lawson, pp. 149–150; and Brickell, p. 357.

34. Brickell, pp. 332 ff., and Lawson, pp. 34 ff.; Brickell, p. 343, and Lawson, pp. 44–45.

35. Pp. 387–393.

36. For the articles, compare Franklin, p. 561, Brickell, pp. 16–17, and Lawson, p. 277; Franklin, p. 357, Brickell, p. 15, and Lawson, p. 76. Compare Crittenden, pp. 148 ff., Brickell, p. 62, and Lawson, pp. 98–99; and Brickell, p. 32, with Lawson, p. 86. For the "full-length history," see Johnson, pp. 14, 48, 738–739; then compare Brickell, pp. 10, 48, 370, with Lawson, pp. 14, 19–20, 88–89. For "another book," compare the paragraph on exports in Lawson, p. 83, with that in Lefler, p. 65, which is quoted from Brickell, pp. 43–44.

37. Lefler and Newsome, p. 71.

38. The following account of Crèvecoeur's misuse of Franklin's name is a reworking of the present author's article, "Crèvecoeur and Franklin," *Pennsylvania History*, XIV, no. 4 (October, 1947), 2–8. For other information about Crèvecoeur's peculiar methods, as well as about his originality, see chapter vi.

39. See the *Voyage*, III, 349, and Carver, *Travels through the Interior Parts of North America* (Philadelphia: 1796), p. 85. Crèvecoeur borrowed from Carver more than once. For example, see chap. iii of the present book, note 36.

40. See *The Works of Benjamin Franklin* (Boston: 1838), VI, 485–488.

41. For the complete evidence of Crèvecoeur's use of Imlay, see the article mentioned in note 38, above.

42. James Parton, *Life and Times of Benjamin Franklin* (Boston: 1884), II, 559.

43. For the "popular anthology," see Evert A. Duyckinck and George L. Duyckinck, *Cyclopedia of American Literature*, I (New York: 1856), 175–177; the "biography" was that by Parton; one other writer who employed the false story was Bernard Faÿ, *Franklin, the Apostle of Modern Times* (Boston: 1939), p. 507.

44. Carl Van Doren, *Benjamin Franklin* (New York: 1938), p. 741.

45. *A Letter by Dr. Benjamin Rush Describing the Consecration of the German College at Lancaster in June, 1787*, edited by L. H. Butterfield (Lancaster, Pennsylvania: 1945), p. 35.

CHAPTER IX: TRAVEL CONTROVERSIES

1. Bishop Berkeley, *Alciphron* (1732), III, 52.

2. William H. Bonner, *Captain William Dampier: Buccaneer-Author. Some account of English Travel Literature in the Early Eighteenth Century* (Palo Alto: 1934), devotes two chapters to the influence on Defoe and one to that on Swift. For more on Dampier, see Clennel Wilkinson, *William Dampier* (London: 1929); Sir Albert Gray, introduction to *A New Voyage Round the World* (London: 1927); and J. C. Beaglehole, *The Exploration of the Pacific* (London: 1934), pp. 199 ff.

3. Beaglehole, p. 212.

4. Funnell's charges, the "Vindication," and the "Answer" are to be found in *William Dampier, Voyages,* edited by John Masefield (London: 1906), II, 576 ff.

5. *Ibid.,* p. 582.

6. For Welbe see *ibid.,* pp. 586 ff.

7. Smyth, *United Service Journal and Magazine,* parts 3 and 4 (1837); Bonner, p. 25; Masefield, II, 593; and Wilkinson, p. 188.

8. Wilkinson, p. 198; Masefield, II, 593.

9. Quoted in George Collingridge, *The Discovery of Australia, A critical investigation concerning the priority of discovery in Australasia by Europeans* (Sydney: 1895), p. 301. Welbe's exorbitant claims caused Collingridge to believe his story of being a captain. See also Burney, IV, 517, especially for the last part of this paragraph.

10. By John Philips, midshipman of the *Centurion* (1744); an anonymous "Officer of the Squadron" (1744); Pascoe Thomas, "teacher of the Mathematicks" on board the *Centurion* (1745); and Richard Walter, chaplain aboard the *Centurion* (1748). All of these books could have been ghostwritten. Walter's was the authorized one, going through sixteen editions by 1781 (Cox, I, 49), but the charge has been made that he did not write it. See, for example, the *Massachusetts Magazine,* I (April, 1789), 204, which says that the real author was someone named "Robin," meaning Benjamin Robins, F.R.S. [See also the *Gentleman's Magazine,* L (1780), 322.]

11. John Bulkeley and John Cummins, *A Voyage to the South Seas . . .* (London: 1743); Alexander Campbell, *The Sequel to Bulkeley and Cummins's Voyage to the South Seas . . .* (London: 1748): Isaac Morris, *A Narrative of the Dangers and Distresses Which befel Isaac Morris and Seven more of the Crew, Belonging to the Wager Store-Ship . . . A Supplement to Mr. Bulkeley's Journal, Campbell's Narrative, and Lord Anson's Voyage* (London: 1750); and Hon. John Byron, *The Narrative of the Hon. John Byron* (London: 1768). Campbell and Morris are rare, Byron was reissued in 1769 and was translated into other languages, while Bulkeley and Cummins were popular, with an edition of 1757 (London and Philadelphia) and modern editions, for example, that in New York, 1927, and London, 1928, with an introduction by Arthur D. Howden Smith, which also contains the papers on the court-martial proceedings, Morris' *Supplement,* and Bulkeley's statements in his defense.

12. Those by Thomas and Morris.

13. For only a few examples of this and the following assertions, see Bulkeley and Cummins (1757), pp. 29, 74–75.

14. *Ibid.,* p. 30.

15. Because Campbell's book is very rare, having been called in and suppressed. See Burney, V, 100.

16. For example, compare Byron, in Kerr, XVII, 333, with Bulkeley and Cummins, pp. 30–31; and Byron (1768), p. 218, with Frézier (London: 1717), p. 99.

17. (15th ed.; London: 1776), pp. 146–155.

18. For the complete story of this controversy, see the *Critical Review,* I (January, February, March, 1791), 84 ff.; William Ray Manning, *The*

Nootka Sound Controversy (Washington: 1905), which is a reprint of a 1904 Chicago dissertation; Sir J. K. Laughton, "Dixon, George," and "Meares, John," DNB; David Lavender, *The Drive for the Pacific Northwest* (New York: 1958); and especially, F. W. Howay, introduction to *The Dixon-Meares Controversy* (Toronto: 1929). Dixon's *Voyage Round the World* (London: 1789) was written by William Beresford, who accompanied him.

19. Howay, pp. 12, 19.

20. P. 87.

21. Quoted by Howay, p. 8.

22. *Ibid.*, p. 22.

23. The literature on the *Bounty* story is, of course, voluminous. The following account is most indebted to George Mackaness, introduction to the Everyman edition, *A Book of the Bounty* (London: 1938), which contains the "Minutes of the Court Martial" and the affidavits referred to here; the several books by Bligh himself; *The Saga of the Bounty; Its Strange History as related by the Participants Themselves,* edited by Irvin Anthony (New York: 1935); James Michener and A. Grove Day, *Rascals in Paradise* (New York: 1957), pp. 147–179; and A. G. L. Shaw, *The Story of Australia* (New York: 1956). See also Mackaness, *Life of Vice-Admiral William Bligh* (rev. ed.; New York: 1936; Sydney: 1951); and Owen Ritter, *Turbulent Journey: A Life of William Bligh* (London: 1936). For many other, especially earlier, references, see Cox, II, 305.

24. See James Norman Hall, *The Tale of a Shipwreck* (Boston and New York: 1934), p. 69, as taken from Sir John Barrow. See also Sir J. K. Laughton, "Christian, Fletcher," DNB.

25. Nearly all students of the *Bounty* affair, Mackaness, for example, agree that these highly romantic letters are "entirely fictitious" (Cox, II, 486) or "an impudent imposture" (Laughton, in DNB). But see Irvin Anthony, editor of *The Saga of the Bounty* (New York: 1935), who prints three of the spurious letters as being authentic.

26. Mackaness, introduction to *A Book of the Bounty*, treats most of these points at length, as do Michener and Day.

27. For example, Anthony [note 25], p. xii, who not only blames Bligh for this mutiny but for the later mutiny when he was Governor of New South Wales, as does Laughton in the DNB, article "Bligh, William." See Shaw, pp. 55 ff., and Michener and Day, pp. 167 ff., however, for the abundant evidence that the revolt in Australia was the result of Bligh's high-principled and determined attack on corruption and theft. See the article "Bounty, Mutiny of the," in both the *Encyclopædia Britannica* (1959) and the *Encyclopædia Americana* (1958), for examples of the popular reference books referred to.

28. See Cox, I, 47, for complete titles and for more details, including the fact that this voyage supplied the inspiration for the Ancient Mariner's albatross.

29. XLIII, 290.

30. See Cox, I, 11, 27, 63, who must be supplemented by F. W. Howay, "Authorship of the anonymous account of Captain Cook's Last Voyage,"

Washington Historical Quarterly, XII (January, 1921), 51–59. Without Howay's evidence, Jared Sparks, *The Life of John Ledyard* (Cambridge and New York: 1828), p. 116, was able to admire Ledyard's style and believe that "the confidence and particularity with which he speaks would seem to indicate actual observation."

31. For the complete story, with quotations from letters and archives, see R. Foulché-Delbosc, *Bibliographie des Voyages en Espagne et Portugal* (Paris: 1896), pp. 122–124; P. Fournier, *Les Voyageurs naturalistes du Clergé français avant la revolution* (Paris: 1932), pp. 39–40, tells of a similar situation involving J.-B. du Tertre and the Chevalier de Rochefort.

32. *Recueil de voiages . . . au nord* (Paris: 1725–1738), VIII.

33. *Ibid.*, pp. 3, 5.

34. Note, however, that Cox, I, 330, without offering evidence, believes that Brand showed himself to be "full of inconsistencies and improbabilities."

35. See the title page of *Examen critique des Voyages dans l'Amérique septentrionale de M. le Marquis de Chastellux . . .* (London: 1786).

36. Brissot's *Réponse à une critique des "Lettres d'un cultivateur américain, des quakers," . . .* (Paris: 1788), was one of the numerous answers to those who on both sides of the Channel charged Crèvecoeur with making America too attractive, for example, the anonymous *Remarks on the letters from an American Farmer; or, a Detection of the Errors of Mr. J. Hector St. John, pointing out the pernicious tendencies of these Letters to Great Britain* (London: 1782).

37. *Nouveau voyage dans les Etats-Unis* (Paris: 1791), II, 116.

38. Chastellux, I, 264; Brissot, I, 174–175.

39. Chastellux, I, 25; Brissot, I, 124.

40. Brissot had pursued this line of attack even harder in the *Examin critique* (1786), calling Chastellux's reports "poison" (p. 1) and writing long defenses of both Blacks and Quakers against what were considered the prejudices of the Marquis (pp. 48–65, 82 ff., for example). For the periodical war that resulted between the friends of Brissot and the friends of Chastellux, see Bernard Faÿ, *Bibliographie critique des ouvrages français relatifs aux Etats-Unis (1770–1800)* (Paris: 1925), p. 63.

41. *A View of . . . Italy . . . described . . . by Mr. Baretti; compared with the Letters from Italy, written by Mr. Sharp* (London: 1768). See Cox, I, 137–140, for many of these details.

42. *Political Register*, III (1768), 189. For other examples of controversy over national prejudice see the battle of the Figaros in chapter i of the present book; and for the periodical war, involving such writers as Ashe, Janson, and Weld on one side, and Dwight, Cooper, and Irving on the other, see Jane Louise Mesick, "Famous Controversies," *The English Traveler in America, 1785–1835* (New York: 1922), pp. 270–298.

43. Grace A. Gill-Mark, *Une Femme de lettres au XVIIIe siècle, Anne-Marie du Boccage* (Paris: 1927), p. 80, who gathered her impression largely from the attitude of J.-J. Lefrançais de La Lande, *Voyage d'un français en Italie* (Venice: 1769). The best evidence for its popularity is to note the many editions of the *Nouveau voyage*.

44. De Blainville, *Travels through Holland* . . . *but especially Italy* (London: 1757), II, 409–410, 454.

45. P. Jean Baptiste Labat, *Voyages* . . . *en Espagne et en Italie* (London: 1757), II, 222, 225–226. The quotation from Pinkerton that follows is in Cox, I, 116.

46. R. Murris, *La Hollande et les Hollandais au XVIIe et au XVIIIe siècle vues par les français* (Paris: 1925), pp. 14–15.

47. See Camille Von Klenze, *The Interpretation of Italy during the Last Two Centuries* (Chicago: 1907), pp. 13–14, who believes that Misson's "information is often unreliable" and then offers as evidence from the two volumes two stories that Misson had heard and passed on, neither connected directly with religion.

48. Brebner, pp. 168, 182–183.

49. IV, 257.

50. Falkener's work, entitled *A Description of Patagonia* (Hereford: 1774), was published thirty years after his stay in South America. See chapter ii of the present book for his part in the affair of the Patagonian giants. For more details on Bougainville, the encyclopedists, and the Jesuits in Argentina, see Chinard, *L'Amérique*, pp. 368, 377, for example.

51. Henry Ward Church, "Corneille De Pauw, and the Controversy over his *Recherches philosophiques sur les américains*," PMLA, LI, no. 1 (March, 1936), 185.

52. Dom Pernetty, p. 34, made this just observation in his reply to the *Recherches*. Their controversy over the size of the Patagonians was one facet of the greater debate stemming from Buffon.

53. For more details of the early tradition, see Cawley, pp. 368–369.

54. P. 61.

55. P. 62.

56. *Nouveau voyage dans l'Amérique septentrionale en l'année 1781* (Paris: 1782), pp. 15, 39–40. See Faÿ, *Bibliographie critique*, p. 16, for the charge that Robin borrowed "a thousand details" from previous travelers, and for information about the public controversy between Robin and other French officers in the American army as reported in the *Mercure de France* (March, 1783), pp. 195–202. Charles H. Sherrill, *French Memories of Eighteenth Century America* (New York: 1915), pp. 224–25, gives the reports of all the French travelers cited here except Bayard and Bossu, but he does not relate the disagreements among them to the then current controversy over Buffon.

57. Bayard, *Voyage dans l'intérieur des Etats-Unis* . . . *pendant l'été de 1791* (Paris: 1797), pp. 130–131, 143. For the other travelers referred to in this paragraph, see Sherrill, pp. 124–125. The translation of St Méry employed here is that by Kenneth and Anna M. Roberts (Garden City, New York: 1947), p. 303.

58. (Amsterdam: 1777), pp. 196 ff. See also p. 204 for reports of very old natives of Amboina. Bossu also wrote *Nouveaux voyages aux Indes occidentales* (Paris: 1768). Rusk, I, 83, judges him "somewhat akin" to Hennepin and Lahontan because he adds "wonders" to others reported by his imaginative predecessors.

59. I, 96 ff. For other travelers on this side of the controversy—Mazzei, La Rochefoucauld, and Bonnet—see Sherrill, p. 125.

60. See Michael Kraus, "America and the Utopian Ideal," *Mississippi Valley Historical Review*, XXII (1936), 499. Mr. Kraus's excellent discussion does not, however, remind the reader of the very popular tradition that provided anti-Utopian statistics and opinions.

CHAPTER X: PREJUDICED TRAVELERS

1. Washington Irving, "English Writers on America."

2. De Pauw, quoted by Church, p. 189; Bernard, I, clv; and Bowen, agreeing with Charlevoix, p. 630; see also the *Journal des Sçavans* (July, 1739), p. 442.

3. Gilbert Chinard points this out in his edition of Chateaubriand, *Les Natchez* (Baltimore: 1932), pp. 52–53. See George Bancroft in the *North American Review* (April, 1824), p. 398, for an illustration of the continuance of this tradition.

4. J.-M. Carré, I, 69–70.

5. Paul Franklin Kirby, *The Grand Tour in Italy (1700–1800)* (New York: 1952), pp. 135–137.

6. Muralt, pp. 72, 83 ff. See Robson-Scott, pp. 129, 165 for some of the influence of these charges.

7. Quoted in Gill-Mark, p. 54, which uses the French original.

8. I, 358, 361; also see I, 3, 12, 14.

9. Robson-Scott, pp. 163 ff., 182, for these details and others on the German Anglophobia.

10. See Bamboat, pp. 75–77.

11. Frantz, p. 62, and, more particularly, H. M. Jones, "The Colonial Impulse: An Analysis of the 'Promotion' Literature of Colonization," *Proceedings of the American Philosophical Society*, XC (1946), 131–161.

12. Reprinted by W. K. Boyd in the *North Carolina Historical Review*, III (October, 1926), 599–621.

13. Douglass, *Summary . . . and Present State of the British Settlements in America* (London: 1755), 2 vols. See Henry Theodore Tuckerman, *America and Her Commentators* (New York: 1864), p. 185; the Marquise du Pin, *Journal d'une femme du cinquante ans* (Paris: 1914), 2 vols., translated by Walter Greer as *Recollections of the Revolution and the Empire* (New York: 1920).

14. Knox, *An Historical Journal of the Campaigns in North America for the years 1757 . . . 1760* (London: 1769), I, 12, 24.

15. Smythe, *A Tour in the United States of America* (London: 1784), 2 vols.; also see Tuckerman, pp. 188–192; for only some of Cobbett's reactions to America, see *A Year's Residence in the United States of America,* (2nd ed.; London: 1819); Bentham's charge is in Tuckerman, p. 208; for much more evidence that the British travelers of that period were prejudiced, see Mesick: Irving's five reasons are in the famous "English Writers on America."

16. Ashe, *Travels in America, performed in the year 1806* . . . (London: 1809), pp. 5–6. The British periodical was the *Quarterly Review,* I (May, 1809), 300, as quoted by Rusk, I, 103.

17. Beverley, p. 300, and the translation by Pierre Ribou, a reworking, apparently pirated, of that by Lombrail (Amsterdam: 1707).

18. Frantz, pp. 86, 87, 99. The three English anti-Catholics cited were John Ovington, Nathaniel Uring, and Alexander Hamilton.

19. See *Five Travel Scripts commonly attributed to Edward Ward,* with a bibliographical note by Howard William Troyer, The Facsimile Text Society (New York: 1933), pp. 5, 6, 7, 11.

20. For Misson, see chap. ix; for Coreal, see chap. vi of the present book.

21. Fleuriot, p. 139; Massias, *Le Prisonnier en Espagne, ou Coup d'oeil philosophique et sentimentale sur les Provinces de Catalogne et de Grenade* (Paris: 1798), p. 119.

22. For Feüillée and Bernard, see Bernard, I, clii; for Delisle, see Pernetty, *Histoire d'un voyage aux Isles Malouines* (Paris: 1770), I, 230–231n.

23. Macaulay is quoted, for example, by N. L. Torrey in a review of *Les Natchez,* edited by Gilbert Chinard, MLN, LI (1936), 472; Addison, *The Freeholder,* no. 7; *The American Magazine* (March, 1769) pp. 83–87.

24. Pinkerton, XIII, 255.

25. Published finally in 34 vols. in 1776 by Du Halde as *Lettres édifiantes et curieuses,* after having been started by Le Gobien in 1702. For two such reviews, see the *Journal des Sçavans* (August, 1738), pp. 481–484, and the *Mercure de France* (April, 1773).

26. Lockman, *Travels of the Jesuits into Various Parts of the World* (London: 1743), I, vi; and Bowen, II, 623.

27. De Pauw, *Recherches philosophiques sur les égyptiens et les chinois* (Berlin: 1773), II, 24–28. De Pauw also pounced gleefully on Du Halde's *Description de la Chine.*

28. Lawrence C. Wroth, "The Jesuit Relations from New France," *The Papers of the Bibliographical Society of America,* XXX, part 2 (1936), 110–150.

29. Pinot, *La Chine et la formation de l'esprit philosophique en France (1640–1740)* (Paris: 1932), pp. 159–180 especially; also see *The Jesuit Relations and Allied Documents* . . . *(1610–1791),* edited by Thwaites (Cleveland: 1896–1901), and Chinard, *L'Amérique et le rêve exotique.* For unqualified praise of the Jesuits, see Père Fournier and *La Grande Encyclopédie.*

30. Hoxie Neal Fairchild, *The Noble Savage, A Study in Romantic Naturalism* (New York: 1928). Also see Benjamin Bissell, *The American Indian in English Literature of the Eighteenth Century* (New Haven: 1925); and the writings of Gilbert Chinard and Lois Whitney.

31. A. O. Lovejoy, "The Supposed Primitivism of Rousseau's Discourse on Inequality," *Modern Philology,* XXI (November, 1923), 165–186; and Fairchild, pp. 120 ff.

32. P. 56.

33. For Beverley, see Wright, p. xxv; Lawson, p. 119; Colden, *History*

of the Five Indian Nations (New York: 1727), p. lv, as quoted in Frantz, p. 79; Bartram, *The Travels of William Bartram,* edited by Mark Van Doren; introduction by John Livingstone Lowes (New York: 1940), pp. 289–290.

34. Lahontan, in Pinkerton, XIII, 255–256; Michel Adanson, *Histoire naturelle du Senegal . . . 1749–1757,* translated in 1759 as *A Voyage to Senegal,* as quoted in Fairchild, pp. 146–147; Bossu, p. 219, for example; Le Vaillant, (London: 1790), pp. 130–131; and Cooper, preface to *Afloat and Ashore.*

35. See Chinard, *L'Amérique,* p. 186, for the possible indebtedness of Rousseau to Lahontan; Lawson's foreshadowing of Shaftesbury is noted by Frantz, p. 108.

36. See Colden, I, xlvii. Chinard, *L'Amérique,* pp. 167–187, gives a discussion of the contents and the versions of the *Dialogues.* The Adario motif has been discussed briefly by Chinard and Atkinson.

37. Hazard, II, 145.

38. Clark B. Firestone, *The Coasts of Illusion: A Study of Travel Tales* (New York: 1924), p. 353.

39. Chinard, *L'Amérique,* p. 170.

40. Pinkerton, XV, 421. Also see Frantz, p. 80.

41. Atkinson, *The Extraordinary Voyage . . . 1700 to 1720,* p. 31.

42. Drury (1890), p. 150; for Marshall see Sencourt, p. 168, and *John Marshall in India: notes and observations in Bengal 1668–1672,* edited by Shafaat Ahmad Khan (London: 1927); Bossu, pp. 272–276; Bayard, pp. 144–171; for Crèvecoeur, see Percy G. Adams, "Notes on Crèvecoeur," *American Literature,* XX (November, 1948), 27–33.

CHAPTER XI: MORE SINNED AGAINST THAN SINNING

1. Quoted by Dr. Johnson in *Idler,* no. 87, December 15, 1759. See also Boileau, *L'Art poétique,* Chant III, l. 48.

2. See George Bancroft, *History of the United States* (Boston: 1866), III, 167; Sparks, *Life of Cavelier de la Salle* (Boston: 1848), p. xviii; and Delanglez, *Journal of Jean Cavelier* (Chicago: 1938), p. 20 ff., who reviews the entire question of the mistreatment of Tonty.

3. For a detailed account of the Dobbs–Middleton controversy, see Crouse, *In Quest of the Western Ocean,* pp. 425 ff.

4. The details of Lederer's life may be found in these sources: Dieter Cunz, *The Maryland Germans, a History* (Princeton: 1948), and "John Lederer, Significance and Evaluation," *William and Mary Historical Magazine,* 2nd S. XXII (1942), 175–185; Douglas Rights, *The American Indian in North Carolina* (Durham: 1947); Lyman Carrier, "The Veracity of John Lederer," *William and Mary Historical Magazine,* 2nd S. XIX (1939), 435 ff.; and W. P. Cumming, "Geographical Misconceptions of the Southeast in the Cartography of the Seventeenth and Eighteenth Centuries," *Journal of Southern History,* IV (1938), 476–493. The latest and best

treatment is that by Professor Cumming in his edition of *The Discoveries of John Lederer* (Charlottesville: 1958).

5. There have been numerous reprintings of this journal, the original Latin of which has been lost. It is in Harris' *Navigantium bibliotheca* of 1705; appeared three times in the late nineteenth century, including one printing in German; and appeared four times since 1900, for example, in C. W. Alvord and L. Bidgood, *The First Explorations of the Trans-Allegheny Region by the Virginians, 1650–1674* (Cleveland: 1912), pp. 131–171; and W. P. Cumming (note 4).

6. See appendix in Cumming, "Geographical Misconceptions."

7. Thomas, V, 724–727 (See Alvord and Bidgood, p. 151); Ashe, "Was Lederer in Bertie County?" *The North Carolina Booklet,* XV (July, 1915), 33–38; and Cox, II, 71.

8. See note 5.

9. Francis Lister Hawks, *History of North Carolina* (Fayetteville, N. C.: 1857–1858), II, 43; and for Rattermann, see Cumming, "Geographical Misconceptions," p. 477.

10. "Geographical Misconceptions," note 4.

11. P. 482. See also *The Discoveries,* edited by Cummings, pp. 85–86.

12. "Geographical Misconceptions," p. 477.

13. XXXVI, 223–224, 325.

14. LIX, 544. Also see *Johnsonian Miscellanies,* edited by J. Birkbeck Hill (Oxford: 1897), II, 12.

15. Quoted in Sir Francis Head, *The Life of Bruce the Abyssinian Traveller* (London: 1830), pp. 298–299.

16. *Travels to Discover the Source of the Nile* (Edinburgh: 1790), III, 144.

17. Head, pp. 531–532.

18. *Travels,* III, 142–144.

19. III, 301–304.

20. See Thomas Seccombe, introduction to *The Adventures of Baron Munchausen* (New York: 1928).

21. *Ibid.,* p. xxxv.

22. See, for example, Walpole's letter to Miss Mary Berry, April 4, 1791, and another to the Rev. Robert Nares, December 14, 1792. It is true, however, that these letters were written after the publication of Bruce's book and after Munchausen had begun to make use of the incident.

23. Quoted by Seccombe.

24. *Gentleman's Magazine,* LIX (June, 1789), 543–546, for a full-length review.

25. The review in the *Chronicle* extended from June 10 to July, 1790. That in the *Critical Review* began in September, 1790, and lasted into December.

26. LXV (March, 1795), 205–207.

27. See the preface, *An Interesting Narrative of the Travels of James Bruce . . . To which are added notes and extracts, from the Travels of Dr. Shaw, M. Savary, and Memoirs of Baron de Tott* (2nd Amer. ed.; Boston: 1798), pp. iv–xv.

28. *Voyages and Travels to India, Ceylon, the Red Sea, Abyssinia, and Egypt in 1802–1806* (London: 1809–1811), in 4 vols.

29. *A Voyage to Abyssinia* (London: 1814).

30. *Ibid.*, pp. 295–297.

31. P. 244

32. Edward Daniel Clarke, Ll.D., *Travels in Various Countries of Europe, Asia and Africa* (4th ed.; London: 1816–1824), V, 88.

33. In a review of Thaddeus Mason Harris, *Natural History of the Bible* (Boston: 1820), *North American Review*, XIX (July, 1824), 88.

34. Major W. Cornwallis Harris, *The Highlands of Aethiopia* (London: 1844), III, 172–173.

35. Mansfield Parkyns, *Life in Abyssinia* (London: 1853), I, 372–373.

36. See, for example, Henry Dufton, *Narrative of a Journey through Abyssinia* (London: 1867), pp. 174–175; Augustus Wylde, *Modern Abyssinia* (London: 1901), p. 153; and Charles F. Rey, *The Real Abyssinia* (London: 1935), p. 61.

37. David Matthew, *Ethiopia, the Study of a Polity, 1540–1935* (London: 1947).

38. See note 1 above.

CHAPTER XII: THE VOYAGE ENDS

1. Lenglet Dufresnoy, *Méthode pour étudier l'histoire* (1713), paraphrased by Hazard, p. 35.

2. The Frenchman was Jean Chapelain, *Lettres*, edited by Tamizey de Larroque (Paris: 1880–1883), II, 340–341, as quoted by Atkinson, *Extraordinary Voyage*, p. 10; the bibliographer was Boucher, *Bibliographie universelle de voyages* (Paris: 1808), I, v. For further corroboration of this point, see Edward Arber, *Term Catalogues, 1668–1709 A.D.* (London: 1903–1906), III, viii; Bonner's chapter, "The Silver Age of Travel," and Kraus, *Literary Relations*, p. 212.

3. See Lane Cooper, *The Cambridge History of American Literature* (New York: 1943), I, 185; and, for the Elizabethans, Kraus, *Literary Relations*, p. 211, quoting Sir Walter Raleigh. For much on the kinds of fiction inspired by travel literature, see Atkinson, *Extraordinary Voyage*, pp. 6–7; and Harold Francis Watson, *The Sailor in English Fiction* (New York: 1931), pp. 98 ff.

4. This is an important thesis of Frantz, p. 71, for example, and is approved by Louis A. Landa in a review of Frantz, *Bibliography of Modern Studies Compiled for Philological Quarterly* (Princeton: 1950), I, 162. For contrary opinions see Hazard, p. 11, for example; Kraus, *Literary Relations*, p. 213; Atkinson, *Les Relations de voyages du XVIIᵉ siècle et l'évolution des idées* . . . (Paris: 1924); and the books of Chinard.

5. Chardin quoted in Hazard, p. 10; for Crèvecoeur, see Percy G. Adams, "The Historical Value of Crèvecoeur's *Voyage dans la haute Pensylvanie et dans New York*," *American Literature*, XXV, no. 2 (May, 1953), 155 ff.

6. For this and certain other facts in the present paragraph, see Frantz, pp. 159 ff., and von der Mühl, pp. 32 ff.

7. A short history of travel literature, by Professor George B. Parks, is in progress and should make this changing nature of voyage literature more apparent.

8. H. G. von Bretschneider was in England in 1772 [see Scott-Robson, pp. 184–186]; Crèvecoeur, *Letters from an American Farmer* (London: 1782), letter xi [see Howard C. Rice, *Le Cultivateur américain* (Paris: 1932), pp. 118 ff., for a discussion of the wide influence of this anecdote]; Cagliostro, *Confessions du comte de C——, avec l'histoire de ses voyages en Russie, Turquie, Italie et dans les Pyramides d'Egypte* (Cairo and Paris: 1787); and A. N. Radischev, *A Journey from St. Petersburg to Moscow* (St. Petersburg: 1790), p. 200. [There is much more to the Radischev story, for all of which I am indebted to Professor Roderick P. Thaler of Bishop's University.]

9. The chief thesis of Professor Frantz is that after the founding of the Royal Society and the pleas of Boyle "the average voyager strove to see clearly and record objectively." See especially pp. 38, 44, 48, 71. But for only one contrary opinion, see Moore, *Defoe*, p. 164.

10. P. cxlv.

11. For Le Comte, see Adolph Reichwein, *China and Europe, Intellectual and Artistic Contacts in the Eighteenth Century,* translated by J. C. Powell (New York: 1925), p. 21; and, for two other examples of the same charge, the criticisms of Careri given by Smollett and the historian John Adams.

12. For Shaftesbury, see Frantz, pp. 139–140; for Ashe, see John Grahame Brooks, *As Others See Us* (New York: 1908), p. 35; for Sterne, see *The Sentimental Journey,* Classics edition, p. 50; also see the *French Journals of Mrs. Thrale and Dr. Johnson,* edited by Tyson and Guppy (Manchester: 1932), p. 8.

13. For example, Captain John Covant of Portbury after reading Dampier [Bonner, p. 31]; J.-M. Carré, I, 53; Chinard, *l'Amérique,* p. 425.

14. *Gentleman's Magazine,* XXXVI (February, May, 1766), 80, 218–219; LIX (March, 1789), 237–238; LX (1790), 830.

15. Ricardo Quintana, *The Mind and Art of Jonathan Swift* (New York: 1936), p. 304.

16. Compare, for example, *The Narrative of the Hon. John Byron* (London: 1768), p. 218, with Frézier (London: 1717), p. 99.

17. Goethe, *Wilhelm Meister,* translated by T. Carlyle, Everyman edition, I, 249. Note Professor Moore's reference to the "considerable amount of cribbing . . . without which no eighteenth-century book of travel in England would be complete" [*Defoe,* p. 76].

18. For other examples of editorial errors caused by travel lies, see Tuckerman, pp. 379–381, 387–388; and Samuel Cole Williams, *Early Travelers in the Tennessee Country* (Johnson City, Tennessee: 1928), p. 323, who was still assuming that Chateaubriand had visited Tennessee.

19. Francis Edwards, Limited, *Voyages and Travels,* Catalogue 810, 1960, pp. 20, 90.

20. *Emile,* II, 423, as translated by Peter Beckford, *Familiar Letters from Italy to a Friend in England* (Salisbury: 1805), I, 2.

21. *Travels in North America,* edited by John Reinhold Forster (London: 1770–1771), I, 116–117. First published in Sweden, 1753–1761.

22. Masterson, p. 187. See Masterson's interesting attempt to "weigh the elements of folklore, mendacity, and humor in the compound known as the traveler's tale," as well as his theory that these stories of nature were the real beginning of the tall tale.

23. Some of these marvels, as well as many others, are to be found in *ibid.*, whose long essay has made it unnecessary for the present book to treat the question in a special chapter. For Weld's oft-repeated story, see Mesick, p. 271; Bossu (Paris: 1777), pp. 85–86; Benoît de Maillet, I, 58, II, 31; Rusoe, *Mémoires* (1800), as quoted by Rusk, I, 93; Bartram (Philadelphia: 1791), p. 277; Dumont, *Mémoires sur la Louisiane* (Paris: 1753), I, 103; Labat, *Nouveau voyage aux Isles de l'Amérique* (Paris: 1742), I, 316–318; for the snake stories see Masterson and Lucas, *Voyage au Levant* (Paris: 1704), I, 46; Brickell, p. 180; Bossu, I, 27n, as repeated by Masterson.

24. Dudley's three mistakes are in Masterson, pp. 54 ff.; Brickell was one who reported the whale strangling, p. 221; for Sloane see Masterson, p. 66; for Linnaeus see Ingersoll, p. 63; for Maupertuis see his "Origine des animaux," *Oeuvres* (Paris: 1752), p. 266.

25. *Histoire naturelle* (Paris: 1845). For Leguat, Careri, and Struys, see II, 307 ff.; for the Patagonians and dwarves, see Firestone's discussion, pp. 132 ff.; for the beaver's tale, see Masterson, p. 53. For other errors that Buffon fell into, see Ingersoll, p. 78, and Firestone, pp. 111, 128–132.

26. III, 310–328.

27. William Bosman, *A New and Accurate Description of the Coast of Guinea . . . written originally in Dutch* (London: 1705).

28. For a discussion of the myth of Russian wealth, see, especially, Albert Lortholary, *Le Mirage Russe en France au XVIIIᵉ siècle* (Paris: 1951), p. 281.

29. See Clara Marburg, *Sir William Temple: A Seventeenth Century "Libertine"* (New Haven: 1932), pp. 56–71, and Frantz, p. 146.

INDEX

A CATALOGUE OF
SELECTED DOVER BOOKS
IN ALL FIELDS OF INTEREST

A CATALOGUE OF SELECTED DOVER
BOOKS IN ALL FIELDS OF INTEREST

RACKHAM'S COLOR ILLUSTRATIONS FOR WAGNER'S RING. Rackham's finest mature work—all 64 full-color watercolors in a faithful and lush interpretation of the *Ring*. Full-sized plates on coated stock of the paintings used by opera companies for authentic staging of Wagner. Captions aid in following complete Ring cycle. Introduction. 64 illustrations plus vignettes. 72pp. 8⅝ x 11¼.   23779-6 Pa. $6.00

CONTEMPORARY POLISH POSTERS IN FULL COLOR, edited by Joseph Czestochowski. 46 full-color examples of brilliant school of Polish graphic design, selected from world's first museum (near Warsaw) dedicated to poster art. Posters on circuses, films, plays, concerts all show cosmopolitan influences, free imagination. Introduction. 48pp. 9⅜ x 12¼.
23780-X Pa. $6.00

GRAPHIC WORKS OF EDVARD MUNCH, Edvard Munch. 90 haunting, evocative prints by first major Expressionist artist and one of the greatest graphic artists of his time: *The Scream, Anxiety, Death Chamber, The Kiss, Madonna*, etc. Introduction by Alfred Werner. 90pp. 9 x 12.
23765-6 Pa. $5.00

THE GOLDEN AGE OF THE POSTER, Hayward and Blanche Cirker. 70 extraordinary posters in full colors, from Maitres de l'Affiche, Mucha, Lautrec, Bradley, Cheret, Beardsley, many others. Total of 78pp. 9⅜ x 12¼.   22753-7 Pa. $5.95

THE NOTEBOOKS OF LEONARDO DA VINCI, edited by J. P. Richter. Extracts from manuscripts reveal great genius; on painting, sculpture, anatomy, sciences, geography, etc. Both Italian and English. 186 ms. pages reproduced, plus 500 additional drawings, including studies for *Last Supper*, Sforza monument, etc. 860pp. 7⅞ x 10¾. (Available in U.S. only)
22572-0, 22573-9 Pa., Two-vol. set $15.90

THE CODEX NUTTALL, as first edited by Zelia Nuttall. Only inexpensive edition, in full color, of a pre-Columbian Mexican (Mixtec) book. 88 color plates show kings, gods, heroes, temples, sacrifices. New explanatory, historical introduction by Arthur G. Miller. 96pp. 11⅜ x 8½. (Available in U.S. only)   23168-2 Pa. $7.50

UNE SEMAINE DE BONTÉ, A SURREALISTIC NOVEL IN COLLAGE, Max Ernst. Masterpiece created out of 19th-century periodical illustrations, explores worlds of terror and surprise. Some consider this Ernst's greatest work. 208pp. 8⅛ x 11.   23252-2 Pa. $5.00

DRAWINGS OF WILLIAM BLAKE, William Blake. 92 plates from Book of Job, *Divine Comedy, Paradise Lost,* visionary heads, mythological figures, Laocoon, etc. Selection, introduction, commentary by Sir Geoffrey Keynes. 178pp. 8⅛ x 11.   22303-5 Pa. $4.00

ENGRAVINGS OF HOGARTH, William Hogarth. 101 of Hogarth's greatest works: *Rake's Progress, Harlot's Progress, Illustrations for Hudibras, Before and After, Beer Street and Gin Lane,* many more. Full commentary. 256pp. 11 x 13¾.   22479-1 Pa. $7.95

DAUMIER: 120 GREAT LITHOGRAPHS, Honore Daumier. Wide-ranging collection of lithographs by the greatest caricaturist of the 19th century. Concentrates on eternally popular series on lawyers, on married life, on liberated women, etc. Selection, introduction, and notes on plates by Charles F. Ramus. Total of 158pp. 9⅜ x 12¼.   23512-2 Pa. $5.50

DRAWINGS OF MUCHA, Alphonse Maria Mucha. Work reveals drafts-man of highest caliber: studies for famous posters and paintings, render-ings for book illustrations and ads, etc. 70 works, 9 in color; including 6 items not drawings. Introduction. List of illustrations. 72pp. 9⅜ x 12¼. (Available in U.S. only)   23672-2 Pa. $4.00

GIOVANNI BATTISTA PIRANESI: DRAWINGS IN THE PIERPONT MORGAN LIBRARY, Giovanni Battista Piranesi. For first time ever all of Morgan Library's collection, world's largest. 167 illustrations of rare Piranesi drawings—archeological, architectural, decorative and visionary. Essay, detailed list of drawings, chronology, captions. Edited by Felice Stampfle. 144pp. 9⅜ x 12¼.   23714-1 Pa. $7.50

NEW YORK ETCHINGS (1905-1949), John Sloan. All of important American artist's N.Y. life etchings. 67 works include some of his best art; also lively historical record—Greenwich Village, tenement scenes. Edited by Sloan's widow. Introduction and captions. 79pp. 8⅜ x 11¼.
                          23651-X Pa. $4.00

CHINESE PAINTING AND CALLIGRAPHY: A PICTORIAL SURVEY, Wan-go Weng. 69 fine examples from John M. Crawford's matchless private collection: landscapes, birds, flowers, human figures, etc., plus calligraphy. Every basic form included: hanging scrolls, handscrolls, album leaves, fans, etc. 109 illustrations. Introduction. Captions. 192pp. 8⅞ x 11¾.
                          23707-9 Pa. $7.95

DRAWINGS OF REMBRANDT, edited by Seymour Slive. Updated Lipp-mann, Hofstede de Groot edition, with definitive scholarly apparatus. All portraits, biblical sketches, landscapes, nudes, Oriental figures, classical studies, together with selection of work by followers. 550 illustrations. Total of 630pp. 9⅛ x 12¼.   21485-0, 21486-9 Pa., Two-vol. set $14.00

THE DISASTERS OF WAR, Francisco Goya. 83 etchings record horrors of Napoleonic wars in Spain and war in general. Reprint of 1st edition, plus 3 additional plates. Introduction by Philip Hofer. 97pp. 9⅜ x 8¼.
                          21872-4 Pa. $3.75

THE EARLY WORK OF AUBREY BEARDSLEY, Aubrey Beardsley. 157 plates, 2 in color: *Manon Lescaut, Madame Bovary, Morte Darthur, Salome,* other. Introduction by H. Marillier. 182pp. 8⅛ x 11. 21816-3 Pa. $4.50

THE LATER WORK OF AUBREY BEARDSLEY, Aubrey Beardsley. Exotic masterpieces of full maturity: *Venus and Tannhauser, Lysistrata, Rape of the Lock, Volpone,* Savoy material, etc. 174 plates, 2 in color. 186pp. 8⅛ x 11. 21817-1 Pa. $4.50

THOMAS NAST'S CHRISTMAS DRAWINGS, Thomas Nast. Almost all Christmas drawings by creator of image of Santa Claus as we know it, and one of America's foremost illustrators and political cartoonists. 66 illustrations. 3 illustrations in color on covers. 96pp. 8⅜ x 11¼. 23660-9 Pa. $3.50

THE DORÉ ILLUSTRATIONS FOR DANTE'S DIVINE COMEDY, Gustave Doré. All 135 plates from Inferno, Purgatory, Paradise; fantastic tortures, infernal landscapes, celestial wonders. Each plate with appropriate (translated) verses. 141pp. 9 x 12. 23231-X Pa. $4.50

DORÉ'S ILLUSTRATIONS FOR RABELAIS, Gustave Doré. 252 striking illustrations of *Gargantua and Pantagruel* books by foremost 19th-century illustrator. Including 60 plates, 192 delightful smaller illustrations. 153pp. 9 x 12. 23656-0 Pa. $5.00

LONDON: A PILGRIMAGE, Gustave Doré, Blanchard Jerrold. Squalor, riches, misery, beauty of mid-Victorian metropolis; 55 wonderful plates, 125 other illustrations, full social, cultural text by Jerrold. 191pp. of text. 9⅜ x 12¼. 22306-X Pa. $6.00

THE RIME OF THE ANCIENT MARINER, Gustave Doré, S. T. Coleridge. Dore's finest work, 34 plates capture moods, subtleties of poem. Full text. Introduction by Millicent Rose. 77pp. 9¼ x 12. 22305-1 Pa. $3.00

THE DORE BIBLE ILLUSTRATIONS, Gustave Doré. All wonderful, detailed plates: Adam and Eve, Flood, Babylon, Life of Jesus, etc. Brief King James text with each plate. Introduction by Millicent Rose. 241 plates. 241pp. 9 x 12. 23004-X Pa. $5.00

THE COMPLETE ENGRAVINGS, ETCHINGS AND DRYPOINTS OF ALBRECHT DURER. "Knight, Death and Devil"; "Melencolia," and more—all Dürer's known works in all three media, including 6 works formerly attributed to him. 120 plates. 235pp. 8⅜ x 11¼. 22851-7 Pa. $6.50

MAXIMILIAN'S TRIUMPHAL ARCH, Albrecht Dürer and others. Incredible monument of woodcut art: 8 foot high elaborate arch—heraldic figures, humans, battle scenes, fantastic elements—that you can assemble yourself. Printed on one side, layout for assembly. 143pp. 11 x 16. 21451-6 Pa. $5.00

THE COMPLETE WOODCUTS OF ALBRECHT DURER, edited by Dr. W. Kurth. 346 in all: "Old Testament," "St. Jerome," "Passion," "Life of Virgin," Apocalypse," many others. Introduction by Campbell Dodgson. 285pp. 8½ x 12¼.   21097-9 Pa. $6.95

DRAWINGS OF ALBRECHT DURER, edited by Heinrich Wolfflin. 81 plates show development from youth to full style. Many favorites; many new. Introduction by Alfred Werner. 96pp. 8⅛ x 11. 22352-3 Pa. $4.00

THE HUMAN FIGURE, Albrecht Dürer. Experiments in various techniques—stereometric, progressive proportional, and others. Also life studies that rank among finest ever done. Complete reprinting of *Dresden Sketchbook*. 170 plates. 355pp. 8⅜ x 11¼.   21042-1 Pa. $6.95

OF THE JUST SHAPING OF LETTERS, Albrecht Dürer. Renaissance artist explains design of Roman majuscules by geometry, also Gothic lower and capitals. Grolier Club edition. 43pp. 7⅞ x 10¾   21306-4 Pa. $2.50

TEN BOOKS ON ARCHITECTURE, Vitruvius. The most important book ever written on architecture. Early Roman aesthetics, technology, classical orders, site selection, all other aspects. Stands behind everything since. Morgan translation. 331pp. 5⅜ x 8½.   20645-9 Pa. $3.75

THE FOUR BOOKS OF ARCHITECTURE, Andrea Palladio. 16th-century classic responsible for Palladian movement and style. Covers classical architectural remains, Renaissance revivals, classical orders, etc. 1738 Ware English edition. Introduction by A. Placzek. 216 plates. 110pp. of text. 9½ x 12¾.   21308-0 Pa. $7.50

HORIZONS, Norman Bel Geddes. Great industrialist stage designer, "father of streamlining," on application of aesthetics to transportation, amusement, architecture, etc. 1932 prophetic account; function, theory, specific projects. 222 illustrations. 312pp. 7⅞ x 10¾.   23514-9 Pa. $6.95

FRANK LLOYD WRIGHT'S FALLINGWATER, Donald Hoffmann. Full, illustrated story of conception and building of Wright's masterwork at Bear Run, Pa. 100 photographs of site, construction, and details of completed structure. 112pp. 9¼ x 10.   23671-4 Pa. $5.00

THE ELEMENTS OF DRAWING, John Ruskin. Timeless classic by great Viltorian; starts with basic ideas, works through more difficult. Many practical exercises. 48 illustrations. Introduction by Lawrence Campbell. 228pp. 5⅜ x 8½.   22730-8 Pa. $2.75

GIST OF ART, John Sloan. Greatest modern American teacher, Art Students League, offers innumerable hints, instructions, guided comments to help you in painting. Not a formal course. 46 illustrations. Introduction by Helen Sloan. 200pp. 5⅜ x 8½.   23435-5 Pa. $3.50

THE ANATOMY OF THE HORSE, George Stubbs. Often considered the great masterpiece of animal anatomy. Full reproduction of 1766 edition, plus prospectus; original text and modernized text. 36 plates. Introduction by Eleanor Garvey. 121pp. 11 x 14¾. 23402-9 Pa. $6.00

BRIDGMAN'S LIFE DRAWING, George B. Bridgman. More than 500 illustrative drawings and text teach you to abstract the body into its major masses, use light and shade, proportion; as well as specific areas of anatomy, of which Bridgman is master. 192pp. 6½ x 9¼. (Available in U.S. only) 22710-3 Pa. $2.50

ART NOUVEAU DESIGNS IN COLOR, Alphonse Mucha, Maurice Verneuil, Georges Auriol. Full-color reproduction of *Combinaisons ornementales* (c. 1900) by Art Nouveau masters. Floral, animal, geometric, interlacings, swashes—borders, frames, spots—all incredibly beautiful. 60 plates, hundreds of designs. 9⅜ x 8-1/16. 22885-1 Pa. $4.00

FULL-COLOR FLORAL DESIGNS IN THE ART NOUVEAU STYLE, E. A. Seguy. 166 motifs, on 40 plates, from *Les fleurs et leurs applications decoratives* (1902): borders, circular designs, repeats, allovers, "spots." All in authentic Art Nouveau colors. 48pp. 9⅜ x 12¼. 23439-8 Pa. $5.00

A DIDEROT PICTORIAL ENCYCLOPEDIA OF TRADES AND INDUSTRY, edited by Charles C. Gillispie. 485 most interesting plates from the great French Encyclopedia of the 18th century show hundreds of working figures, artifacts, process, land and cityscapes; glassmaking, papermaking, metal extraction, construction, weaving, making furniture, clothing, wigs, dozens of other activities. Plates fully explained. 920pp. 9 x 12. 22284-5, 22285-3 Clothbd., Two-vol. set $40.00

HANDBOOK OF EARLY ADVERTISING ART, Clarence P. Hornung. Largest collection of copyright-free early and antique advertising art ever compiled. Over 6,000 illustrations, from Franklin's time to the 1890's for special effects, novelty. Valuable source, almost inexhaustible.
Pictorial Volume. Agriculture, the zodiac, animals, autos, birds, Christmas, fire engines, flowers, trees, musical instruments, ships, games and sports, much more. Arranged by subject matter and use. 237 plates. 288pp. 9 x 12. 20122-8 Clothbd. $13.50

Typographical Volume. Roman and Gothic faces ranging from 10 point to 300 point, "Barnum," German and Old English faces, script, logotypes, scrolls and flourishes, 1115 ornamental initials, 67 complete alphabets, more. 310 plates. 320pp. 9 x 12. 20123-6 Clothbd. $13.50

CALLIGRAPHY (CALLIGRAPHIA LATINA), J. G. Schwandner. High point of 18th-century ornamental calligraphy. Very ornate initials, scrolls, borders, cherubs, birds, lettered examples. 172pp. 9 x 13. 20475-8 Pa. $6.00

ART FORMS IN NATURE, Ernst Haeckel. Multitude of strangely beautiful natural forms: Radiolaria, Foraminifera, jellyfishes, fungi, turtles, bats, etc. All 100 plates of the 19th-century evolutionist's *Kunstformen der Natur* (1904). 100pp. 9⅜ x 12¼. 22987-4 Pa. $4.50

CHILDREN: A PICTORIAL ARCHIVE FROM NINETEENTH-CENTURY SOURCES, edited by Carol Belanger Grafton. 242 rare, copyright-free wood engravings for artists and designers. Widest such selection available. All illustrations in line. 119pp. 8⅜ x 11¼.
23694-3 Pa. $3.50

WOMEN: A PICTORIAL ARCHIVE FROM NINETEENTH-CENTURY SOURCES, edited by Jim Harter. 391 copyright-free wood engravings for artists and designers selected from rare periodicals. Most extensive such collection available. All illustrations in line. 128pp. 9 x 12.
23703-6 Pa. $4.00

ARABIC ART IN COLOR, Prisse d'Avennes. From the greatest ornamentalists of all time—50 plates in color, rarely seen outside the Near East, rich in suggestion and stimulus. Includes 4 plates on covers. 46pp. 9⅜ x 12¼. 23658-7 Pa. $6.00

AUTHENTIC ALGERIAN CARPET DESIGNS AND MOTIFS, edited by June Beveridge. Algerian carpets are world famous. Dozens of geometrical motifs are charted on grids, color-coded, for weavers, needleworkers, craftsmen, designers. 53 illustrations plus 4 in color. 48pp. 8¼ x 11. (Available in U.S. only) 23650-1 Pa. $1.75

DICTIONARY OF AMERICAN PORTRAITS, edited by Hayward and Blanche Cirker. 4000 important Americans, earliest times to 1905, mostly in clear line. Politicians, writers, soldiers, scientists, inventors, industrialists, Indians, Blacks, women, outlaws, etc. Identificatory information. 756pp. 9¼ x 12¾. 21823-6 Clothbd. $40.00

HOW THE OTHER HALF LIVES, Jacob A. Riis. Journalistic record of filth, degradation, upward drive in New York immigrant slums, shops, around 1900. New edition includes 100 original Riis photos, monuments of early photography. 233pp. 10 x 7⅞. 22012-5 Pa. $6.00

NEW YORK IN THE THIRTIES, Berenice Abbott. Noted photographer's fascinating study of city shows new buildings that have become famous and old sights that have disappeared forever. Insightful commentary. 97 photographs. 97pp. 11⅜ x 10. 22967-X Pa. $4.50

MEN AT WORK, Lewis W. Hine. Famous photographic studies of construction workers, railroad men, factory workers and coal miners. New supplement of 18 photos on Empire State building construction. New introduction by Jonathan L. Doherty. Total of 69 photos. 63pp. 8 x 10¾.
23475-4 Pa. $3.00

THE DEPRESSION YEARS AS PHOTOGRAPHED BY ARTHUR ROTH-STEIN, Arthur Rothstein. First collection devoted entirely to the work of outstanding 1930s photographer: famous dust storm photo, ragged children, unemployed, etc. 120 photographs. Captions. 119pp. 9¼ x 10¾.
23590-4 Pa. $5.00

CAMERA WORK: A PICTORIAL GUIDE, Alfred Stieglitz. All 559 illustrations and plates from the most important periodical in the history of art photography, Camera Work (1903-17). Presented four to a page, reduced in size but still clear, in strict chronological order, with complete captions. Three indexes. Glossary. Bibliography. 176pp. 8⅜ x 11¼.
23591-2 Pa. $6.95

ALVIN LANGDON COBURN, PHOTOGRAPHER, Alvin L. Coburn. Revealing autobiography by one of greatest photographers of 20th century gives insider's version of Photo-Secession, plus comments on his own work. 77 photographs by Coburn. Edited by Helmut and Alison Gernsheim. 160pp. 8⅛ x 11.
23685-4 Pa. $6.00

NEW YORK IN THE FORTIES, Andreas Feininger. 162 brilliant photographs by the well-known photographer, formerly with Life magazine, show commuters, shoppers, Times Square at night, Harlem nightclub, Lower East Side, etc. Introduction and full captions by John von Hartz. 181pp. 9¼ x 10¾.
23585-8 Pa. $6.00

GREAT NEWS PHOTOS AND THE STORIES BEHIND THEM, John Faber. Dramatic volume of 140 great news photos, 1855 through 1976, and revealing stories behind them, with both historical and technical information. Hindenburg disaster, shooting of Oswald, nomination of Jimmy Carter, etc. 160pp. 8¼ x 11.
23667-6 Pa. $5.00

THE ART OF THE CINEMATOGRAPHER, Leonard Maltin. Survey of American cinematography history and anecdotal interviews with 5 masters—Arthur Miller, Hal Mohr, Hal Rosson, Lucien Ballard, and Conrad Hall. Very large selection of behind-the-scenes production photos. 105 photographs. Filmographies. Index. Originally Behind the Camera. 144pp. 8¼ x 11.
23686-2 Pa. $5.00

DESIGNS FOR THE THREE-CORNERED HAT (LE TRICORNE), Pablo Picasso. 32 fabulously rare drawings—including 31 color illustrations of costumes and accessories—for 1919 production of famous ballet. Edited by Parmenia Migel, who has written new introduction. 48pp. 9⅜ x 12¼. (Available in U.S. only)
23709-5 Pa. $5.00

NOTES OF A FILM DIRECTOR, Sergei Eisenstein. Greatest Russian filmmaker explains montage, making of Alexander Nevsky, aesthetics; comments on self, associates, great rivals (Chaplin), similar material. 78 illustrations. 240pp. 5⅜ x 8½.
22392-2 Pa. $4.50

CATALOGUE OF DOVER BOOKS

HOLLYWOOD GLAMOUR PORTRAITS, edited by John Kobal. 145 photos capture the stars from 1926-49, the high point in portrait photography. Gable, Harlow, Bogart, Bacall, Hedy Lamarr, Marlene Dietrich, Robert Montgomery, Marlon Brando, Veronica Lake; 94 stars in all. Full background on photographers, technical aspects, much more. Total of 160pp. 8⅜ x 11¼. 23352-9 Pa. $5.00

THE NEW YORK STAGE: FAMOUS PRODUCTIONS IN PHOTO-GRAPHS, edited by Stanley Appelbaum. 148 photographs from Museum of City of New York show 142 plays, 1883-1939. *Peter Pan, The Front Page, Dead End, Our Town,* O'Neill, hundreds of actors and actresses, etc. Full indexes. 154pp. 9½ x 10. 23241-7 Pa. $4.50

MASTERS OF THE DRAMA, John Gassner. Most comprehensive history of the drama, every tradition from Greeks to modern Europe and America, including Orient. Covers 800 dramatists, 2000 plays; biography, plot summaries, criticism, theatre history, etc. 77 illustrations. 890pp. 5⅜ x 8½. 20100-7 Clothbd. $10.00

THE GREAT OPERA STARS IN HISTORIC PHOTOGRAPHS, edited by James Camner. 343 portraits from the 1850s to the 1940s: Tamburini, Mario, Caliapin, Jeritza, Melchior, Melba, Patti, Pinza, Schipa, Caruso, Farrar, Steber, Gobbi, and many more—270 performers in all. Index. 199pp. 8⅜ x 11¼. 23575-0 Pa. $6.50

J. S. BACH, Albert Schweitzer. Great full-length study of Bach, life, background to music, music, by foremost modern scholar. Ernest Newman translation. 650 musical examples. Total of 928pp. 5⅜ x 8½. (Available in U.S. only) 21631-4, 21632-2 Pa., Two-vol. set $9.00

COMPLETE PIANO SONATAS, Ludwig van Beethoven. All sonatas in the fine Schenker edition, with fingering, analytical material. One of best modern editions. Total of 615pp. 9 x 12. (Available in U.S. only) 23134-8, 23135-6 Pa., Two-vol. set $13.00

KEYBOARD MUSIC, J. S. Bach. Bach-Gesellschaft edition. For harpsichord, piano, other keyboard instruments. English Suites, French Suites, Six Partitas, Goldberg Variations, Two-Part Inventions, Three-Part Sinfonias. 312pp. 8⅛ x 11. (Available in U.S. only) 22360-4 Pa. $5.50

FOUR SYMPHONIES IN FULL SCORE, Franz Schubert. Schubert's four most popular symphonies: No. 4 in C Minor ("Tragic"); No. 5 in B-flat Major; No. 8 in B Minor ("Unfinished"); No. 9 in C Major ("Great"). Breitkopf & Hartel edition. Study score. 261pp. 9⅜ x 12¼. 23681-1 Pa. $6.50

THE AUTHENTIC GILBERT & SULLIVAN SONGBOOK, W. S. Gilbert, A. S. Sullivan. Largest selection available; 92 songs, uncut, original keys, in piano rendering approved by Sullivan. Favorites and lesser-known fine numbers. Edited with plot synopses by James Spero. 3 illustrations. 399pp. 9 x 12. 23482-7 Pa. $7.95

PRINCIPLES OF ORCHESTRATION, Nikolay Rimsky-Korsakov. Great classical orchestrator provides fundamentals of tonal resonance, progression of parts, voice and orchestra, tutti effects, much else in major document. 330pp. of musical excerpts. 489pp. 6½ x 9¼.   21266-1 Pa. $6.00

TRISTAN UND ISOLDE, Richard Wagner. Full orchestral score with complete instrumentation. Do not confuse with piano reduction. Commentary by Felix Mottl, great Wagnerian conductor and scholar. Study score. 655pp. 8⅛ x 11.   22915-7 Pa. $12.50

REQUIEM IN FULL SCORE, Giuseppe Verdi. Immensely popular with choral groups and music lovers. Republication of edition published by C. F. Peters, Leipzig, n. d. German frontmaker in English translation. Glossary. Text in Latin. Study score. 204pp. 9⅜ x 12¼.
23682-X Pa. $6.00

COMPLETE CHAMBER MUSIC FOR STRINGS, Felix Mendelssohn. All of Mendelssohn's chamber music: Octet, 2 Quintets, 6 Quartets, and Four Pieces for String Quartet. (Nothing with piano is included). Complete works edition (1874-7). Study score. 283 pp. 9⅜ x 12¼.
23679-X Pa. $6.95

POPULAR SONGS OF NINETEENTH-CENTURY AMERICA, edited by Richard Jackson. 64 most important songs: "Old Oaken Bucket," "Arkansas Traveler," "Yellow Rose of Texas," etc. Authentic original sheet music, full introduction and commentaries. 290pp. 9 x 12.   23270-0 Pa. $6.00

COLLECTED PIANO WORKS, Scott Joplin. Edited by Vera Brodsky Lawrence. Practically all of Joplin's piano works—rags, two-steps, marches, waltzes, etc., 51 works in all. Extensive introduction by Rudi Blesh. Total of 345pp. 9 x 12.   23106-2 Pa. $13.50

BASIC PRINCIPLES OF CLASSICAL BALLET, Agrippina Vaganova. Great Russian theoretician, teacher explains methods for teaching classical ballet; incorporates best from French, Italian, Russian schools. 118 illustrations. 175pp. 5⅜ x 8½.   22036-2 Pa. $2.00

CHINESE CHARACTERS, L. Wieger. Rich analysis of 2300 characters according to traditional systems into primitives. Historical-semantic analysis to phonetics (Classical Mandarin) and radicals. 820pp. 6⅛ x 9¼.
21321-8 Pa. $8.95

EGYPTIAN LANGUAGE: EASY LESSONS IN EGYPTIAN HIERO-GLYPHICS, E. A. Wallis Budge. Foremost Egyptologist offers Egyptian grammar, explanation of hieroglyphics, many reading texts, dictionary of symbols. 246pp. 5 x 7½. (Available in U.S. only)
21394-3 Clothbd. $7.50

AN ETYMOLOGICAL DICTIONARY OF MODERN ENGLISH, Ernest Weekley. Richest, fullest work, by foremost British lexicographer. Detailed word histories. Inexhaustible. Do not confuse this with *Concise Etymological Dictionary*, which is abridged. Total of 856pp. 6½ x 9¼.
21873-2, 21874-0 Pa., Two-vol. set $10.00

A MAYA GRAMMAR, Alfred M. Tozzer. Practical, useful English-language grammar by the Harvard anthropologist who was one of the three greatest American scholars in the area of Maya culture. Phonetics, grammatical processes, syntax, more. 301pp. 5⅜ x 8½.　　　　23465-7 Pa. $4.00

THE JOURNAL OF HENRY D. THOREAU, edited by Bradford Torrey, F. H. Allen. Complete reprinting of 14 volumes, 1837-61, over two million words; the sourcebooks for *Walden,* etc. Definitive. All original sketches, plus 75 photographs. Introduction by Walter Harding. Total of 1804pp. 8½ x 12¼.　　　　20312-3, 20313-1 Clothbd., Two-vol. set $50.00

CLASSIC GHOST STORIES, Charles Dickens and others. 18 wonderful stories you've wanted to reread: "The Monkey's Paw," "The House and the Brain," "The Upper Berth," "The Signalman," "Dracula's Guest," "The Tapestried Chamber," etc. Dickens, Scott, Mary Shelley, Stoker, etc. 330pp. 5⅜ x 8½.　　　　20735-8 Pa. $3.50

SEVEN SCIENCE FICTION NOVELS, H. G. Wells. Full novels. *First Men in the Moon, Island of Dr. Moreau, War of the Worlds, Food of the Gods, Invisible Man, Time Machine, In the Days of the Comet.* A basic science-fiction library. 1015pp. 5⅜ x 8½. (Available in U.S. only)
20264-X Clothbd. $8.95

ARMADALE, Wilkie Collins. Third great mystery novel by the author of *The Woman in White* and *The Moonstone.* Ingeniously plotted narrative shows an exceptional command of character, incident and mood. Original magazine version with 40 illustrations. 597pp. 5⅜ x 8½.
23429-0 Pa. $5.00

MASTERS OF MYSTERY, H. Douglas Thomson. The first book in English (1931) devoted to history and aesthetics of detective story. Poe, Doyle, LeFanu, Dickens, many others, up to 1930. New introduction and notes by E. F. Bleiler. 288pp. 5⅜ x 8½. (Available in U.S. only)
23606-4 Pa. $4.00

FLATLAND, E. A. Abbott. Science-fiction classic explores life of 2-D being in 3-D world. Read also as introduction to thought about hyperspace. Introduction by Banesh Hoffmann. 16 illustrations. 103pp. 5⅜ x 8½.
20001-9 Pa. $1.50

THREE SUPERNATURAL NOVELS OF THE VICTORIAN PERIOD, edited, with an introduction, by E. F. Bleiler. Reprinted complete and unabridged, three great classics of the supernatural: *The Haunted Hotel* by Wilkie Collins, *The Haunted House at Latchford* by Mrs. J. H. Riddell, and *The Lost Stradivarious* by J. Meade Falkner. 325pp. 5⅜ x 8½.
22571-2 Pa. $4.00

AYESHA: THE RETURN OF "SHE," H. Rider Haggard. Virtuoso sequel featuring the great mythic creation, Ayesha, in an adventure that is fully as good as the first book, *She.* Original magazine version, with 47 original illustrations by Maurice Greiffenhagen. 189pp. 6½ x 9¼.
23649-8 Pa. $3.00

UNCLE SILAS, J. Sheridan LeFanu. Victorian Gothic mystery novel, considered by many best of period, even better than Collins or Dickens. Wonderful psychological terror. Introduction by Frederick Shroyer. 436pp. 5⅜ x 8½.   21715-9 Pa. $4.00

JURGEN, James Branch Cabell. The great erotic fantasy of the 1920's that delighted thousands, shocked thousands more. Full final text, Lane edition with 13 plates by Frank Pape. 346pp. 5⅜ x 8½.
                                                          23507-6 Pa. $4.00

THE CLAVERINGS, Anthony Trollope. Major novel, chronicling aspects of British Victorian society, personalities. Reprint of Cornhill serialization, 16 plates by M. Edwards; first reprint of full text. Introduction by Norman Donaldson. 412pp. 5⅜ x 8½.   23464-9 Pa. $5.00

KEPT IN THE DARK, Anthony Trollope. Unusual short novel about Victorian morality and abnormal psychology by the great English author. Probably the first American publication. Frontispiece by Sir John Millais. 92pp. 6½ x 9¼.   23609-9 Pa. $2.50

RALPH THE HEIR, Anthony Trollope. Forgotten tale of illegitimacy, inheritance. Master novel of Trollope's later years. Victorian country estates, clubs, Parliament, fox hunting, world of fully realized characters. Reprint of 1871 edition. 12 illustrations by F. A. Faser. 434pp. of text. 5⅜ x 8½.   23642-0 Pa. $4.50

YEKL and THE IMPORTED BRIDEGROOM AND OTHER STORIES OF THE NEW YORK GHETTO, Abraham Cahan. Film *Hester Street* based on *Yekl* (1896). Novel, other stories among first about Jewish immigrants of N.Y.'s East Side. Highly praised by W. D. Howells—Cahan "a new star of realism." New introduction by Bernard G. Richards. 240pp. 5⅜ x 8½.   22427-9 Pa. $3.50

THE HIGH PLACE, James Branch Cabell. Great fantasy writer's enchanting comedy of disenchantment set in 18th-century France. Considered by some critics to be even better than his famous *Jurgen*. 10 illustrations and numerous vignettes by noted fantasy artist Frank C. Pape. 320pp. 5⅜ x 8½.   23670-6 Pa. $4.00

ALICE'S ADVENTURES UNDER GROUND, Lewis Carroll. Facsimile of ms. Carroll gave Alice Liddell in 1864. Different in many ways from final Alice. Handlettered, illustrated by Carroll. Introduction by Martin Gardner. 128pp. 5⅜ x 8½.   21482-6 Pa. $2.00

FAVORITE ANDREW LANG FAIRY TALE BOOKS IN MANY COLORS, Andrew Lang. The four Lang favorites in a boxed set—the complete *Red, Green, Yellow* and *Blue* Fairy Books. 164 stories; 439 illustrations by Lancelot Speed, Henry Ford and G. P. Jacomb Hood. Total of about 1500pp. 5⅜ x 8½.   23407-X Boxed set, Pa. $14.00

HOUSEHOLD STORIES BY THE BROTHERS GRIMM. All the great Grimm stories: "Rumpelstiltskin," "Snow White," "Hansel and Gretel," etc., with 114 illustrations by Walter Crane. 269pp. 5⅜ x 8½.
21080-4 Pa. $3.00

SLEEPING BEAUTY, illustrated by Arthur Rackham. Perhaps the fullest, most delightful version ever, told by C. S. Evans. Rackham's best work. 49 illustrations. 110pp. 7⅞ x 10¾.
22756-1 Pa. $2.00

AMERICAN FAIRY TALES, L. Frank Baum. Young cowboy lassoes Father Time; dummy in Mr. Floman's department store window comes to life; and 10 other fairy tales. 41 illustrations by N. P. Hall, Harry Kennedy, Ike Morgan, and Ralph Gardner. 209pp. 5⅜ x 8½.
23643-9 Pa. $3.00

THE WONDERFUL WIZARD OF OZ, L. Frank Baum. Facsimile in full color of America's finest children's classic. Introduction by Martin Gardner. 143 illustrations by W. W. Denslow. 267pp. 5⅜ x 8½.
20691-2 Pa. $3.50

THE TALE OF PETER RABBIT, Beatrix Potter. The inimitable Peter's terrifying adventure in Mr. McGregor's garden, with all 27 wonderful, full-color Potter illustrations. 55pp. 4¼ x 5½. (Available in U.S. only)
22827-4 Pa. $1.10

THE STORY OF KING ARTHUR AND HIS KNIGHTS, Howard Pyle. Finest children's version of life of King Arthur. 48 illustrations by Pyle. 131pp. 6⅛ x 9¼.
21445-1 Pa. $4.00

CARUSO'S CARICATURES, Enrico Caruso. Great tenor's remarkable caricatures of self, fellow musicians, composers, others. Toscanini, Puccini, Farrar, etc. Impish, cutting, insightful. 473 illustrations. Preface by M. Sisca. 217pp. 8⅜ x 11¼.
23528-9 Pa. $6.00

PERSONAL NARRATIVE OF A PILGRIMAGE TO ALMADINAH AND MECCAH, Richard Burton. Great travel classic by remarkably colorful personality. Burton, disguised as a Moroccan, visited sacred shrines of Islam, narrowly escaping death. Wonderful observations of Islamic life, customs, personalities. 47 illustrations. Total of 959pp. 5⅜ x 8½.
21217-3, 21218-1 Pa., Two-vol. set $10.00

INCIDENTS OF TRAVEL IN YUCATAN, John L. Stephens. Classic (1843) exploration of jungles of Yucatan, looking for evidences of Maya civilization. Travel adventures, Mexican and Indian culture, etc. Total of 669pp. 5⅜ x 8½.
20926-1, 20927-X Pa., Two-vol. set $6.50

AMERICAN LITERARY AUTOGRAPHS FROM WASHINGTON IRVING TO HENRY JAMES, Herbert Cahoon, et al. Letters, poems, manuscripts of Hawthorne, Thoreau, Twain, Alcott, Whitman, 67 other prominent American authors. Reproductions, full transcripts and commentary. Plus checklist of all American Literary Autographs in The Pierpont Morgan Library. Printed on exceptionally high-quality paper. 136 illustrations. 212pp. 9⅛ x 12¼.
23548-3 Pa. $7.95

AN AUTOBIOGRAPHY, Margaret Sanger. Exciting personal account of hard-fought battle for woman's right to birth control, against prejudice, church, law. Foremost feminist document. 504pp. 5⅜ x 8½.

20470-7 Pa. $5.50

MY BONDAGE AND MY FREEDOM, Frederick Douglass. Born as a slave, Douglass became outspoken force in antislavery movement. The best of Douglass's autobiographies. Graphic description of slave life. Introduction by P. Foner. 464pp. 5⅜ x 8½. 22457-0 Pa. $5.00

LIVING MY LIFE, Emma Goldman. Candid, no holds barred account by foremost American anarchist: her own life, anarchist movement, famous contemporaries, ideas and their impact. Struggles and confrontations in America, plus deportation to U.S.S.R. Shocking inside account of persecution of anarchists under Lenin. 13 plates. Total of 944pp. 5⅜ x 8½.

22543-7, 22544-5 Pa., Two-vol. set $9.00

LETTERS AND NOTES ON THE MANNERS, CUSTOMS AND CONDITIONS OF THE NORTH AMERICAN INDIANS, George Catlin. Classic account of life among Plains Indians: ceremonies, hunt, warfare, etc. Dover edition reproduces for first time all original paintings. 312 plates. 572pp. of text. 6⅛ x 9¼. 22118-0, 22119-9 Pa.. Two-vol. set $10.00

THE MAYA AND THEIR NEIGHBORS, edited by Clarence L. Hay, others. Synoptic view of Maya civilization in broadest sense, together with Northern, Southern neighbors. Integrates much background, valuable detail not elsewhere. Prepared by greatest scholars: Kroeber, Morley, Thompson, Spinden, Vaillant, many others. Sometimes called Tozzer Memorial Volume. 60 illustrations, linguistic map. 634pp. 5⅜ x 8½.

23510-6 Pa. $7.50

HANDBOOK OF THE INDIANS OF CALIFORNIA, A. L. Kroeber. Foremost American anthropologist offers complete ethnographic study of each group. Monumental classic. 459 illustrations, maps. 995pp. 5⅜ x 8½.

23368-5 Pa. $10.00

SHAKTI AND SHAKTA, Arthur Avalon. First book to give clear, cohesive analysis of Shakta doctrine, Shakta ritual and Kundalini Shakti (yoga). Important work by one of world's foremost students of Shaktic and Tantric thought. 732pp. 5⅜ x 8½. (Available in U.S. only)

23645-5 Pa. $7.95

AN INTRODUCTION TO THE STUDY OF THE MAYA HIEROGLYPHS, Syvanus Griswold Morley. Classic study by one of the truly great figures in hieroglyph research. Still the best introduction for the student for reading Maya hieroglyphs. New introduction by J. Eric S. Thompson. 117 illustrations. 284pp. 5⅜ x 8½. 23108-9 Pa. $4.00

A STUDY OF MAYA ART, Herbert J. Spinden. Landmark classic interprets Maya symbolism, estimates styles, covers ceramics, architecture, murals, stone carvings as artforms. Still a basic book in area. New introduction by J. Eric Thompson. Over 750 illustrations. 341pp. 8⅜ x 11¼.

21235-1 Pa. $6.95

GEOMETRY, RELATIVITY AND THE FOURTH DIMENSION, Rudolf Rucker. Exposition of fourth dimension, means of visualization, concepts of relativity as Flatland characters continue adventures. Popular, easily followed yet accurate, profound. 141 illustrations. 133pp. 5⅜ x 8½.
23400-2 Pa. $2.75

THE ORIGIN OF LIFE, A. I. Oparin. Modern classic in biochemistry, the first rigorous examination of possible evolution of life from nitrocarbon compounds. Non-technical, easily followed. Total of 295pp. 5⅜ x 8½.
60213-3 Pa. $4.00

THE CURVES OF LIFE, Theodore A. Cook. Examination of shells, leaves, horns, human body, art, etc., in *"the* classic reference on how the golden ratio applies to spirals and helices in nature . . . . "—Martin Gardner. 426 illustrations. Total of 512pp. 5⅜ x 8½.   23701-X Pa. $5.95

PLANETS, STARS AND GALAXIES, A. E. Fanning. Comprehensive introductory survey: the sun, solar system, stars, galaxies, universe, cosmology; quasars, radio stars, etc. 24pp. of photographs. 189pp. 5⅜ x 8½. (Available in U.S. only)   21680-2 Pa. $3.00

THE THIRTEEN BOOKS OF EUCLID'S ELEMENTS, translated with introduction and commentary by Sir Thomas L. Heath. Definitive edition. Textual and linguistic notes, mathematical analysis, 2500 years of critical commentary. Do not confuse with abridged school editions. Total of 1414pp. 5⅜ x 8½.   60088-2, 60089-0, 60090-4 Pa., Three-vol. set $18.00

DIALOGUES CONCERNING TWO NEW SCIENCES, Galileo Galilei. Encompassing 30 years of experiment and thought, these dialogues deal with geometric demonstrations of fracture of solid bodies, cohesion, leverage, speed of light and sound, pendulums, falling bodies, accelerated motion, etc. 300pp. 5⅜ x 8½.   60099-8 Pa. $4.00

Prices subject to change without notice.

Available at your book dealer or write for free catalogue to Dept. GI, Dover Publications, Inc., 180 Varick St., N.Y., N.Y. 10014. Dover publishes more than 175 books each year on science, elementary and advanced mathematics, biology, music, art, literary history, social sciences and other areas.